TO SPEAK OF EASTER WEEK

FAMILY MEMORIES OF THE IRISH REVOLUTION

HÉLÈNE O'KEEFFE

MERCIER PRESS

IRISH PUBLISHER – IRISH STORY

For my family, Barra, Jane, Maurice, Claire, David and Brigid: the makers of memory and champions of dreams.

MERCIER PRESS

Cork

www.mercierpress.ie

© Hélène O'Keeffe, 2015

ISBN: 978 1 78117 221 6

10 9 8 7 6 5 4 3 2 1

This publication is supported by

**An Roinn
Ealaíon, Oidhreachta agus Gaeltachta
Department of
Arts, Heritage and the Gaeltacht**

A CIP record for this title is available from the British Library

Printed and bound in the EU.

Contents

INTRODUCTION

⇝ INDIVIDUAL TRUTHS ⇜

Early on the morning of Friday 28 April 1916, as O'Connell Street burned around him, Patrick Pearse, the commander-in-chief of the Army of the Irish Republic, composed a final manifesto:

> I desire now, lest I may not have an opportunity later, to pay homage to the gallantry of the soldiers of Irish Freedom who have, during the last four days, been writing with fire and steel the most glorious chapter in the later history of Ireland. Justice can never be done to their heroism … Let me who have led them into this … ask those who come after to remember them.[1]

In this Decade of Centenaries (2012–22), the Irish nation is once again confronted by the imperative to remember the men and women who staged a week-long uprising against the British Empire and laid the foundations for the revolutionary period that followed. However, as we reflect on the significance and the political legacy of the Easter Rising, it is also worth considering the personal legacies of 1916 and its aftermath for the children and grandchildren of the participants. Only they can testify to the reality of a revolutionary inheritance; they are also the custodians of memory, the caretakers of stories, which, like the medals and faded photographs, have been handed down from one generation to the next. Their recollections resonate with many Irish families and, as such, are as important an emblem of that complex period in Irish history as any official act of commemoration.

This book tells the story of the Easter Rising from the perspective of those for whom the lines of family history converge with the national narrative. The details are drawn from three different layers of memory. The first layer comprises eyewitness accounts of the 1916 Rising and its aftermath; the second is provided by those who recount the stories told to them by their parents and grandparents; and the final layer comes from family members who never knew the people about whom they speak, but share inherited memories, reimagined and diluted by distance.

Many of the first generation committed their memories to print or submitted witness statements to the Bureau of Military History (BMH). The second- and third-generation memories reproduced in these pages are drawn primarily from the oral histories relating to the 1916 Rising and its aftermath recorded for the Irish Life and Lore series.[2] The idea for this project originated in 2005, when independent oral historian Maurice O'Keeffe embarked on a self-sponsored local study of the 1916 Rising in Kerry entitled 'Recollections of 1916 and its Aftermath: Echoes from History'.[3] The interest generated by this early collection provided the impetus for him to pursue a more elaborate and further-reaching oral-history project in 2012. Having compiled a cross-section of twenty recordings, he was encouraged by the 'historical potential of the collection' to approach the Department of Arts, Heritage and the Gaeltacht for sponsorship.[4] Patronage of the project was consistent with the government's expressed commitment to 'a measured and reflective' commemoration of the Decade of Centenaries, and its contribution, together with additional funding from South Dublin County Council, allowed O'Keeffe to compile an oral-history collection comprising ninety-nine interviews with the descendants of participants in the revolutionary period in Ireland. They each speak from their own family's unique labyrinth of loyalties and idiosyncrasies, but their stories share a starting point in 1916 and their protagonists were all present at the moment of myth making.

We should not, however, confuse memory with history. As Richard White observes:

> History is the enemy of memory. The two stalk each other across the fields of the past, claiming the same terrain. History forges weapons from what memory has forgotten or suppressed … but there are regions of the past that only memory knows. If historians wish to go into this dense and tangled terrain, they must accept memory as a guide.[5]

Even as we accept memory as a guide, we must ask the same questions about its origins as we would of a more traditional source. Established by the Fianna Fáil government in 1947, the Bureau of Military History was a state-sponsored body created to facilitate an oral-history project, which inevitably influenced the range and depth of the contributions. The Treaty negotiations and the Civil War were excluded from its remit in order to secure testimony from both sides of the Civil War divide. The Irish Life and Lore project differs in that it was an independent enterprise and Maurice O'Keeffe was unhindered by any particular remit other than a personal commitment to 'collect as many interesting stories connected to the Rising as possible, from as many different perspectives as possible before they vanish from living memory'.[6] The Civil War, which for years has represented an unspoken gap in the official narratives of the state, is addressed on a personal level by the second generation, who witnessed its most bitter legacies.

This is not to say that the source of the contemporary collection is unproblematic. The project was undertaken by an independent historian, limited by deficits in personnel, time and resources, which means that the collection lacks the breadth and balance of an academic or an official enterprise. The pool of interviewees was confined to those whom O'Keeffe was able to source through word of mouth; consequently there is an obvious Dublin-centricity and gender imbalance in the final compilation of interviews. The value of this collection in comparison to that of the Bureau of Military History, however, lies in the unmediated, unscripted nature of the final interviews.

These oral-history projects, conducted almost sixty years apart, also had obvious differences in terms of methodology. The Bureau's investigators – primarily military officers – were given clear procedural guidelines. Should testimony be given orally, the investigators were directed 'to steer witnesses away from obvious fantasy or exaggeration, but under no circumstances to induce testimony'.[7] They were urged to take 'copious notes', which would subsequently be converted into a coherent statement and submitted to the witness for approval. Where there was evidence of unreliability through 'failing memory', or 'self-glorification', a report to that effect should be appended. Statements could be as long or short as the witness desired, and no disclosure would be made to anyone outside the Bureau except with the permission of the donor.[8] In March 1959, 1,770 witness statements were sealed in eighty-three steel boxes and locked in the archives in Government Buildings, where they remained until 2003, after the last witness had died.[9]

This meticulous procedure contrasts with the more informal approach of the independent oral historian, who explained that his method is 'born of twenty-five years of experience'. His interviews are generally conducted in the interviewee's home, allowing for an ease of exchange, and are characterised by an unhurried, conversational tone. O'Keeffe has honed an unobtrusive, straightforward and sympathetic interviewing style, which he likens to 'engaging in conversation over a cup of tea'. While the interviews are often circuitous and lack the focus of a formal interview, the casual context nurtures candid discussion and facilitates the recollection of the finer details of a family anecdote.[10]

Questions about origin and procedure reveal the disparate nature of the projects, but both are collections of oral history and, as such, raise similar issues of reliability. Fearghal McGarry, who sifted through the tens of thousands of submissions to the Bureau of Military History to 'distil the vast testimony of the statements into a coherent readable narrative', cautioned that they do not represent a perfect record of events. Rather, they are the witnesses' imperfect memory of the events from a remove of several decades and are often rendered unconvincing by retrospective judgements and factual flaws.[11] As autobiographical accounts, the testimonies were inevitably informed by human impulses to shift blame, justify actions or even by modesty.

The testimonies in the Irish Life and Lore collection are by no means pure or unfiltered. Despite the informal nature of the interview process, an interviewee's awareness of the act of recording a testimony for public consumption will always incur a form of self-censorship, and the same human impulses to exonerate or exalt apply to the second and third generations, perhaps to an even greater extent. Furthermore, human beings are inherently storytellers and, in the context of an oral history interview, will employ narrative conventions such as drama, climax and resolution, often sacrificing accuracy for cohesion. In terms of factual historical reliability, therefore, oral testimony from each of the three layers of memory should be approached with caution and in conjunction with documentary source material.

For the purposes of this book, however, the value of oral testimony from the second and third layers of memory lies less in its potential for yielding an unvarnished truth about the revolutionary period, and more in its revelations about the long-term impact of political activism on the participants and their families. Equally significantly, the oral history testimonies provide an insight into how memory is transferred from one generation to the next, and reveal the personal motives for remembering, and forgetting, 1916.

SELECTIVE MEMORY

Commemoration was Thomas Derham's primary motive for remembering. He recently penned a poetic tribute to his father, Joseph Derham, the garrison timekeeper in the General Post Office (GPO) during the 1916 Rising, because he wanted to see his father take his place among Ireland's celebrated patriots:

> Now my father, we could set our watches by the sound of his key in the hall door
>   on his return home each evening,
> His homeward stride interrupted by the Stations of the Cross.
> A man of great faith and infinite patience, dedicated to the care of a large family.
> He died an unsung Volunteer hero fiercely carrying his 1916 story to the grave,
> His brave sacrifice is now being told,
> His hero status now firmly enshrined in our memories.

Derham's intention was mirrored in the interviews provided by many from the second and third generations. Some of the descendants of participants in the 1916 Rising, for example, emphasised details that singled out their relatives from the other names on the Roll of Honour. Éamonn Bulfin was the man who 'raised the flag on the roof of the GPO'. Charlie Bevan was, according to his son, 'the first man into the Four Courts', and Diarmuid Lynch was the 'last to leave the GPO'. Fifteen-year-old Peter O'Connor 'was one of the youngest members of the GPO garrison', and Captain Seán Connolly of the Irish Citizen Army (ICA) was 'the first rebel to be shot in Easter Week'.

Éamon Ó Cuív's motives for remembering were largely corrective. He was anxious to dispel the various myths that surround the legacy of his grandfather, Éamon de Valera, including those relating to his conduct and demeanour as commandant of the 3rd Battalion in Boland's Mills in 1916. Historian Tim Pat Coogan, for example, has suggested that de Valera's leadership was erratic and contradictory, and that he seemed to be 'a man on or over the threshold of a nervous breakdown'.[12] Coogan quoted eyewitnesses who reported seeing a 'tall gangling figure in green Volunteer uniform and red socks running around day and night without sleep, getting trenches dug, giving contradictory orders and forgetting the password so that he nearly got himself shot'.[13]

Among de Valera's papers in the UCD archives at Belfield, Ó Cuív discovered what he considered to be absolute proof of his grandfather's presence of mind. When they 'got the [Treaty] ports back' in 1938, a sergeant major 'who had been in the arresting party' in 1916 wrote to him and said, 'You've now achieved everything that you spoke about on the march away from Boland's Mills.'[14] That does not 'smack of somebody who has lost control of themselves', Ó Cuív declared. On the contrary, 'that looks like somebody who was marching down the road … very much aware of what they were doing [and] why they were doing it, and actually made a huge impression in a casual encounter with the arresting sergeant'.

Richard Mulcahy in Free State uniform, 1922 (*courtesy of Dr Risteárd Mulcahy*)

Thomas Ashe's niece, Eileen Quinn, and Richard Mulcahy's son, Risteárd Mulcahy, were similarly concerned with addressing what they considered to be inconsistencies in the historical record regarding their relatives' respective roles in the Ashbourne engagement. On Friday 28 April 1916, forty men of the 5th (Fingal) Battalion, Dublin Brigade, under Commandant Thomas Ashe, engaged a convoy of Royal Irish Constabulary (RIC) officers at Rath Cross, a mile outside the village of Ashbourne in County Meath. After five hours of intense, close-quarter fighting, the RIC men surrendered to the North County Dublin Volunteers. In the words of Eileen Quinn, it was 'one of the successes of the Easter Rising. It was the one place they could say we had a battle … and won. They just walked away.'

The story passed into legend as a daring, well-organised Volunteer ambush of a larger, better-equipped enemy force, and Commandant Thomas Ashe emerged as an exemplary rebel leader. More recently, commentators have suggested that the reality of the events that afternoon lies more in the realm of chaotic accident, with Ashe being demoted to the position of indecisive leader in favour of his more practical and steadfast second-in-command, Lieutenant Richard Mulcahy.[15]

This was certainly the opinion of Section Commander Joseph Lawless from Swords, who told his son, Colm, that 'Tom Ashe was very brave [but] when Dick Mulcahy arrived [on Monday evening] he actually took over as more of a military commander.' Lawless expressed the same opinion to the Bureau of Military History:

> What fortuitous circumstances guide our destiny! The officer who thus made accidental contact [on Monday] and remained with us was Dick Mulcahy, without whose presence with us on the Friday following, there might have been a very different story to tell.[16]

In 1952 Thomas Ashe's sister, Nora Ashe, took issue with suggestions by Joseph Lawless and Desmond Ryan that her brother held only nominal command at Ashbourne. She insisted that the former had 'given a wrong impression on every occasion he has spoken of it' and the latter had 'not been fair to Tomás'. She claimed that Ashe 'had sent a despatch to Lieutenant Mulcahy with instructions as to where to place his men and outlining his own position'.[17] Eileen Quinn is similarly convinced that her uncle 'stayed in command out there'.

Richard Mulcahy often paid tribute to his commanding officer at Ashbourne. In 1985, for example, he said: 'All through the week the presence of Ashe was to be felt, erect, composed, confident ... The influence of his calm, unquestioning alertness seemed to pervade the whole force; he was the fulcrum against which difficulties were levered out of the way.'[18] Dr Risteárd Mulcahy, however, is inclined to believe that his father's effusive praise for Ashe was actually evidence of his own humility: 'He was embarrassed when people said that he was the brains behind the whole thing, [and it was] typical of him that he'd give the whole credit to Ashe.' He also identified his father's modesty as the primary reason for his absence at the unveiling of the Ashbourne memorial in 1959: 'My mother [Min Mulcahy] was very upset [but] he was quite implacable … adamant not to go. [And yet] the people who went to that, the people who were in Ashbourne, knew that my father had been the main influence behind [their] success.'

These very human impulses to protect a relative's historical reputation and to challenge his detractors are compelling reasons for remembering. Equally worthy of consideration, however, are the motives for forgetting. Among the first generation these motives included humility and self-censorship. Éamonn Bulfin, for example, never told his daughter 'hero stories', and Jack Shouldice, a lieutenant in the 1st Battalion in 1916, was a 'very quiet, modest, gentle kind of guy and not one for courting the limelight'. This resonates with Fearghal McGarry's observation that the BMH witness statements were 'characterised by modesty rather than vanity or self-interest'.[19]

The interviewees' parents had been, in many cases, members of the Irish Republican Brotherhood (IRB) or Cumann na mBan (the Irishwomen's Council) and, as such, inculcated with the imperative of secrecy. Chris Shouldice, for instance, never asked his father about his membership of the IRB: 'The secrecy was such a heavy cult among them all.' Eleanor Burke, whose mother, Rosalie Rice, and grandmother, Kathleen Ring, were members of Cumann na mBan in Kenmare, only latterly learned the full extent of her family's involvement in the republican movement. When Eleanor eventually asked her grandmother why she never spoke about her experiences, she replied, 'We learned not to speak or say anything because one idle word during that time could cause somebody's death.'

The continuity between the Easter Rising and the Civil War meant that in Dan Holland's family 'there was a moratorium' on talking about 1916.[20] The fraternal conflict in which erstwhile comrades became bitter enemies was symbolic of frustrated ideals and, according to Chris Shouldice, 'the traumas were so intense and so deep' that they drove his father, 'and a lot of his contemporaries, into a kind of silence'.

There was an added complexity for the women who participated in Ireland's struggle for independence. ICA member Brigid Davis was proud to have stood with Seán Connolly's garrison in City Hall on Easter Monday 1916, but her daughter, Mary Dawson, felt that her mother's pride was atypical: 'It was frowned upon – what [women] did at that time.' For most women, the motives for forgetting were linked specifically to traditional gender roles, and the Civil War, in particular, was taboo. This was unsurprising, considering the 'atmosphere of bitterness following the defeat of the republicans when women were condemned by the victorious Free State as "furies" and blamed for having set brother against brother'.[21] It was also 'a source of extreme embarrassment to some families that their women-folk had been in prison'.[22] The subject was avoided in both the domestic and social spheres, and so all-encompassing was the silence that, for some of the interviewees, the discovery of their mothers' participation in the revolutionary period was delayed, accidental or even posthumous.

In a letter to the secretary of the Pensions Department Group in May 1962, Bridie O'Rahilly (née Clyne) simply wrote: 'Dear Sir, I want a medal. Here is my record.' A copy of the enclosed typed record was among the documents she had carefully concealed in the wine cellar for years. After her death, in November 1971, her son, Proinsias Ó Rathaille, discovered 'a briefcase full of papers' and, for the grandson of The O'Rahilly, the discovery that his mother had been involved in republican activities was shocking. The papers included details about her work for the republican underground in Dublin and Wicklow during the Civil War, and her son discovered that she 'was in the Four Courts when it was shelled' by Free State forces in June 1922: 'She drove an ambulance through the barricades and brought in arms … but she never said it and my father [Niall O'Rahilly] never knew it.'

The pattern that has emerged from the selection of interviews is that a combination of reserve, regret and practised restraint proved to be a deterrent to conversation about the revolutionary period. The continuity between insurrection and Civil War discouraged discussion about the Rising, and narrow gender roles further limited disclosure. There is also evidence to suggest that a parent's very understandable impulse to protect a child from exposure to unsettling truths or inherited biases limited what they were willing to discuss. 'The generation that goes through a civil war,' said Máire MacSwiney Brugha in 2009, 'should not impose it on the next generation. They should be allowed to make their own decisions and to do their own thinking.'

While the participants might not have wanted to engage in discussion about their revolutionary pasts, in many cases their children were complicit in the

Bridie Clyne - record

Joined Cumann na mBan in Scotland 1919/20. Came to Dublin and joined staff of Dermot O'Hegarty in Middle Abbey Street about 1920. Did occasional work with Gearoid O'Sullivan. Transferred from there to Belfast Boycott and worked with Miceal Staines. From there went to Department of Labour in North Frederick Street and worked with Dick Cotter, Madame Markievicz. Travelled through the country on Arbitration cases and was in Cork on the big railway disoute at time of Treaty. Worked in Labour De artment under Joe McGrath until the Four Courts.

On the morning of the attack on the Four Courts I rushed the Free State barricade and got into the garrison. I came out with guns durin the whole of the attack and took in messages from Oscar Traynor and Dublin Brigade, also medical supplies which were needed and clothing. In the closing scenes was asked by Rory O'Connor and Liam Mellowes if I though I could break through to get news back as to the outside situation - things were then desperate. Made several attempts to get back into the Courts and finally after a second attempt with an Ambulance I ot through and took in the last reports. Came out at the surrender and was arrested for a few hours.

Went to the Gresham until the attack. Went to Blessington and was with the army until it moved south. Walked back to Dublin with Fr. Dominic and the wounded. Work with Frank Henderson in the Dublin Brigade. Later was moved to Intelligence Department and ran a flat forthem for activities. Wohrked with Michael Carolan and Joe Griffin. The Department went underground and I was with them until arrested in a raid on the "secret" house in Strand Road, Merrion. Spent 3 months in jail under the name of Anny Hardwicke. Did a hungerstrike of a month - not sure of length. Was released from Kilmainham and had got a damaged knee there (which is still with me). Joined Chief of Staff Department with Frank Aiken and Paddy Ruttledge. Worked underground in secret houses with them until formation of Fianna ail.

Remained with IRA until about 1926. Not sure of date

Was with deValera when he was attacked at Ennis. Had been sent down with warning of attack. Returned to Dublin in his car to his hideout in Mount Street. Was sent with 2 others on special trip to Cork to take back the lads who had done the Cobh shooting of British army soldiers. Very special trip through the country which was looking for them.

Letter from Bridie O'Rahilly (née Clyne) to the secretary of the Pensions Department in May 1962 (*courtesy of Prionsias O'Rathaille*)

cultivation of silence. Their questions, when they asked them, were often met with evasion or the provision of a sanitised anecdote to entertain a child. More usually, the questions were not asked at all. Many of the interviewees from the second generation admitted to being caught in what W. B. Yeats called 'that sensual music' of youth, and regretted deeply the passing of a parent and the realisation that they knew only part of the story.[23] Captain Frank Henderson's son, Fr Éanna Henderson, for example, confessed that he 'didn't know an awful lot' about 'F' Company, 2nd Battalion, in 1916 'until later years because [he] had more interest in girls and a bit of roguery'. Paddy Weston also regretted not asking questions about his family's integral involvement in the Battle of Ashbourne in 1916: 'It's always when you get older,' he sighed, 'that you know all the questions you should have asked.'

The social context in which the second generation grew up is also significant in terms of how memory was transmitted and received. For the children of the 1930s, 1940s and 1950s, the masculine ideal was that of 'upright' and 'dignified' fortitude. In deeply conservative Catholic Ireland, the family was defined by a 'strong, silent', often emotionally unavailable paternal figure, and a mother restrained by the traditional restrictive gender roles ascribed to women by an enduringly patriarchal society. So many of the interviewees from that generation used interchangeable phrases to denote emotional detachment when describing their fathers. Colonel Joseph Lawless was described by his son Colm as 'a very strong man in every way' and Dr Gearóid Lynch remembered his father, Fionán Lynch, Captain of 'F' Company, 1st Battalion in 1916 as 'a quiet man' who was very 'contained'. Thomas Derham's father was a 'straight-backed man of honour'.

For a cohort of men who engaged in acts of revolutionary violence and who often found it difficult to rebuild a civilian career, the detachment may also have been a means of self-preservation, an unwillingness to indulge in emotional excavation. For Charlie Dalton, it was a façade that crumbled spectacularly, resulting in a nervous breakdown. According to his daughter, Carol Mullan, Dalton had always been 'totally silent' about his membership of Michael Collins' Special Intelligence Unit when, 'at just eighteen', he participated in and witnessed some of the most harrowing violence of the War of Independence. 'It deeply affected his life,' she said, and, in retrospect, Carol is convinced that he was suffering from post-traumatic stress, which 'wasn't recognised at the time ... Nobody took these young men to just check were they okay afterwards ... I can't believe my father was the only one who was so damaged.'

For other veterans, such as Mairéad de hÓir's father, Éamonn Dore, association with the events of 1916–21 was the highlight of their lives. As historian Michael Hopkinson points out, participation in the 1916 Rising in particular 'made historically significant men and women who would otherwise have been

May Gibney
(*courtesy of Kilmainham Gaol
Museum, 20PC-1B55-01*)

unremarkable' and 'they loved to talk about it'.[24] Yet it was a topic reserved for discussion in the company of fellow veterans in the pub or around the card table. The experiences were not shared with their children, many of whom remarked on the fragments of information gleaned while eavesdropping on private conversations between comrades.

If the first generation subscribed to the expectations accorded to their gender, so too did their children. The male interviewees from the second generation seemed particularly reluctant to romanticise their mothers' involvement in any aspect of the revolutionary period. In many cases, the sons of that generation struggled to reconcile the roles of mother and revolutionary. Con O'Neill's mother, May Gibney, volunteered in the GPO in 1916 and spent the week attending to the wounded and performing any other duties required of her. Con simply said, 'She wasn't a member of Cumann na mBan, she wasn't a member of any of the warring parties there, so she was an odd-ball in the place.'

At the end of the week, Pearse ordered the evacuation of the wounded Volunteers and the women from the GPO, and Con's cousin, 'who was down there just to see what was happening', saw May Gibney 'leading one small group of the women out carrying a white flag'. Her son does not feel that May was 'leading' them as such:

> I'd say somebody just said, 'Look there's a flag, go out that way and they won't shoot at you.' She didn't rally the people, they were rallied for her and that's all it was … [My family] didn't sit down around the table and discuss it [because] she herself would feel that she had nothing much to speak about. She didn't glory in the thing at all, it was just what happened and that was it.

Con's understanding is in line with Margaret Ward's observation that too few of the revolutionary women felt 'that their lives would be of interest to future generations'.[25] But it is also revealing of the fact that the interviewee, born in 1936, grew up in a generation when women were very much relegated to the realm of the domestic, and the idea of revolutionary proactivity was incongruous with the ideal of 1940s motherhood.

The daughters of the insurgents seemed more willing to embrace the idea of their mothers as revolutionaries. Kathleen Boland's daughter, Eileen Barrington, for example, testified to being 'very proud' of her mother's participation in the 1916 Rising, and Eleanor Burke clearly admired her mother, Rosalie Rice, for her bravery: 'She worked at the post office in Kenmare and it was she who filed the telegram to her cousins Eugene and Tim Ring at the cable station in Valentia which alerted America and the world that the Irish had risen.' Her grandmother, Kathleen Ring, similarly impressed Eleanor, and she described her as a 'bold woman' who 'didn't take any nonsense ... When they used to be raided by the Black and Tans, she used to make them all wipe their feet before they came in. The family were afraid that they'd pick up a gun and shoot her, because she wasn't a bit afraid of them.'

The women who knew the details of their mothers' revolutionary records tended to celebrate their involvement, but they often shied away from the idea of a father wielding a gun. Éamonn Bulfin's daughter, Jeanne, preferred to think that he 'shot over the heads' of the looters on O'Connell Street in 1916 and Joseph Leonard's daughter, Clare Duffy, is unwilling to sully with violent truth the memory of her 'lovely Daddy', who would 'catch [her] in his arms and swing [her] around'.[26]

While all the interviews are individual and unique, and some of the interviewees are in possession of more information than others, similar threads are evident in the tapestries of inherited memory. There are clear gender differences and generational differences in the ways that these revolutionary men and women are remembered, and compelling reasons existed to preclude the disclosure of troubling or discordant memories. The domestic silence, together with the fact that, until the 1960s, the History curriculum in schools 'stopped with the Act of Union' meant that 'the revolutionary decade' was 'an era hopelessly beyond imaginative reach'.[27] So emerged a generation once removed from revolution.

THE BURDEN OF INHERITANCE

While in some cases, the children of revolutionaries were sheltered from realities they could not understand, in others, they were traumatised by association or carried the heavy burden of expectation. It was their duty, many felt, to build on the impossible ideals of the previous generation.

It is her grand-nephew's opinion that, for Nora Connolly, the burden of expectation was immense. James Connolly Heron explained: 'I imagine because she was so closely identified with her father [James Connolly] that his shadow was in the background. He was on her shoulder so she remained always committed to a Workers' Republic.' Nora's brother, Roddy Connolly, who stood with his father in the GPO at the age of fifteen, was equally invested with the custodianship of the Connolly legacy. He went on to found the Communist Party of Ireland and support the anti-Treaty republicans during the Civil War. As a representative of the fourth generation, James Connolly Heron claimed, 'There is a lot of pride, obviously. But it's difficult as well trying to live up to the ideal.'[28]

Tomás MacCurtain
(*courtesy of Mercier Archive*)

According to Cathal Brugha's granddaughter, Deirdre Stuart, her father Ruairí inherited a 'very, very strong sense of serving his country', and Micheline Sheehy-Skeffington, in conversation about her father Eoin, said: 'I think he felt a sense of duty to honour what his father [Francis Sheehy-Skeffington] would have done had he lived.' While some of the family members of the fallen rebels fulfilled their duty, as they saw it, in the realms of politics, literature and administration, others, such as George Plunkett and Tomás Óg MacCurtain, carried on the military campaign. Fionnuala MacCurtain's father, Tomás Óg, was four years old in March 1920 when he witnessed the assassination of his father, Tomás MacCurtain, Ireland's first republican lord mayor, which 'must have made a huge impression on a child'. Tomás Óg was active in the republican movement until the late 1950s and 'was officer in command of the 1st Cork Brigade, exactly the same role as his father had'. His story is not dissimilar to that of Séamus Mallin, son of Michael Mallin, who commanded the St Stephen's Green garrison in 1916. Séamus fought on the republican side in the Civil War and narrowly escaped execution in 1922 for his part in an armed attack on Free State troops in Dublin.

As well as an innate sense of duty, there is evidence in the interviews of a deep emotional legacy. Interestingly, the full weight of the emotional inheritance was more obvious in the interviews from the third layer of memory. The second generation tended more towards respect for their parents' stoicism and loyalty, and their personal grief seemed more muted. Henry Coyle of 'F' Company, 2nd Battalion, died with The O'Rahilly in Moore Street on Friday 28 April 1916. His son, also called Henry, grew up without a father, but accepted that 'it was a product of the times and [his father] was doing what he felt should be done'. With the perspective that distance offers, the grandsons and granddaughters were more willing to articulate the pain, and often the resentment, felt by their parents – the children of the revolutionaries. In conversation about his grandmother, Ina Connolly, James Connolly Heron explained:

> You couldn't actually discuss James Connolly with my granny because she found it so upsetting. So you were reluctant to engage in a conversation about [her father] because you didn't want to witness this breaking down. That told you how extraordinarily brutal the execution of her father was in terms of her memory bank … I recall that when she was writing her memoirs in our house in Ballymun, you would hear her sobbing in the bedroom as she wrote. There was extraordinary closeness for her still. As an elderly person so many years later, the brutality of the loss was still felt to that extent by her.

There was a clear generational difference too in terms of awareness about a family member's involvement in the revolutionary period. That extra layer of distance, together with different cultural and educational experiences, meant that the third and fourth generations were generally more conscious of the complexities of the period, and almost universally proud of their antecedents' achievements. They were less concerned, as Thomas MacDonagh's granddaughter, Lucille Redmond, put it, 'with baton handing'. Eoin MacNeill's grandson, Michael McDowell, agreed: 'I think I'm sufficiently far away enough from all of those events not to believe that I am some kind of clone of him … I take history as a complex mosaic, not as an unbreakable thread coming from the past.'

The responsibility of the third generation, as many of them see it, is to plumb the family archives to uncover the truth of their place at the fountainhead of modern Ireland. In many cases their motivation is less to protect or emulate the person; rather, it is to correct or supplement the historical record and to commemorate their ancestors' achievements and sacrifices. The centenary of the Rising offers an opportunity for them to tell the stories of the men and women at the barricades in Church Street and North King Street, on the roof of the GPO, standing with Thomas Ashe at Ashbourne, or with The O'Rahilly in Moore Street. Many of their stories diverge at the surrender and again at the signing of the Anglo-Irish Treaty in 1921, and represent the complex cocktail of allegiances during the revolutionary period.

There can be no clear strand of inherited memory uncomplicated by affinity and subsequent experience for those who share a name and an inheritance with our revolutionaries and state-builders. But, as John Waters observed, 'If the anniversary of the Easter Rising has any meaning, it must surely offer them the right to their individual truths.'[29]

The chapters in this book are organised according to the dominant themes in the interviews. In some cases, the interviewees prioritise their relatives' roles at a particular location during the Rising, while, in others, the circumstances of an antecedent's death take precedence. In all the chapters the voices are those of the interviewees, and intrusion by the author is minimal, but for the sake of coherency and continuity, the account is bolstered by documentary evidence and first-hand eyewitness accounts. The voices presented do not reflect the author's bias or affiliation, and the collection of interviews dictated the breadth and balance of the study. The full interviews are available to download at www.irishlifeandlore.com.

Memories in Context

↠ Ireland 1890–1923 ↞

The men and women whose stories are told here by their descendants were born into a generation presented with increased educational opportunities and influenced by concurrent streams of cultural and social radicalism at the turn of the twentieth century. Theirs was a generation alienated from British rule and the values and ambitions of their parents, and 'bent on self-transformation'.[1] While the experience of every individual is unique, the stories of Jack Shouldice and Frank Henderson, as told by their sons, are broadly representative of the complex web of often-conflicting influences on the generation that reached adulthood between the fall of Charles Stewart Parnell in 1890 and the outbreak of the First World War in 1914. In conversation about his father, Chris Shouldice explained:

> You see, they were looking across a couple of centuries of famine, emigration, deprivation back to 1798, the last time that a serious blow had been struck for independence, and they considered themselves the generation that were going to do it, whether it was the Parnell way [or] the Thomas Clarke way.[2]

In the late 1890s Frank Henderson was a student at St Joseph's Christian Brothers' School in Fairview in the north-east of inner-city Dublin. 'Family traditions on both sides gave [him] an early separatist and physical force outlook',[3] and according to his son, Fr Éanna Henderson, the family was very 'republican minded'. The 'Fenian Faith' inherited from his ancestors was augmented in Henderson's adolescence by the heady mix of a Christian Brothers education, 1798 centenary literature and the separatist propaganda surrounding royal visits to Ireland at the beginning of the twentieth century.

Kevin Whelan contends that the road to the 1916 Rising began with Queen Victoria's Jubilee, 'zealously marked in Belfast and Dublin in 1897'. The celebrations represented the 'very zenith of the Empire, seeming to show an imperial community of loyalty so cohesive that the British Empire was unassailable'.[4] Eleven-year-old Frank Henderson accompanied his father in the procession around the city and recalled 'the huge crowd' and the 'great excitement'.[5] The 'city was decorated by loyalists', and nationalists held protest meetings and demonstrations against those who tried to welcome 'the Famine Queen' to Dublin. Henderson was particularly affected by one protest, which included throwing a coffin labelled 'The British Empire' into the River Liffey.[6]

In the following year, the attention of 'the rising generation' was focused on centenary celebrations for the 1798 Rebellion.[7] During the carefully stage-managed anniversary events in Dublin, the rival factions of constitutional nationalism shared a platform with socialists, Irish-language revivalists and republicans. The growth of literacy and the spread of nationalist reading rooms meant that competitive claims to heredity with the patriots of 1798, together with dramatic accounts of the battles of 1798, were published and circulated by the expanding nationalist press. For Jack Shouldice, the son of an RIC officer in Ballaghaderreen, County Roscommon, the public spectacles and stories proved a powerful radicalising influence. The centenary year also prompted the establishment, by William O'Brien, of the United Irish League (UIL), a rural grass-roots movement that injected new dynamism into popular politics.[8] The reform of local government in 1899 provided a platform for aspiring nationalist politicians, and Irish women were enfranchised in local elections. Henderson and Shouldice were growing up in an era of political innovation and intellectual energy that would ultimately light the torch of revolt.

In 1899 Arthur Griffith began his editorship of *The United Irishman*, the newly founded advanced nationalist newspaper. Thirteen-year-old Frank Henderson was an appreciative reader of the 'well-written' publication which, in his opinion, made 'many converts' to separatism.[9] The weekly newspaper proved to be an effective vehicle for anti-imperialist and pro-Boer sentiment when, in the closing months of the year, Britain went to war with the two South African republics of the Transvaal and the Orange Free State. The military successes of the small states against the might of the British Empire had a strong resonance in Ireland and pro-Boer sentiment served to galvanise nationalist opinion. Henderson recalled that Major John MacBride, who headed the Irish Brigade in the Transvaal, 'became the popular hero about whom songs were sung'.[10]

Jack Shouldice (*courtesy of the Shouldice family*)

In the same year, Jack Shouldice, a 'quiet' and 'reserved' seventeen-year-old, left his native Ballaghaderreen in search of employment with the civil service in London, where, in his son's words, he 'got caught up in the ferment of all

23

things national that were happening'. Like so many Irish emigrants at the turn of the century, 'revolted by the anti-Boer triumphalism', Shouldice was drawn to the playing fields of the Gaelic Athletic Association (GAA) and the Irish classes and *feiseanna* (festivals) of the Gaelic League. Both organisations were facets of the late-nineteenth-century Gaelic revival, which asserted the importance of an Irish cultural identity and promoted 'an awareness of the baleful impact of Anglicisation'.[11] Shouldice was introduced to 'Sam Maguire and Peadar Kearney and all of these people' in the London Hibernians Gaelic football team, his son explained, and so began his 'involvement in the national movement'.

While Shouldice was 'proving a tricky customer' on the sports pitches in London, Frank Henderson continued his education in St Joseph's in Fairview. The Irish Christian Brothers had shunned the state curriculum in favour of one that placed more emphasis on Catholic nationalist values and imbued their students with a patriotic Gaelic ethos. In fact, Éanna Henderson credits his father's 'inclination towards nationality' to 'some Christian Brother way back [in] about 1900, [who] got my father and a few others fired up'. Brother Casey's rousing 'Faith and Fatherland' version of Irish history stimulated Henderson's appetite for Gaelic sports and the Irish language, and instigated his membership of the GAA and Gaelic League in Clontarf, where he met his future wife, Josephine Ni Bhraonáin (Brennan).

After he left school in 1903, Frank Henderson 'flatly refused' to take the civil service entrance examination, because employment in the British system was incompatible with his increasingly nationalist politics. 'This was a heavy blow for my parents,' he wrote, 'who had spent a lot of money to provide me with a suitable education.'[12] Instead, he found employment as a clerk in a solicitor's office in inner-city Dublin and became intensely aware of the extreme poverty of Dublin's labouring classes. Dangerously overcrowded tenements, high mortality rates and discontent about the pitiable state of workers' rights gave rise at the start of the twentieth century to socialist and labour movements under the leadership of James Larkin and James Connolly.[13] In Éanna's words:

> [My father] would have had a strong sympathy with the poor and down-trodden …
> [and] he had strong leanings towards a type of National Socialism … I asked him

one time, down here in Roscrea, 'Who was your favourite member of Irish politics or history?' He thought for a moment and then he said, 'James Connolly.'

Chris Shouldice explained that, although his father 'had great sympathy with Connolly's people', he was 'more of a farming type of guy from rural Ireland', and less influenced by the socialist agenda. Shouldice, for whom Thomas Clarke was 'a great idol', was drawn to the secret oath-bound IRB and was sworn into the movement by Sam Maguire in London in 1901. Formed in 1858 with the aim of establishing an Irish Republic by revolutionary means, the separatist movement had experienced a decline in the late 1800s as a result of the successes of constitutional nationalism; at the beginning of the twentieth century the IRB was a marginal force that lacked credibility.[14] The movement was revitalised in the early 1900s by the new and dynamic leadership of Bulmer Hobson, Denis McCullough, Seán MacDermott and Tom Clarke, and drew fresh recruits from the ranks of cultural nationalism, by now frustrated by the perceived failures of the Irish Parliamentary Party (IPP) and possessing a more assertive sense of national identity. On his return to Dublin in 1907, Shouldice became attached to the Bartholomew Teeling Circle, but Frank Henderson rejected overtures from Seán O'Casey, among others, to join the movement.[15] As a devout Catholic, he found it difficult to reconcile his faith with membership of a secret society of which the Catholic Church expressly disapproved.

Jack Shouldice told his son that 'even though he had been involved in the physical force side of things, he had a great respect for John Redmond', under whom the IPP had reunited in 1900. Shouldice was not unusual in that respect, as 'most of those who joined cultural nationalist movements continued to support the Irish Party's drive for Home Rule', particularly after 1909, when the majority of Irish attention was focused firmly on Westminster, where Redmond's party seemed set to achieve Home Rule for Ireland after nearly twenty years of trying.[16] Liberal Prime Minister Henry Asquith, conscious of the likely necessity for Irish nationalist support in the upcoming general election, gave a public commitment to Home Rule in December 1909, and Arthur Griffith's Sinn Féin party, perceived as a rallying point for more extreme nationalists, withdrew into political inactivity, facilitating Redmond's pursuit of legislative independence.[17]

In the same year, aristocrat and former debutante Countess Constance Markievicz, together with Bulmer Hobson, a leading GAA, IRB and Sinn Féin activist from Belfast, established a pseudo-military youth organisation, Na Fianna Éireann (Warriors of Ireland). The movement provided an important source of radicalisation and Con Colbert and Seán Heuston were among the early recruits. Jack Shouldice's younger brother, Bertie, later joined a local branch of the Fianna in Roscommon.

After the general election of 1910, the IPP held the balance of power between the Conservatives and Liberals in the House of Commons and was in a position to force the Liberal Party to commit to a new Home Rule Bill. In the following year, the power of the House of Lords to veto any bill permanently was removed under the Parliament Act and, by 1912, Asquith was in a much stronger position to carry Home Rule than his predecessor, William Gladstone, had ever been.[18] Jack Shouldice resigned his membership of the IRB on the eve of the introduction of the Third Home Rule Bill in the British House of Commons, because 'suddenly it seemed as if the prospects for Home Rule and the Nationalist Party had never been so bright and Ireland warmed to both'.[19] He told his son that on 31 March 1912 he attended that 'very interesting Monster Meeting in O'Connell Street, when [John] Redmond spoke in support of the Home Rule Bill from the same platform as Patrick Pearse' and the various Irish nationalist bodies were united in optimism.[20] However, after the passage of the Home Rule Bill through the House of Commons in January 1913, *The Irish Times* accurately predicted that 'extremists would never be satisfied by such half measures' and that the passage of the Bill into law would open 'a terrible vista of strife and discontent'.[21]

The very real prospect of Home Rule for Ireland caused alarm among the majority Unionist Protestant population in the north. Its resolve to oppose an Irish Home Rule parliament found forcible expression in the half a million signatures – many in blood – on Edward Carson's Solemn League and Covenant on 28 September 1912, and the formation of a volunteer militia – the Ulster Volunteer Force (UVF) – by Edward Carson and James Craig in January 1913. The southern nationalists responded by establishing their own paramilitary force to secure the implementation of the Home Rule legislation. Eoin MacNeill's grandson, Michael McDowell, explained:

[My grandfather] was co-founder of the Gaelic League with Douglas Hyde and editor of *An Claidheamh Soluis*, the movement's newspaper. In that capacity in 1913 … he wrote an article called the 'The North Began', effectively saying that if the Ulster Volunteers could come into force to support their rights the nationalists should do likewise … The IRB people said, 'This is our chance. He is a respectable man, not from the Fenian tradition, suggesting the establishment of a counter force to the UVF.' [So] he was approached by various people on behalf of the IRB asking would he participate and become President … which brought about the foundation of the Irish Volunteers.

Frank Henderson's socialist sympathies were subsumed by the allure of Eoin MacNeill's Irish Volunteers, and he distributed handbills 'at masses' in Glasnevin advertising the inaugural meeting at the Rotunda Rink in Dublin on 25 November 1913. 'I well understood that the IRB were behind this movement,' he wrote, 'but they had now openly asked the young men of Ireland to unite together and to take their stand in the political life of the country.'[22] Jack Shouldice was also among the 180,000 men recruited to the Volunteers and committed to its expressed aims 'to secure and maintain the rights and liberties common to all the people of Ireland. The duties will be defensive and protective and they will not contemplate either aggression or domination.'[23] His sister, Christina, and Frank Henderson's sister, Nora, later joined the women's auxiliary league, Cumann na mBan, founded on 2 April 1914 at Wynn's Hotel in Dublin. Jack Shouldice rejoined his IRB circle almost immediately. According to his son:

He ended up fetching up on the physical force side because, even though they had passed Home Rule in 1912, he felt that it was never going to happen because the people in the north were very firmly determined against it. He felt that there was going to be [an] eventual struggle against the unionists in the north and that's what he dreaded more than anything and that's why he did it – the physical force … So, you see, there was a whole ferment of things. It was an extraordinary time to be alive, I would have thought.

In 1913 Patrick Pearse joined the IRB, was co-opted onto the Supreme Council and elected to the Provisional Committee of the newly formed Irish Volunteers.

In the same year, James Larkin, Jack White and James Connolly established the ICA to defend striking workers from police during the 'Dublin Strike and Lockout'.[24] The working-class militia was much more radical in spirit than the conservative nationalist Irish Volunteers, which drew its membership mainly from the Catholic middle classes and, in contrast to the Volunteers, 'women were involved in the organisation from the outset'.[25]

A year of crisis followed in 1914 when the Home Rule Bill was given royal assent and the UVF armed its recruits with 24,000 German rifles imported in the Larne gun-running on 24 April. In July and August 1914 the Volunteers' director of arms, Michael J. O'Rahilly (The O'Rahilly), together with Erskine Childers and Darrell Figgis, organised the importation of approximately 1,500 vintage Mauser single-shot rifles and 45,000 rounds of ammunition from Germany. The arms were taken from Hamburg by tugboat and transferred to two yachts off the Irish coast. Erskine Childers piloted the *Asgard* into Howth harbour on 26 July, where Frank Henderson, newly appointed non-commissioned officer (NCO) of 'F' Company, 2nd Battalion, Dublin Brigade, was among the Volunteers who 'helped to load lorries of the rifles on to the pier'.[26]

As the Volunteers left Howth and began their march back to Dublin, they encountered 'police and military' on the Malahide Road. The column halted, and while the leaders 'parleyed with the police', Bulmer Hobson ordered Henderson's rearguard to 'get away through the fields as quietly as possible'[27] According to Éanna Henderson 'some [arms] were dumped into my father's own house in Fairview. They took up the boards and dumped them there. And my uncle, a younger brother of my father's, [was] playing the pipes when this was going on. Now, [Frank] was well prepared,' his son smiled. 'He had a uniform and a rifle' and was engaged in 'intensive' drilling, marching and 'mock battles' in the Dublin mountains under the instruction of his officers and 'some ex-British soldiers'.

In the summer of 1914, Jack Shouldice was appointed 1st lieutenant of 'F' Company, in Edward Daly's 1st Battalion, Dublin Brigade. His son suggested that his appointment as an officer was influenced by the fact that, at the age of thirty-three, Shouldice 'was slightly older than a lot of the other guys and also he was "a name" because of his prowess with the GAA'. 'Half of the company,'

Jack Shouldice noted, 'were members of the Gaelic League, and about one-third were members of the GAA.' 'Practically all' of the brigade, battalion and company officers of the Volunteers were members of the IRB.[28] As a captain in the 2nd Battalion, Frank Henderson was atypical in that he continued to refuse requests from the IRB to join its ranks.

Frank Henderson and Josephine Ní Bhraonáin 1918 (*courtesy of Fr Éanna Henderson*)

The outbreak of war in Europe in August 1914 temporarily defused the Ulster situation, and Home Rule was suspended for the duration of the conflict. In a gesture calculated to galvanise Asquith into placing Home Rule on the statute books, John Redmond rallied Irish recruits to the British war effort. His words precipitated a split in the Volunteer movement. The majority of approximately 181,000 Volunteers who supported Redmond's recruitment policy became known as the National Volunteers, while the dissenting 11,000 under Eoin MacNeill retained the name Irish Volunteers.[29] 'It was heartbreaking,' wrote

Henderson, who estimated that sixty of the 100 members of 'F' Company 'went with Redmond'.[30]

The IRB retained almost complete control of the Irish Volunteers and, on 9 September 1914, a small inner circle of the IRB (the Supreme Council) decided in principle that 'difficulty' for Britain presented by war in Europe offered the 'opportunity' to launch a nationwide rebellion, using Eoin Mac-Neill's Volunteers. In the words of P. S. O'Hegarty: 'it was the Supreme Council of the IRB which decided the insurrection, planned it, organised it, led it and financed it'.[31] They sought financial support from Clan na Gael, an Irish republican organisation in America, and military assistance from Imperial Germany. In May 1915 the Executive of the Supreme Council of the IRB established a military committee (the Military Council) consisting initially of Pearse, Joseph Plunkett and Éamonn Ceannt, and later Thomas Clarke, Seán MacDermott, James Connolly and Thomas MacDonagh.[32] The planning was placed in the hands of a few men, and shrouded in secrecy.

Membership of the Irish Volunteers remained small following the split, so the IRB seized the occasion of the funeral of veteran Fenian Jeremiah O'Donovan Rossa on 1 August 1915 to manufacture a large public demonstration. Patrick Pearse, dressed in the fern-green Volunteer uniform, delivered the oration at the graveside and, claiming to speak on behalf of the new generation 're-baptised in the Fenian faith', he made a defiant statement of revolutionary intent:

> Life springs from death and from the graves of patriot men and women spring living nations ... The defenders of this realm ... think they have pacified Ireland ... the fools, the fools, the fools, they have left us our Fenian dead and while Ireland holds these graves Ireland unfree shall never be at peace.[33]

For Jack Shouldice, Pearse's rhetoric was rather 'remote,' but for many in attendance his words were 'an outstanding statement of the gospel of Irish freedom and nationality'.[34] The text of the oration was disseminated in the nationalist press and 'soon became a favourite recitation at [nationalist] concerts and social entertainments all around the country', thus provoking a 'renewed interest in the Volunteers'.[35]

By January 1916 the Military Council had decided on Sunday 23 April as the date for the planned insurrection, but most of the IRB Supreme Council was oblivious to the specifics of the plan. Eoin MacNeill, who was not a member of the IRB, was kept in the dark because they felt he would not call his small force into action except in the event of a crisis. In the words of MacNeill's grandson, Michael McDowell:

> He wasn't a person who was interested in violence for its own sake … He was not interested in making a blood sacrifice … His view was that you could only issue force if it was morally justified, but to be morally justified it had to have a reasonable chance of succeeding.

MacNeill became alarmed during the first week of April 1916, when Patrick Pearse, as the Volunteers' director of military organisation, issued orders for three days of manoeuvres at Easter. Pearse, however, allayed his fears, denying that an insurrection was planned. In the meantime, Henderson and Shouldice were involved in the 'nitty gritty' of training and organising. Chris Shouldice explained, 'My father was responsible for drilling his corps of men. … They met regularly and had lectures and that kind of thing', but for the rank and file of the Volunteers the prospect of an armed insurrection was still remote. As the Military Council finalised plans for an insurrection, the lectures became more practical in nature and Shouldice's company 'had lessons on street fighting.' Meetings were held at brigade headquarters at No. 2 Dawson Street in the spring of 1916, during which 'discipline was emphasised' and 'the importance of the closed mouth was very successfully instilled into the men'.[36] Without 'being told in actual words', the officers in attendance gradually came to the realisation that there 'would be a rising soon'.[37] According to Éanna Henderson:

> My father wasn't terribly keen about parting with too much information or speaking about himself, but he did tell me about an occasion a few weeks before the Rising when [the officers] were addressed by Pearse. He said, 'Is every man here prepared to meet his God? … If not, now is the time to get out' … They knew this could be life or death, and they were prepared to do it. That shows that there was a great sense of purpose.

The Military Council continued to deceive MacNeill. On 17 April its seven members approved both the draft Proclamation of the Irish Republic and the circulation of the so-called 'Castle Document' – a secret document, purported to have been leaked from Dublin Castle, which set out a plan to suppress the Volunteers and arrest its leadership.[38] On Wednesday 19 April, while this sensational document distracted public attention, the Volunteer officers received word that the Rising would begin on Easter Sunday.

Jack Shouldice told his son that when Harry Boland informed him of the plans, he never imagined that it would end in failure:

> He got quite irritated when people talked about the 'blood sacrifice'. The men that were fighting didn't see it that way at all. They were making a stand and they were part of a national movement. They were well trained, and fighting against what was largely a conscripted army unfamiliar with street fighting. [Furthermore] their initial instructions provided for a retreat to the country. My father was part of the key route up from the quays … past the Broadstone station and out to the north side, where they [would] link up with the people in Ashbourne. So, in fact, they didn't see themselves as being hemmed in or cooped up in buildings. That was kind of forced on them by the loss of the *Aud* and MacNeill's countermanding order.

The events which ultimately led to the Volunteers' 'complete immobilisation' in buildings in the city were set in train when Bulmer Hobson informed MacNeill on Holy Thursday of the preparations for insurrection.[39] Incensed, the Volunteer leader confronted Patrick Pearse who, on this occasion, confirmed the Military Council's plans. MacNeill immediately wrote a series of orders cancelling the manoeuvres organised for Easter Sunday. Seán MacDermott, however, argued convincingly that the planned countrywide uprising had every prospect of success, because of the imminent arrival of Sir Roger Casement in Kerry with a consignment of 20,000 German rifles. Realising that he was too late to prevent the uprising, and still convinced of the veracity of the Castle Document, MacNeill ordered Hobson to hold the countermanding orders.

On Saturday morning, Frank Henderson's brother Leo, also an officer in the 2nd Battalion and – unlike his brother – a member of the IRB, told him that Roger Casement had been arrested at Banna Strand in Tralee Bay.

James Connolly summoned an emergency meeting of the Military Council and in the afternoon they learned that the *Aud* had been scuttled near Cork Harbour and its precious cargo lost. Michael J. O'Rahilly gave Eoin MacNeill the news and also conveyed his suspicions that the Castle Document was a forgery and that Hobson had been kidnapped by the IRB.[40] After a third confrontation with Pearse at St Enda's, MacNeill convened an emergency meeting of members of the central executive and the headquarters staff of the Volunteers. He told them that 'the enterprise was madness and would mean the slaughter of unarmed men and that it was his bounden duty to try and stop it'.[41] Accordingly, he dispatched couriers, including The O'Rahilly and Min Ryan, to deliver an order countermanding the nationwide mobilisation, and he personally organised its publication in the *Sunday Independent*:

> Owing to the very critical position, all orders given to Irish Volunteers for tomorrow, Easter Sunday, are hereby rescinded, and no parades, marches or other movement of Irish Volunteers will take place. Each individual Volunteer will obey this order strictly in every particular.[42]

Michael McDowell feels that his grandfather, Eoin MacNeill, would have considered the deception dishonourable, but for the Military Council it was 'a small sideshow in the greater project of staging a revolution against British rule'.

For Shouldice and the other Volunteer officers, the countermanding order provoked 'surprise and disappointment' and caused 'complete disorganisation'.[43] Determined not to abandon the plans for an insurrection, the Military Council resolved to postpone the planned rising until the following day, and sent dispatch carriers, mainly women, with messages to that effect around the country. At the same meeting in Liberty Hall, they finalised the draft Proclamation of the Irish Republic and Patrick Pearse was appointed to the posts of president of the Provisional Government of the Irish Republic and commandant general of the Army of the Irish Republic. Early on Easter Monday morning, Captain Frank Henderson received orders from his vice-commandant, Tom Hunter, 'to set the mobilisation scheme in order'. 'There was no doubt then,' Henderson wrote, 'as to what was going to happen.'[44] The Volunteers would go out at midday, seize a number of public buildings and proclaim an Irish Republic. The confusion caused by the conflicting orders, however, meant that the Rising was confined almost exclusively to the capital city, Dublin.

The Easter Rising in Dublin
Monday 24 April 1916

On Easter Monday morning, approximately 1,500 Volunteers and more than a hundred members of the ICA gathered at their prearranged assembly points in the city. Their numbers were severely depleted because of the confusion of the countermand, and only 'a quarter' of Jack Shouldice's company paraded at Colmcille Hall in Blackhall Street. The Women's Section of the ICA assembled as combatants, and members of Cumann na mBan offered their valuable services as couriers and nurses and in the provision of food for the rebels. Some would also take up arms during Easter Week, relieving exhausted or wounded Volunteers at their posts.

The Dublin Division of the Irish Volunteers was organised into four battalions. Fifty men of the 1st Battalion mustered at the Gaelic League hall in Blackhall Street under Commandant Edward Daly. Seán Heuston took the depleted 'D' Company to occupy the Mendicity Institution on the south quays of the River Liffey, and Jack Shouldice was among those who moved out to occupy the area around the Four Courts on Inns Quay to the north of the city. According to Chris Shouldice:

> They had lessons in street fighting in the weeks before 1916, and Daddy got to know the area around North King Street very well … they had it all worked out beforehand so they knew exactly where they were supposed to build the barricade and post the snipers … So on the Monday they were able to get stuck in straight away.

Most of Thomas MacDonagh's 2nd Battalion gathered at St Stephen's Green. Their orders were to occupy Jacob's Biscuit Factory (now the National Archives) and Bishop Street to the south of the city centre. In the meantime, Tom Weafer prepared to lead a column of the 2nd Battalion, which included the Henderson brothers, from Father Mathew Park in Fairview into the city centre. In the afternoon Leo Henderson's advance guard engaged British troops approaching from Dollymount, and Frank's rearguard seized premises commanding Tolka Bridge. Just before midday, Éamon de Valera led the 130 men of the 3rd Battalion from Earlsfort Terrace towards Boland's Mills and Bakery to the south-east of the city, while the 4th Battalion, under Éamonn Ceannt, moved out from Emerald Square to occupy the South Dublin Union to the south-west. Con Colbert's men seized an outpost at Watkins' Brewery, and Captain Séamus Murphy took command at Jameson's Distillery in Marrowbone Lane. The people of Dublin, familiar with the sight of 'men, going around carrying arms in military formation', no doubt assumed that this was just another exercise.[45]

The ICA gathered at Liberty Hall under Commandant James Connolly. Commandant Michael Mallin led 100 men and women of the ICA towards St Stephen's Green, and a small detachment under Captain Seán Connolly was deployed to occupy City Hall and its surrounding streets. Those who remained followed James Connolly, Joseph Plunkett, Patrick Pearse, Tom Clarke and Seán MacDermott, now styled as the Provisional Government of the Irish Republic, to the General Post Office (GPO) on O'Connell Street, which had been selected as Volunteer headquarters.

At midday, Paddy O'Daly and thirty men who had been selected from the ranks of Na Fianna Éireann, the Volunteers and the ICA disarmed the guards at the Magazine Fort in the Phoenix Park. Their intention was to seize the weapons and blow up the building as a signal that the uprising had begun. They failed, however, to gain access to the main arms store and the endeavour resulted only in a muted explosion and the death of the Fort commander's son, George Playfair.[46] As O'Daly's men dispersed to their positions, Seán Connolly's unit attacked Dublin Castle, shooting an unarmed guard and overpowering the six soldiers in the guardroom, but their momentary hesitation allowed time for the gates to be closed and the rebels retreated to the City Hall, where they took up positions on the roof.

Michael Mallin began the occupation of St Stephen's Green at midday. His second-in-command, Constance Markievicz, arrived shortly afterwards and the garrison began digging trenches and commandeering vehicles to build barricades. They secured the Royal College of Surgeons, but the depleted ranks made the proposed occupation of the Shelbourne Hotel at the north-east corner of the park untenable. While Mallin's men secured the Green, 'F' Company, under Frank Fahy, had gained entry to the Four Courts, and Jack Shouldice and his men were erecting barricades at the junction of Church Street and North King Street. He told his son that his company 'was among the first to see action' when a troop of fifty mounted cavalrymen of the 5th and 12th Lancers came under fire from the rebels and took refuge in the Medical Mission in Chancery Place: 'Daddy said he claimed the lance [of one of the fallen soldiers], wedged it into a grate … tied their tricolour to the top of it [and] … was very proud' of the fact that 'it was still fluttering' even after the surrender.

Joseph Plunkett's sister, Geraldine, and her new husband, Thomas Dillon, watched from their window in the Imperial Hotel in O'Connell Street as the headquarters battalion charged the GPO, expelled its frightened staff and took a number of prisoners. As George Plunkett led the Kimmage garrison towards the Volunteer headquarters, Desmond Ryan, Éamonn Bulfin and Frank Burke of 'E' Company (Pearse's Own), 4th Battalion were making their way to the city by tram from Rathfarnham. They arrived in O'Connell Street in time to see a troop of the 6th Reserve Cavalry Regiment withdraw in the face of rebel fire. Less than an hour later, Lieutenant Bulfin hoisted the green flag bearing the inscription 'Irish Republic' over the GPO, just as Desmond FitzGerald arrived at Volunteer headquarters. Like The O'Rahilly, FitzGerald had been unconvinced by the decision to proceed with the rebellion but, according to his son, Garret FitzGerald, 'the fact that they opposed the Rising was irrelevant [because] once they had trained people knowing they were going out to fight, they had to be there too'. The O'Rahilly took command of the prisoners in the GPO, and FitzGerald became the guardian of the garrison's provisions. At 12.45 p.m. Pearse emerged from the GPO under a guard provided by Diarmuid Lynch and George Plunkett and read the Proclamation of the Provisional Government of the Irish Republic to the surprised citizens gathered in the spring sunshine.[47] The Irish Republic 'as a sovereign Independent State' was thus proclaimed and a provisional government declared.

By Monday afternoon the rebels had fortified six garrisons in the city with relatively little bloodshed. Captain Seán Connolly was a notable exception. As dusk settled over the city, he was 'mortally wounded by a sniper's bullet from the Castle'.[48] ICA member Brigid Davis never washed her uniform afterwards because, according to her daughter, it bore a 'faded stain marking the place where she had cradled [Connolly's] body on her shoulder'.

Tuesday 25 April

After darkness fell, the garrison in City Hall was besieged by troops from Dublin Castle: 'Bullets and bursting grenades smashed and exploded into the ground floor' and Dr Kathleen Lynn, as the senior ICA officer, was forced to surrender.[49] Overnight, the military authorities reinforced their Dublin garrison with 3,000 reserves from Belfast and the Curragh. At dawn, British forces in the Shelbourne Hotel opened fire on Mallin's men in St Stephen's Green and forced their retreat to the College of Surgeons. MacDonagh's garrison in Jacob's was surrounded by an angry mob of civilians who shouted abuse at the rebels, but all was relatively quiet in the GPO except for the looters' 'boisterous carnival of destruction' in the streets outside.[50]

On Tuesday afternoon Connolly realised that he needed more men to secure the Metropole Hotel and to reinforce the garrisons in the city. He sent a request for reinforcements to Thomas Ashe, commandant of the 5th (Fingal) Battalion in Finglas, who sent twenty men into the city. At his outpost in Fairview, Captain Frank Henderson received a similar handwritten request. As he and his sixty-six men arrived under the portico of Volunteer headquarters, with their khaki-clad British prisoners, they came under fire from the garrison in the Imperial Hotel. The shooting stopped only when Connolly, 'dressed in the dark green uniform of the Citizen Army', dashed out into O'Connell Street shouting and waving his hands over his head.[51]

On Connolly's orders, the Henderson brothers took twenty men to occupy outposts in Henry Street and the remainder were sent to reinforce the garrisons in the Imperial and Metropole hotels. The brothers were directed to create entries at two different points into the buildings flanking the GPO. 'Of course, there was danger from then on,' Éanna Henderson said. They worked through the night and by Wednesday morning they 'had a passage right through to the post office'.[52] The creation of this interior communications line gave the rebels a strategic position in the Coliseum Theatre commanding the approach from Moore Street and with a view up to Parnell Street.[53]

Éanna Henderson was surprised to learn that his mother, Josephine, 'paid a visit' to the GPO that Tuesday. 'My father knew that there was going to be a rising and I suppose he must have told [her] that they might not survive the arrest.' When her son inquired about how she got to the GPO, Josephine told him:

> She just went down to Church Street with some medals and a crucifix from Stanhope Street Convent. When she reached the position of the Four Courts garrison she met [Captain] Fionán Lynch, who she knew through the Gaelic League, and he allowed her through the barricades. She ran up Mary Street, running all the time. She heard the shots but just kept going. She was that type of person.
>
> When she reached the GPO she knocked on the door and Dad came down and said, 'Would you get the hell out of here, there's going to be holy murder', or something like that. He appointed one of the Volunteers to guide her across to the side door of the GPO and Moore Street and left her there to fend for herself after that. So it's lucky she got away because the intensity began then. She was a very brave woman, even in later life … She would do anything, you know.

More British reinforcements arrived on Tuesday afternoon, and by evening there were over 6,000 British officers and men in the city. Martial law was declared in both Dublin city and county, and that evening Captain J. C. Bowen-Colthurst arrested three civilians, including pacifist and journalist Francis Sheehy-Skeffington. All three were shot at Portobello Barracks the next day. According to Micheline Sheehy-Skeffington, her grandfather had simply been 'trying to prevent people looting. It was a real tragedy and I can still feel the tragedy of it all.'

Wednesday 26 April

A British gunboat sailed up the Liffey on Tuesday night, and early on Wednesday morning it began shelling the empty Liberty Hall. On the same day martial law was extended throughout the country for an indefinite period and official orders were issued instructing soldiers to shoot any individual suspected of being a rebel, uniformed or otherwise, who was armed and not surrendering.[54]

On Wednesday morning Seán Heuston's men, trapped inside the Mendicity

Institution, were forced to surrender. There was also vicious fighting at Mount Street Bridge on the south side of the city, where a handful of Volunteers from Éamon de Valera's 3rd Battalion engaged two battalions of Sherwood Foresters from Kingstown for five hours, with heavy casualties on both sides.

Paddy O'Daly was wounded in the Four Courts in the afternoon and taken to Richmond Hospital, while the men on the barricades in Church Street and North King Street were subjected to sustained sniper fire. Incendiary shells in O'Connell Street set the street ablaze, and fires raged through large parts of Dublin for the next three days.

Thursday 27 April

By Thursday the crown forces had regained a strong grip on the city. They had recaptured the Mendicity Institution, laid siege to the Four Courts, and the men in North King Street were engaged in intensive house-to-house fighting with the South Staffordshire Regiment. Éamonn Ceannt's garrison at the South Dublin Union also came under fierce attack on Thursday, during which Vice-Commandant Cathal Brugha was severely wounded. He would not have survived his 'twenty-five' shrapnel wounds, his grandson Cathal Brugha observed, 'except that he was extraordinarily fit'. Jameson's Distillery was surrounded, while in the GPO, Pearse maintained morale with the fiction that the country was in general insurrection, German U-boats were on their way and the 'vast bulk' of Dubliners were behind the republicans. This illusion began to shatter in the afternoon, however, when James Connolly was wounded twice and the area around the GPO came under heavy artillery fire. On Thursday night Frank Henderson received an order to withdraw to the GPO 'as an attack on the main positions appeared to be imminent'. He and his men were posted to various positions 'facing O'Connell Street' which appeared to be 'a blazing inferno'.[55]

Friday 28 April

By Friday morning, Major Sir John Maxwell had arrived in Dublin as commander-in-chief of the forces in Ireland. Lines of communication between rebel outposts were fractured, and the men and women in Jacob's, who had seen little action, believed they were winning the battle. Michael Mallin's sustained optimism and competent leadership similarly encouraged the men and women in the College of Surgeons. On Friday afternoon, Thomas Ashe and his second-in-command, Richard Mulcahy, led the men of the 5th Battalion at the Battle of Ashbourne. The men of North County Dublin captured the police barracks and engaged RIC reinforcements at Rath Cross before taking ninety prisoners. At the same time, Jack Shouldice's small garrison of twenty men was struggling to defend its outpost at 'Reilly's Fort', a public house at the junction of Church Street and North King Street. From Friday morning until noon the next day, they came under incessant fire from the South Staffordshire Regiment under Lieutenant Colonel Henry Taylor. The gunfire was relentless, Shouldice recalled, and their rifles 'jammed from the continuous firing'.[56]

The shelling on O'Connell Street continued on Friday, and Éamonn Bulfin remembered that, after the first direct hit at 3 p.m., the upper floors of the GPO were quickly engulfed by fire. The 'hoses were useless', Henderson recalled, and when the fires became uncontainable, it was clear to the garrison that the prospect of a glorious last stand was impossible.[57] The evacuation was organised in three stages. The O'Rahilly led a front guard to secure possession of a new headquarters at the Williams and Woods factory on Parnell Street. In a charge down Moore Street, many of his men, including Henry Coyle, Patrick O'Connor, Paddy Shortis and Michael Mulvihill, were killed, while The O'Rahilly himself slowly bled to death in a lane off Moore Street. Frank Burke was among the second batch of evacuees 'who dashed in one's and two's into Henry Lane … the bullets like hailstones, hopping on the street'.[58] In the meantime, Frank Henderson had answered MacDermott's request to ensure that any remaining men in the Metropole Hotel were evacuated to the GPO, and on his return he helped James Connolly's aide-de-camp, Diarmuid Lynch, to move explosives to the basement, before evacuating with the Pearse brothers and George Plunkett.[59] He told his son that he was 'among the last twelve to escape'.

The evacuating Volunteers came under heavy fire from the British barricades as they crossed to Moore Lane, and seventeen men were wounded. The remainder of the rebels were led into Moore Street by the young Fianna Éireann officer Seán McLoughlin, who directed them to the relative safety of a terrace of houses under the cover of a large van pulled from a nearby yard. Seventeen-year-old future Taoiseach Seán Lemass would never forget his entry into Moore Street, which 'was littered with dead people, including … men, women, and children who had tried to leave their homes'.[60]

Saturday 29 April

On Saturday morning, the GPO was still smouldering, and its exhausted former garrison continued to break through the internal walls of houses in Moore Street towards Parnell Street. No. 16 was chosen as the rebel headquarters, and Pearse, James Connolly, Joseph Plunkett, Thomas Clarke and Seán MacDermott, the members of the Provisional Government who had escaped from the GPO, assembled a council of war. At midday, they made the decision to seek surrender terms, and shortly afterwards Cumann na mBan member Nurse Elizabeth O'Farrell left under a flag of truce to deliver the message to the commander of the British forces in the O'Connell Street area. At 2.30 p.m. Brigadier General Lowe took Pearse's surrender in Parnell Street, after which he was escorted to meet General John Maxwell.[61] The commandant general of the Army of the Irish Republic signed a general order instructing the rebels to surrender, and Connolly, who had been taken to a Red Cross hospital in Dublin Castle, countersigned the order as commander of the ICA.

According to Éanna Henderson, the head-quarters garrison was marched from Moore Street 'out onto Henry Street, around the corner, up before the Gresham [Hotel] and lined up there. [They were] searched and names taken. My father was beside Plunkett [and] Seán Mac-Dermott.' During Saturday afternoon, Nurse O'Farrell, accompanied by a priest and Captain Henry de Courcy Wheeler, staff captain to General Lowe, carried the surrender order to the various posts in the city. She met Edward Daly at the Four Courts and he led his men, including

Nurse Elizabeth O'Farrell
(*courtesy of Kilmainham Gaol Museum*)

Jack and Frank Shouldice, to the Rotunda, where the military officers in charge were 'aggressive and insulting' and 'responded with the butt of their rifles to any protests'.[62] The Shouldice and Henderson brothers spent Saturday night on the small green outside the Rotunda Gardens. In his witness statement, Henderson recalled the 'night of horror', during which they could hear 'the intermittent firing from the tower of the Rotunda Hospital' and 'the shrieks of the patients inside who appeared to have gone out of their minds'.[63] 'It was cold,' his son added, and 'they [were] not allowed even to relieve themselves. One of the officers was a bit rough with Tom Clarke, [who] I think was half stripped, but the Volunteers got him down in Wexford during the War of Independence.'[64]

The next morning O'Farrell went first to St Stephen's Green and then to Boland's Mills. After consultation with Éamonn Ceannt at the South Dublin Union, Thomas MacDonagh surrendered to General Lowe and the Tricolour at Jacob's was hauled down at about 5 p.m. Richard Mulcahy arrived under escort from the 5th Battalion in Ashbourne to confirm the surrender with an imprisoned Pearse, and returned with the news to Thomas Ashe and his bitterly disappointed North County Dublin Volunteers. 'They were so completely mesmerised by their own success' at Ashbourne, Risteárd Mulcahy explained, 'and they probably projected that onto the whole rebellion'. The Fingal men were arrested and marched under military escort 'like near relatives at a funeral', five miles to Swords for transport to the city.[65]

AFTERMATH

On the morning of Sunday 30 April, the men at the Rotunda were marched through the city to Richmond Barracks in Inchicore. To Jack Shouldice, the 'heart of the city presented a picture of utter desolation'.[66] He and Leo Henderson were among the 'black sheep' separated from the main body of Volunteers in the gymnasium of Richmond Barracks.[67] Chris Shouldice felt that his father 'was singled out [because] he was well known from his GAA record and he was still wearing his uniform. It was afterwards that they found out his rank and that led to his court martial.' Éanna Henderson's father was luckier: 'He still had Connolly's handwritten dispatch order in his pocket' and, knowing that he would be searched, 'he tore it up and put it into the fireplace and hated to have to do it'. Henderson was among the rank and file that marched through the dark city to the North Wall on Sunday night. They were transported to Holyhead by cattle boat and then to Stafford Prison. Henderson remembered seeing the morning newspapers, which declared the end of the 'Seven Days' War'. 'The fact that they referred to our fight as a "War",' he wrote, 'helped to cheer us somewhat.'[68]

During Easter Week 1916, 485 people died, the majority of whom were civilians; much of O'Connell Street was reduced to rubble; and the rebels were perceived by a disapproving public as a small, unrepresentative group who had engaged in 'an inglorious and disgraceful outbreak of organised rowdyism'.[69] Newspapers variously interpreted the Rising as 'a Shinners [Sinn Féin] Rising' or a 'mad orgy' led by nationalist-socialist leader James Connolly.[70] 'The Volunteers were jeered at when they were going to the docks,' Éanna Henderson explained, 'and it was understandable. The people at the time had got so used to the British and here this crowd of yahoos was disturbing it.'

The British Army command was determined to make an example of the leaders, and Jack Shouldice was one of the 'marked men' tried by field general court martial in secret without defence lawyers.[71] Thomas Clarke, Thomas MacDonagh and Patrick Pearse were found guilty of taking part in an armed rebellion and waging war against the King, and sentenced to death on 3 May. *The Irish Times* offered its full support for the execution of the leaders, because 'the safety of the whole kingdom and the peace of Ireland is at stake'.[72] The *Irish Independent* claimed, 'we are not advocates of undue severity but undue leniency to some of the worst firebrands would be just as bad'.[73] Joseph Plunkett, Michael O'Hanrahan, Edward Daly and William Pearse were executed in Kilmainham Gaol in Dublin on 4 May. John MacBride, vice commandant of the 2nd Battalion, was executed on 5 May, and two days later Jack Shouldice was moved to Kilmainham to await the verdict of his court martial. According to his son, he was 'put into the same cell as Mallin and Ceannt', and he said that both 'were fully resigned, and happy in fact, awaiting their fate in the morning'.[74] Michael Mallin, Éamonn Ceannt, Seán Heuston and Con Colbert were executed at dawn on 8 May and on the following day Thomas Kent's sentence of death was carried out by firing squad in Cork. Chris Shouldice has often tried to imagine how his father must have felt in his cell in Kilmainham, 'waiting and listening to the volleys in the stone breakers' yard'. In Jack Shouldice's words:

> Every morning at dawn for the few days I was detained there I was awakened by the executions of two or three of the leaders at a time. We were in doubt as to our own fate until … an officer came along to our cells and read out our sentences. Mine was 'that I was sentenced to death – a pause – but the officer presiding at the court-martial had commuted the sentence to 5 years penal servitude'. That was some relief, though at the time I was prepared for anything after the executions of our comrades and leaders.[75]

The ferocity of the British response shocked the public, and on 11 May, Home Rule MP John Dillon told the House of Commons:

> What is happening is that thousands of people in Dublin, who ten days ago were bitterly opposed to the whole Sinn Féin movement and to the rebellion, are now becoming infuriated against the government on account of these executions, and, as I am informed by letters received this morning, that feeling is spreading throughout the country in a most dangerous degree.[76]

Seán MacDermott and James Connolly were the last to die in Kilmainham, on 12 May. Sir Roger Casement was tried in London for high treason and hanged at Pentonville Prison on 3 August. Irish MP Arthur Lynch's response was representative of the change in popular opinion, when he said that he 'could not withhold [his] admiration for the extraordinary courage and devotion of the young leaders … Whatever politicians may say of their wisdom and judgement, they will inevitably take their place in the gallery of Irish heroes and martyrs.'[77]

Jack Shouldice was transferred to Mountjoy Prison, where he appreciated the relative comfort of a bed, a hot bath and a change of clothes and, following a week of uncertainty, was among 'a batch of twelve' prisoners, including Éamon de Valera and Harry Boland, put on a cargo vessel bound for Holyhead. A train took them to Dartmoor Prison, where Shouldice remained until Christmas, after which he was moved to Lewes Prison for the last six months of his imprisonment. Jack told his son about the arrival at Dartmoor of 'Major General MacNeill, who had originally been a kind of "bad boy" because he had countermanded the order for the Rising on the Easter Sunday':

> [Jack] didn't consider de Valera a marvellous military commander ... [and] was quietly critical of him [for not] reinforcing the people at Clanwilliam House when there was very heavy fighting at Mount Street Bridge. He felt that they had been hung out to dry a bit ... but de Valera, who was the senior officer in charge of the Irish Volunteers [in the prison] at the time, saw MacNeill coming and he called them all to order and saluted MacNeill ... Daddy said that was very strong [and] it sent a very strong message that they were together again as brothers. So he said that he liked de Valera very much for this.

In all, 3,400 people were arrested in the wake of the 1916 Rising, and 1,841 of these were interned.[78] In July 1916 Frank Henderson was transferred to Frongoch Internment Camp in North Wales. 'He survived that too,' his son said, 'and survived it well'. In fact, 'he enjoyed it' and 'got on well with the British', who were apparently 'amazed that the Irish weren't as wild as they were made out to be in the British press'. The internees were also 'planning and regrouping after the Rising' and the remote Welsh prison camp would become colloquially known as 'the University of Revolution'.

REORGANISATION

In Kevin Whelan's words, 'the Rising killed Home Rule and, at a stroke, dramatically widened the horizons of the politically possible'.[79] Redmond's failure to secure the implementation of Home Rule by the summer of 1916, and the continuing conflict with Edward Carson over Ulster's exclusion, increased public disillusionment with the IPP. They did little during the crucial period after the Rising to bolster popular support for constitutional nationalism while, conversely, Arthur Griffith's Sinn Féin party used the 1916 Rising as an effective recruiting and propaganda platform. A key constituent of the party's fresh intake was the tranche of internees released from Frongoch in the General Amnesty at Christmas 1916, and the rebels released from English jails in June 1917. Thus began a period of intense reorganisation, culminating in the Sinn Féin Ard-Fheis in October 1917. The political landscape was changing; faith in the monolithic Home Rule party was beginning to crumble and it would soon become clear that a limited measure of devolved power was no longer sufficient to satisfy nationalist aspirations.

The National Executive of the Volunteers was re-established in March 1917 and in October Éamon de Valera assumed the presidency of both the Volunteers and Sinn Féin. After his release in December 1916, Frank Henderson took command of 'F' Company and, together with Richard Mulcahy and Dick McKee, became a key figure in the reorganisation of the Dublin Volunteers. They procured arms, organised the funeral of Thomas Ashe, who had died while being force-fed on hunger strike in Mountjoy Prison in September 1917, and assisted the emerging Sinn Féin party at by-elections. Jack Shouldice was released in the summer of 1917. 'They got such a fantastic reception in Westland Row,' Chris Shouldice said. 'My father thought it was quite extraordinary considering the way they had been booed and jeered when they were being led off to prison.' He rejoined his company immediately, and in the summer of 1917 returned to Ballaghaderreen with Harry Boland to organise the Volunteers in East Mayo.

When, in March 1918, the decision was taken by Westminster to include Ireland in conscription to the British Army, Sinn Féin, reorganised under the leadership of Éamon de Valera, spearheaded a vigorous anti-conscription campaign. Jack Shouldice and Harry Boland narrowly escaped capture after an anti-conscription rally in Ballaghaderreen in April, but Frank Henderson was not so lucky. He was arrested for drilling in public in March and taken to Dundalk Gaol. After his release in May 1918, Henderson was appointed commandant of the 2nd Battalion under Brigadier Dick McKee, officer commanding the Dublin Brigade.

In the same month, the British uncovered a so-called 'German Plot' and organised the arrest of seventy anti-conscription agitators, most of whom were members of Sinn Féin. Jack Shouldice deputised as adjutant of the Dublin Brigade for Fionán Lynch after his arrest, and represented the brigade on the committee of the Volunteer Dependants' Fund (VDF). The failure of the German offensive in France in November relieved the pressing need for conscription and the alleged plotters were freed some months later. After the

'Conscription Crisis', however, the Sinn Féin party was popularly perceived as the voice of a resurgent nationalist Ireland and, in contrast, the IPP was exposed as, at best, conservative and ineffective.

THE WAR OF INDEPENDENCE

Popular support for Sinn Féin and its demand for an Irish Republic was reflected in its spectacular victory in the general election in December 1918, when it won 73 of a possible 105 parliamentary seats. Having declared that its elected MPs would abstain from Westminster, the thirty elected members of Sinn Féin who were not in prison met in the Mansion House in Dublin on 21 January 1919, declared a sovereign Irish Republic and established a parliament, Dáil Éireann, to legislate for all Ireland. On the same day, two members of the RIC were ambushed and killed at Soloheadbeg in County Tipperary by an Irish Volunteer unit; this marked the beginning of the Irish War of Independence. In February 1919 Michael Collins and Harry Boland organised the rescue of their president, Éamon de Valera, from Lincoln Gaol, and in June, de Valera travelled to America to raise funds and promote international recognition of the new Republic.

The Irish Volunteers and the IRB regrouped as the Irish Republican Army (IRA), a force created to buttress militarily the claim to independence. Michael Collins, the first Minister for Finance, organised a highly successful National Loan (Republican Bond) to finance the government, and the Sinn Féin courts were established as a parallel justice system. In addition to his military activities, Jack Shouldice was appointed a justice of the republican courts. In his son's words: 'He was involved in mostly local things about exporting cattle and butter to England. Firms and companies that were involved in it were gently, and sometimes not so gently, persuaded to stop it and to cut down trade altogether with England.'

The early stage of the Anglo-Irish War was characterised by the assassination of members of the RIC and concerted attacks on various RIC barracks. On 11 September 1919 Dáil Éireann was suppressed as an 'illegal assembly' and warrants were sworn out for all members; likewise, all national movements in Ireland were banned. The year 1920 saw larger-scale engagements with the RIC, which had been supplemented in March with several thousand British recruits dubbed 'The Black and Tans' because of their distinctive uniform, and these, in turn, were reinforced in August by the Auxiliaries ('Auxies'), a paramilitary force of ex-army officers who were attached as auxiliaries to the RIC. Unlike the urban insurrection of 1916, the War of Independence was concentrated in the countryside, where local Volunteer units and 'flying columns' employed hit-and-run guerrilla tactics overseen by the IRA's GHQ. Volunteer ambushes were countered by military reprisals and devastating brutalities were perpetrated by both sides. As IRA director of intelligence, Collins also coordinated an intricate intelligence network, and in July 1919 he established a special intelligence unit or 'Squad' – an elite group of Dublin Volunteers attached to the GHQ intelligence department and tasked with the elimination of spies and informers.

Chris Shouldice feels that his father 'was very active during the War of Independence but he didn't boast about it'. His brother Frank 'was arrested for his activities down in the west of Ireland', but Jack evaded capture because he was 'popular' and, 'like Collins, he was able to wander around Dublin. Although a lot of people knew him, no one ever grassed on him.' Disguise also helped, and 'at one stage he used to go around dressed as a priest'. Jack

Jack Shouldice and Elizabeth Merriman in 1918 (*courtesy of Chris Shouldice*)

Shouldice married Elizabeth Merriman on 31 October 1918, but, because he was 'on the run', the 'only place that he could meet my mother was at 10 o'clock mass in Fairview church'. Their son remembered being surprised when he learned that the old parish priest in Fairview, Fr Walter MacDonald, whom he considered 'a kind of gruff old man', had been a curate there in 1919 and 'made the vestry of the church' available to the newlyweds when 'they wanted to be together'.

Frank Henderson and Josephine Brennan were also married in 1918, and they settled at 75 North Circular Road. It was there, Éanna said, that 'the nine of us were born'. When the War of Independence escalated in June 1920 Henderson was appointed as assistant to Diarmuid O'Hegarty, director of organisation at IRA GHQ. He was an energetic administrator and visited IRA units in Wicklow, south Kildare, Wexford and Laois, and even though he had no first-hand involvement with the events in Dublin at the height of the War of Independence, he kept in close contact with the IRA leadership.[80] He had a close association, for example, with the officer commanding the Dublin Brigade, Dick McKee: 'He and my father would have been kindred spirits,' and 'my mother thought he was a grand fella.'[81]

Frank Henderson's son also recorded his family's shock after the events of what became known as 'Bloody Sunday'. In the early hours of 21 November 1920, Michael Collins' Squad and a unit of the Dublin Brigade assassinated fourteen alleged British intelligence agents in Dublin. In response, IRA prisoners Dick McKee and Peadar Clancy, and student Conor Clune, were killed in Dublin Castle. McKee's sister, Margaret, shared with Fr Éanna her distressing memories of being called down to Dublin Castle to identify his remains: 'She made no hesitation in saying that the whole atmosphere reeked of drink … They said that they were killed trying to escape [and] she saw they bayoneted them.'

The British reprisals continued in the afternoon of 21 November, when Black and Tans opened fire on spectators at a Gaelic football match in Croke Park. As secretary of the Leinster Council, Jack Shouldice had been in charge of the arrangements for the VDF-organised football match between Dublin and Tipperary in Jones Road Ground (Croke Park) at 3 o'clock that day. He recalled that the 'lorries of the raiders swooped down on the grounds and opened fire on the crowd and on the players'. Their scattered bullets found only one target among the players – Michael Hogan – but thirteen of the spectators were killed and up to a hundred more wounded in the 'mad scramble that followed'.[82] Shouldice narrowly escaped arrest when an Auxiliary officer who appeared to Jack 'a decent and sober man' told him quietly: 'There has been enough shooting and bloodshed here to-day and I advise you to get away as quickly as you can.' He 'obeyed the order with alacrity'.[83] They were 'exciting times', said Chris, but they were also 'very difficult' and 'tragic and he saw so many terrible things happening'.

Éamon de Valera returned from America in December 1920 and, concerned by international disapproval of 'the sledge hammer-ambushes' on RIC and military patrols, he advocated a spectacular show of force with which to enter negotiations with the British.[84] On 25 May 1921, in what was essentially a propaganda exercise, the IRA attacked the Custom House, the centre of local government in Dublin. Almost eighty members of the Dublin Brigade were arrested after a ferocious battle with crown forces, during which three civilians and five members of the IRA were killed and many more wounded.[85] The immediate consequence for Frank Henderson was that he was recalled to active duty and replaced the wounded Tom Ennis as commanding officer of the 2nd Battalion. A truce was declared on 11 July 1921, and during the truce period Henderson organised and commanded battalion training camps. In November he was appointed brigade and divisional adjutant.

THE TREATY AND CIVIL WAR

Éamon de Valera's discussions with British Prime Minister David Lloyd George in London in July 1921 resulted in a mutual agreement to engage in treaty negotiations. A sceptical de Valera sent a delegation to the Anglo-Irish conference on 11 October 1921 and, in the face of Lloyd George's 'threat of terrible and immediate war', the Irish plenipotentiaries signed the Articles of Agreement on 6 December 1921.[86] The British military garrison was to be withdrawn from Ireland and the RIC disbanded, but the British would retain three naval bases in Ireland. The Treaty conferred dominion status on the 'Irish Free State' and allowed for the partition of Ireland (instituted under the Government of Ireland Act, 1920), subject to the operation of an inter-governmental Boundary Commission.

The ensuing bitter dispute, which divided Sinn Féin, was not about partition but about the monarchy. The Treaty required that the Irish TDs swear an oath of allegiance to the British monarch. Hard-line republican TDs, such as Cathal Brugha and Éamon de Valera, viewed this as a betrayal of the men and women of 1916 and were most vehemently anti-Treaty. Michael Collins, on the other hand, argued that the Treaty offered 'not the ultimate freedom that all nations desire … but the freedom to achieve it'.[87] After a series of highly charged debates in December 1921 and January 1922, Dáil Éireann ratified the Treaty by a slender 64–57 vote. Éamon de Valera led the anti-Treaty TDs out of the Dáil, and Michael Collins and Arthur Griffith oversaw the establishment of a provisional Free State government and the formation of a National Army.

Like the Dáil, the military wing of the republican movement was split. The majority of IRA officers, including Frank and Leo Henderson, rejected the Treaty and repudiated the authority of the Provisional Government. On 14 April 1922 Rory O'Connor and Liam Mellows led 200 hard-line anti-Treatyites in an occupation of the Four Courts. Their aim was to draw an attack by the British, reignite the War of Independence and reunite Sinn Féin.

On 26 June Leo Henderson was arrested by pro-Treaty forces and the Four Courts garrison responded by abducting a Free State officer, J. J. 'Ginger' O'Connell. This, combined with the assassination of the ultra-loyalist Field Marshal Sir Henry Wilson in London four days earlier, meant that Collins came under significant pressure to respond with force. On 28 June 1922, on the expiration of Collins' ultimatum to the Four Courts garrison to surrender or be attacked, pro-Treaty troops opened fire on the building and ignited a civil war. Frank Henderson led anti-Treaty forces against their erstwhile comrades in O'Connell Street during two days of heavy fighting, before Oscar Traynor, the commandant of the Dublin Brigade IRA, issued the order to surrender. The IRA units around the country fractured, most siding with Chief of Staff Liam Lynch's anti-Treaty faction.

Frank Henderson was involved in the reorganisation of the IRA forces following the outbreak of Civil War and in August, after the arrest of Oscar Traynor, he became Dublin Brigade O/C with responsibility for IRA operations in Dublin. In July and August 1922 anti-Treaty strongholds in Cork and Kerry were taken by sea in a series of landings, which marked the end of the conventional phase of the Civil War. The subsequent guerrilla phase claimed its most prominent victim on 22 August 1922, when Michael Collins, the head of the Provisional Government and commander-in-chief of the National Army, was killed in an ambush in his native County Cork. W. T. Cosgrave was elected president of the Provisional Government and Richard Mulcahy succeeded Collins as commander-in-chief, overseeing the horrific era of reciprocal revenge killings that followed in the wake of Collins' death. Concerned at the continuing threat to the stability of the newly established state, Cosgrave and his Minister for Home Affairs, Kevin O'Higgins, implemented martial law, enacted legislation to set up military courts and embarked on a policy of executions.

The first anti-Treaty prisoners were executed in Dublin in November 1922 and, in response, Liam Lynch gave the order that any member of the Dáil who had voted for the 'murder legislation' was to be shot on sight.[88] Henderson was reluctant, and told Ernie O'Malley:

> Prominent supporters of the Free State government and Parliament were to have been shot and it was left to officers in charge of each area who was to have been shot … I didn't like that order … I could have shot Éamonn Duggan and Fionán Lynch, for they went home every night drunk but I left them alone. Seán McGarry was often drunk on Amiens St and the boys wanted to shoot him and the Staters there but I wouldn't let them.[89]

On 7 December 1922 the IRA assassinated pro-Treaty TD Seán Hales, outside Leinster House. The Free State responded by executing, without trial, IRA prisoners Rory O'Connor, Liam Mellows, Joe McKelvey and Richard Barrett. Kevin O'Higgins' granddaughter, Iseult O'Malley, felt that it was 'an appalling decision for anyone to [have to] make', particularly given the fact that Rory O'Connor had been her grandfather's best man at his wedding to Brigid Cole on 27 October 1921. 'The fratricidal nature of the conflict was appalling,' she said, and both sides 'came away with very bitter memories that took a long, long time to heal'. Frank Henderson explained that the shocking executions had the desired effect of stemming the IRA's executions policy, but he struggled with his conscience and 'over a period of sixteen years he asked his son [Fr Éanna Henderson] to say Mass for Seán Hales'.[90]

The Free State continued with its punitive policy, and by the end of the Civil War, seventy-seven republicans had been officially executed and many more were assassinated or killed in the field; the worst cases occurred in March 1923, when seventeen republican prisoners were killed using trap mines in Ballyseedy, Caherciveen and Killarney in County Kerry.

Neither Jack nor Frank Shouldice took any part in the Civil War, and Chris felt that the death of his father's close friend, Harry Boland, confirmed his neutrality after the Treaty:

> He was absolutely devastated when [anti-treaty TD] Harry was killed [by Free State soldiers] in Skerries in the early part of the Civil War [2 August 1922] … It

certainly drove a lot of the national sentiment out of him. Then, of course, Collins was killed. He had such revulsion at the loss of some of his friends and colleagues [and] the concept of Irishmen fighting Irishmen, and the awful things at Ballyseedy and these other places … absolutely revolted him. He said he never wanted to see a gun again in his life … [and] was glad to leave the political stage to become the full-time secretary to the Leinster Council of the GAA.

By the spring of 1923 the republican campaign had largely been reduced to the destruction of property and communications. Frank Henderson, who was captured on 10 March 1923, was one of approximately 12,000 republicans imprisoned during the Civil War. A month later, Liam Lynch was killed in action and his successor, Frank Aiken, called for a ceasefire and ordered the anti-Treaty forces to 'dump arms'.

In August the pro-Treaty Sinn Féin candidates, now organised as Cumann na nGaedheal, defeated the republican candidates at the polls and the Free State government began the process of rebuilding the shattered economy, infrastructure and confidence of the nascent state. However, the Civil War left damaging legacies, and the Irish nationalist parties were polarised and embittered. This was the setting into which Éanna Henderson was born in 1925. His father had found it difficult to rebuild a civilian career after his release in 1924, but by 1927 '[he] and Oscar Traynor and Cathal Brugha's brother-in-law, Charles Kingston, had founded the Fodhla Printing Company in Parnell Square'.[91]

In the same year, Jack Shouldice rejoined the civil service as a junior executive officer in the fisheries branch of the Department of Agriculture, and the anti-Treaty republicans entered politics as Fianna Fáil. De Valera's party came to power peacefully in 1932, a year after Chris Shouldice was born. By 1939 most of what they considered to be the objectionable features of the Treaty had been removed by acts of parliament, and Éamon de Valera maintained Ireland's neutrality successfully during the Second World War. Frank Henderson's family recorded their father's pleasure at a neutrality meeting in 1940, at which old adversaries shared a platform for the first time since the Civil War.[92]

In January 1950 Frank Henderson finally acquiesced to his son's request to write a personal memoir. The occasion was Fr Éanna Henderson's ordination to the priesthood, and for the devout Catholic 'a request made on such an occasion' was impossible to refuse.[93] Henderson prefaced his personal memoir by saying:

> I hesitate to write the events of my life, as I am not a person who performed any heroic deed. But as I happened to partake from beginning to end in the battle against the British Empire and as I happened to know most of the illustrious men and women who figured in the national movement, it would appear that I have knowledge of things and events which are worthwhile recalling.[94]

Frank Henderson passed away peacefully on 13 January 1959 and Jack Shouldice died six years later, 'just before the 50th anniversary of the 1916 Rising'. His son, Chris, remembered the funeral as a 'pretty huge affair' attended by the 'diminishing band' of the 1916 colleagues, 'quiet, decent men of passionate moderation':

> After the service, I was standing on the steps of the church and looking out across Fairview Strand. I noticed two old men wearing long coats and homburg hats standing close together and talking gravely. [I realised that] one was Éamon de Valera and the other was W. T. Cosgrave. And I just thought to myself what a wonderful final stroke [by] my father to bring together the old foes in commemoration of a former comrade-in-arms. I thought it was a very tearful moment apart from the general sadness.

Frank (*left*) and Jack Shouldice in the 1960s (*courtesy of Frank Shouldice jr*)

LONG SHADOWS

❧ EXECUTED LEADERS ❧

The images of the executed leaders of the 1916 Rising have been appropriated, revised and reimagined, and reside centrally in the collective memory of the Easter Rising. Posthumously, they assumed a potent symbolism that subsumed the reality of their roles as sons and brothers, fathers and uncles.

The stages of popular interpretation began with a sense that the rebel leaders were, in John Dillon's words, 'misguided' and the Rising part of a German plot.[1] It was condemned from the pulpit as 'a senseless, meaningless debauch of blood', and railed against by the conservative press as 'insane' and 'criminal'.[2] After the executions in the first weeks of May, this early interpretation of the rebel leaders was replaced by one of morally upstanding, devout and brave leaders of insurrection, which eased the transition from public hostility to deepest sympathy and moral outrage. It was also the beginning of a kind of popular beatification in the patriotic tradition. The leaders' personal stories were lost in the early hagiographies and depersonalised in post-1969 revisionist histories. In more recent studies, the personalities have been reinvested with humanity and hubris. However, as Michael Mallin's biographer, Brian Hughes, has noted:

> The wives and children left behind by the men executed in May 1916 have been regularly neglected by historiography. How widows coped with the sudden and tragic loss of a husband and a breadwinner, and how children grew up with the legacy of a martyred father, who in many cases they never really knew, are aspects of the history of the Rising that are rarely explored.[3]

Historian Sinéad McCoole has effectively addressed the lacuna in the historical record relating to the lives of the wives in her book, *Easter Widows*, but what

Henry Street in ruins in the aftermath of the 1916 Rising
(*courtesy of Mercier Archive*)

remains largely unexplored is the burden of loss and expectation placed on the children and the extended families of the executed leaders. For the second generation – the children of the revolutionaries – the immediate effect was often an undefined sense of displacement, or the vague awareness of a parent's often unspoken grief. In adulthood, the daughters and sons of a martyred revolutionary were often guided by their father's explicit requests or implicit expectations. For a niece or nephew, the family association was enough to render a childhood home the focus for military raids or stringent supervision, and their parents were often motivated to continue the struggle for independence in the names of their 'martyred' brothers. The potency of the family name was inescapable.

Michael Mallin's son and Con Colbert's niece and nephew, Joseph Plunkett's nephews and Edward Daly's nieces and nephew are at one remove from the generation that forged the path to revolution. Their understanding is derived both from family stories and nationalist narrative; public and private interpretations compete with and complement each other. Thomas MacDonagh's granddaughter, Éamonn Ceannt's grand-niece, Patrick Pearse's grand-nephews and James Connolly's great-grandson are more distantly removed from the personality and the period. Their childhoods were less disturbed by the echoes of war or a parent's imprisonment, and theirs is a diluted version of the story, distilled through subsequent experiences, collective memory and a vast historiography. For the third generation it is a complicated inheritance. A familial connection with the icons of modern Irish history is at once a reason for pride and a source of discomfort; it is both a birthright and a burden. It is in their voices that the stories of these men are now retold.

MICHAEL MALLIN

Silk weaver, musician, socialist and chief of staff of the ICA, Michael Mallin commanded the garrison at St Stephen's Green in 1916. When he was executed on 8 May in Kilmainham Gaol, he left behind a widow and five children, the eldest of whom was thirteen years old. For Agnes Mallin, who was five months pregnant in April 1916, the burden of responsibility and loss was particularly heavy. Mallin's almost unbearably poignant, four-page stream-of-consciousness last letter to his wife conveys the desperate grief endured by these men and their families:

> My darling wife, pulse of my heart, this is the end of all things earthly, sentence of death has been passed … I am prepared but … my heartstrings are torn to pieces when I think of you … of our manly James [Séamus], happy-go-lucky John [Seán], shy warm Una, dady's [*sic*] girl and oh, my little Joseph, my little man, my little man. Wife, dear wife, I cannot keep the tears back when I think of him. He will rest in my arms no more. To think I have to leave you to battle through the world with them without my help.[4]

Agnes Mallin's daughter, Maura Constance Mallin, was born on 19 August 1916 and from the moment of her birth 'the past shaped her future'.[5] There were protests by opponents of the Rising outside the Coombe Hospital on the day she was born, and even her name was reminiscent of her father's twin tenets of Catholicism and socialism. Her middle name was chosen in honour of her father's second-in-command, Constance Markievicz, and her first name was dictated by Mallin in his last moments with her mother. 'If it is a boy, call it "Michael" after me; if a girl, call it "Mary" after the Mother of God.'[6]

If Maura Mallin wore the indelible mark of her heritage, her siblings' destinies were also forged in their father's last moments. In his final letter to Agnes, he made explicit his expectations for their futures:

> God and his blessed mother, again and again, bless and protect you. Oh Saviour of mine, if my dear ones could die and enter Heaven with me how blessed and happy I would be. They would be away from the cares and trials of the world. Una my little one be a nun. Joseph, my little man, be a priest if you can. James and John, to you the care of your mother. Make yourselves good strong men for her sake.[7]

Fr Joseph Mallin explained that his older sister, Una, initially 'fiercely refused to accept' her father's wishes 'but then she suddenly went and joined the Loreto order in 1925'. She was to 'spend the rest of her life living and working in Spain'. For his part, Joseph 'always felt that [joining the priesthood] was not the thing I'd like to do but what I should do' and after his mother died in 1932, he fulfilled his father's last wish and joined the Jesuit order.[8] He insisted, however, that their decisions were not directed by their mother, who 'never spoke' to her children about her husband's last wishes – 'she left it alone completely'.

Neither did Agnes Mallin speak of her sorrow. The public scrutiny directed towards the families of the executed leaders, together with a desire on their part not to impose their grief on their young children, meant that the next generation rarely saw their mothers' tears. Interviewed in 2000, Maura Mallin said, 'my mother sighed, she didn't cry. I used to lie in bed looking at my father's photograph and wonder what would it have been like if he had lived. I always thought that my mother was the heroic one. She was the one left behind.'[9] Joseph also attested to his mother's 'heroism' and resilience, and suggested that perhaps 'it was wise of my mother in those years not to speak of my father … I think she didn't want to take away from my childhood by brooding on these things.'[10] He later said:

> I saw her crying once; that would have been in the early 1920s. My sister and I were playing, and I went into the kitchen and my mother was standing at the window. I can be very clear about the day – it was a fine May day. And I've often thought since, was it 8 May? That was the anniversary of when he was executed. I walked away, told my sister and we both kept quiet.[11]

His mother's anguish, Joseph feels, was born out of a sense of disbelief, 'because she never expected him to be executed', and her obvious love for her husband, which he found manifested in the yellowed pages of their early correspondence. The letters traversed continents because Mallin, who had joined the 21st Royal Scots Fusiliers as a drummer boy at fifteen years of age, was serving with the British Army in India. They kept up a regular, tender correspondence until his return to Dublin in 1902:

> He didn't talk too much [about] politics [in the letters]. It was about family [and] her father [Fenian Joseph Hickey] who died rather early. [But it is clear that] he was terribly fond of my mother … Oh! He would do anything for her.
>
> [You can also see] from his writings, that his time in India provoked a bitter opposition to the Empire business. I think he felt that he had been tricked. He was young [and] he was terribly attracted to the music. He reacted, I suppose, to the things he saw in India. I've seen the old colonial spirit [too] in the early days [as a missionary] in Hong Kong: the complete dismissal of the other peoples there.

Mallin's service with the British Army, during which he witnessed extremes of social injustice and inequality, proved a significant radicalising influence. He returned to Ireland with an anti-imperialistic and socialist agenda, and his military career afforded him the expertise that was to prove so valuable in subsequent years.

Agnes Hickey married Michael Mallin in April 1903 and he secured work as a silk weaver in Atkinson's Poplin factory in Dublin. As was the case in most of Dublin's factories at the turn of the century, the conditions for workers were appalling and, in an effort to effect some improvement, the young socialist from the working-class area of the Liberties became an active trade unionist. Mallin's wholehearted investment in the movement led to his election as secretary of the Dublin Weavers' Trade Society in 1909, and his early association with James Larkin, with whom he became friendly during the weavers' strike in 1911.[12] Joseph Mallin was born 'during Larkin's Strike on 13 September 1913' and in the same year his father joined the ICA. He gained prominence in its ranks after James Larkin's departure for America at the end of 1914, when James Connolly appointed him chief of staff.

By 1914 many of the ICA members who had been attracted by the excitement and glamour of Larkin's presence had drifted away, and the Irish Volunteers were winning recruits who might otherwise have joined the trade union army. Despite this, under Mallin's disciplined leadership, the ICA began to win awards at Volunteer drill competitions. According to one description of the forty-year-old officer during this period:

> He was about 5 feet seven inches in height, with broad shoulders, thick black hair and a finely shaped head. He was neat in appearance as perhaps befitted a former soldier, and although he had a gentle manner he could be firm when the occasion required it. He had boundless energy and an infectious enthusiasm for everything he tackled.[13]

In late 1914 James Connolly asked Mallin to manage Emmet Hall, the premises of the Inchicore branch of the Irish Transport and General Workers' Union. He moved with Agnes and his young children into the apartment attached to the hall, where he and William Partridge drilled their recruits between 1914 and 1916.

Con Colbert, the Fianna Éireann officer and captain of 'F' Company, 4th Battalion, whom Agnes 'liked very much', also used Emmet Hall to drill the Volunteers. Joseph's sister told him that, as a toddler, he had wandered from the adjoining kitchen into the hall and began 'imitating [Colbert] behind his back'. So, Joseph laughed, 'I was fired out of there.'

As well as enforcing high standards of discipline and a rigorous training regime, Mallin used all his ingenuity to obtain weapons for the ICA, which, under Connolly's leadership, was committed to striking against English rule. Emmet Hall was adjacent to Richmond Barracks, and James O'Shea of the ICA, referred to by Joseph as his father's 'guardian', recalled spending 'many nights with Mallin under the walls of Richmond Barracks waiting for "friendlies"'.[14] Joseph explained: 'The [sympathetic] soldier would report that his gun was stolen and the man who was in charge [for the sake of expediency] would say: "Get another one; you're off to the Front".'

Agnes Mallin (*courtesy of Una O'Callanáin*)

The activity was not without risk, and Joseph's brother, Séamus, recalled one 'dark' night when three 'thugs hired by the police' came after his father. Mallin 'handed his coat' to his thirteen-year-old son 'and went for them'. He was a 'good boxer', Joseph recalled and 'very active', so he 'handled three men and knocked out two … The third man ran away.' After the incident, Mallin turned to his son and said: 'Don't say anything about that to your mother.'

Agnes was 'worried all the time' during that period because she 'knew the danger of a gun'. On one occasion, 'my father brought back a rifle and put it on the table. Seán, I think, grabbed it and she nearly died; it was so careless of him to put a gun on the table like that. A loaded gun, you know, can always kill people.' Agnes' fears were realised when her eldest son accidentally shot himself in the foot during manoeuvres. 'Séamus, was the first man shot in 1916,' Joseph said. 'He was bawling ... [but] they couldn't tell people why he had been shot.'

In the months before the Rising, Mallin intensified his efforts to mould his recruits into an efficient fighting unit. He organised field manoeuvres, staged mock attacks on public buildings and gave lectures on tactics. In James O'Shea's opinion, 'we were improved out of all semblance of what we were when Mick Mallon [*sic*] took over. We were now thoroughly trained soldiers.'[15] By 1916 Connolly estimated that he had 300 members in the ICA, all fully armed.[16]

In the days before the Rising, Mallin made arrangements that his brother, Thomas, would take Agnes and the children to his home in Dolphin's Barn, where they would be safer than in Inchicore, so close to Richmond Barracks. Despite his efforts to protect his family, Agnes suffered extreme anxiety and James O'Shea remembered seeing her outside Liberty Hall on Easter Sunday, when she 'appeared as if the weight of the world was on her. And it was. She was pale and very shaken but I admired her courage ... She knew all.'[17]

On 24 April 1916 Mallin and his second-in-command, Countess Markievicz, were given command of the St Stephen's Green area. Their objective was to occupy and hold the park, a central location, which was to be used as a depot area for the envisaged convergence on the city of men and materials from the country. Control of the Green would also provide a link between Thomas MacDonagh's 2nd Battalion in Jacob's Biscuit Factory on Aungier Street and Éamon de Valera's 3rd Battalion in Boland's Bakery in Ringsend.

Directed to secure the Green, an open expanse surrounded on all sides by tall buildings, Mallin's men began to dig trenches and they took the nearby Royal College of Surgeons as a fall-back position. On Monday evening, when the British forces had regained a number of key positions and reinforcements began to arrive to the capital, the British decided to contain Mallin's forces in the area and concentrate on the Volunteer headquarters in the GPO. Troops took up position in the Shelbourne Hotel and in the United Services Club overlooking the Green, and by dawn on Tuesday morning British machine-gun fire rained down on the exposed ranks of the ICA.

In the aftermath of the Rising, Mallin was criticised for the 'critical and surprising tactical blunder' of failing to occupy and secure the surrounding buildings, the Shelbourne Hotel in particular.[18] Brian Barton, for example, observed that, as a commander, 'his military experience served him well, but when it came to strategy, he was unimaginative and this was a grave deficiency'.[19] Considering Mallin's military background, it is unlikely that he would have overlooked such a basic consideration when working out his strategy for the area but, as Frank Robbins pointed out, 'the real problem' was 'the scarcity of men to occupy all the positions set out in the plans'.[20] His son agreed with this analysis and added that the methods employed in St Stephen's Green were 'against all [his father] had learned and written about … but he was working to orders'.

On Tuesday 25 April Mallin ordered the men in the trenches to withdraw from the most dangerous positions and later issued orders for a general evacuation from the Green to the College of Surgeons. 'The danger to our men would certainly have increased much more considerably,' said Robbins, 'had Commandant Mallin not acted promptly.'[21]

Anxious to avoid being encircled in the College of Surgeons, Mallin ordered his men to gain entry into the nearby Turkish Baths and to establish sniper posts in the houses between Kildare Street and Grafton Street.[22] As the week progressed, communication with the GPO was severed, rations were dwindling and rumours were rife. By Thursday British troops had manoeuvred themselves into a position on the south side of the Green, and the remainder of the week passed in violent exchanges of gunfire, apart from during the mutually observed twice-daily ceasefire when the park keeper entered the Green to feed the ducks. Mallin remained calm and methodical. He was respected and trusted by his men, and his efforts to maintain morale proved so successful that when Nurse Elizabeth O'Farrell delivered the order to surrender on Saturday, they wanted to ignore it and fight on. Sergeant James O'Shea testified: 'I did my best to get [Mallin] to take to the hills … He rejected my plea and said, "As soldiers we came into this fight obeying orders. We will now obey this order by James Connolly to surrender".'[23]

The garrison assembled in the College, and Mallin and Markievicz, with their group of approximately 109 men and 10 women, surrendered to Captain Henry de Courcy Wheeler. The British officer's grand-nephew, Grattan de Courcy Wheeler, recalled that 'Mallin gave him a walking stick [as a

Studio portrait of Captain Henry de Courcy Wheeler
(*courtesy of Grattan de Courcy Wheeler*)

memento] which he had for years until it was stolen or vanished' and he kept Markievicz's pistol in a locked drawer in his desk until April 1949, when he presented it to President Seán T. O'Kelly at a ceremony at Áras an Uachtaráin, the official residence of the president of Ireland.

Led by Mallin and Markievicz, the column marched into York Street where, according to de Courcy Wheeler's diary, 'immense crowds of civilians' had assembled. 'The hostile crowds were held back at the point of the bayonet to allow the escort and their prisoners through to the safety of the Castle.'[24] They were subsequently removed to Richmond Barracks to face court martial. Michael Mallin's wife and his brother, Thomas, 'anxiously watched the papers for the results of the trials and … discussed what sentence Mike would get. Agnes spoke in terms of years, even twenty years,'

Thomas recorded. 'She never thought of a sentence of death.'[25]

Mallin had been fully informed about the ICA's preparations for the Rising, but he told the court martial: 'I had no commission whatever in the Citizen Army. I was never taken into the confidence of James Connolly. I was under the impression that we were going out for manoeuvres on Sunday.'[26] He claimed that he had felt obliged to stay with his men once the Rising began, and testified that Countess Markievicz was in command at St Stephen's Green.

'My father did try to avoid execution,' his son explained, 'he defended himself.' This was not an act of cowardice or a shirking of responsibility. Rather it was 'a terrible case of conscience'. 'He couldn't bear to think that he had brought [Agnes] into this. Although she was the daughter of a Fenian, he thought it was too much to ask of her. But what should he do?'[27] Joseph continued:

> He knew that the Countess [Markievicz] could not have been executed, she was a woman, so he said that she was the commander … Of course it wasn't true but what could he do? When you're faced with these things what answer do you give?
>
> [He was] leaving my mother in the state she was [heavily pregnant]. That was a thing he couldn't bear. So I think it was a desperate attempt by my father to save my mother from the life that was going to be ahead of her, and it was a hard life.

Despite his efforts to avoid his fate, Mallin was sentenced to death, and on the night of 7 May Agnes and Thomas were summoned to his cell for a final meeting. Agnes passed through the gates of Kilmainham with her brother-in-law's advice ringing in her ears: 'Even if Mike's sentence was death, she should bear up and not make his sentence harder for him' and in the prison yard they met Éamonn Ceannt's brother, Michael, who told them to 'Stick it!' Thomas entered the cell first and saw his brother standing at the back wall:

> There was a small grid in the wall above his head. There was little light. He had an old green blanket around him and he said it was very cold. He had several days' growth of beard and his eyes appeared to be fixed and glossy [sic]. He said: 'Where is Agnes?' She ran towards him and said: 'What is it?' He replied: 'Death.' She collapsed on the floor.[28]

'My father is supposed to have spoken of a coldness in the air,' Joseph said, but 'I don't think it was a coldness, I think what was at the back of his mind [was] that he was leaving a family destitute.' Brian Hughes finds evidence in Mallin's final letters of a 'developed sense of the loss and sadness that his imminent execution would cause for [his family] and significantly, for which he accepts full responsibility himself'.[29] Yet his letters also reveal his clear conviction that the Rising would be vindicated and that 'Ireland will come out greater and grander'. The implication is that he felt his death was a noble one, and he closed the letter to his wife with a signature that illustrates both his pride and his dual loyalties: 'Your loving husband, Michael Mallin, Commandant, Stephen's Green Command.'[30]

Thomas left the couple to bring his oldest nephews, Séamus and Seán, to see their father for the last time, while two-year-old Joseph waited outside with his sister Una.[31] 'My father had sent for me,' he said, 'and I was brought to Kilmainham, but I was only two [and] I've no memory of it. I know I was asleep on the metal stairway in the main hall. My sister Una told me that. A soldier came over and said he was very sorry for me.'

After the all-too-brief final exchange, Thomas led Agnes and her children from Kilmainham to his mother's house, where the Mallin family had gathered. 'My grandfather [John Mallin] was working in Liverpool during the Rising', but seventy-eight-year-old Sarah Mallin (née Dowling) had been 'to see her boy before they killed him'.[32] She apparently refused the sympathy of an officer in Kilmainham, telling him that 'she was delighted to have a son dying for Ireland'.[33] Her resolve crumbled, however, when she returned to her family and Thomas 'found them all crying'.[34] Among the mourners were Michael's younger brothers, John and Bartholomew, both of whom were later active with the IRA. 'Bart got two or three bullets' during the War of Independence, Joseph said, and 'John was in Wormwood Scrubs [prison in London] after 1916. I liked both of them very much.'

Joseph's memories of the immediate aftermath of his father's death are vague, and he was more certain about 'a feeling' than about any particular event. He remembered being in a 'strange house' and being 'distressed about it'. He assumed that Maura must have been born at that point because he could remember the crib, but the most substantial aspect of Joseph's memory of the summer of 1916 was a profound sense of 'displacement'.

During the War of Independence, the family home in Inchicore was the target of raids by the Black and Tans, and Joseph's fractured memories of his mother's small acts of resistance during this period mean more to him than the stories of a father he never knew. 'How cool she was in an emergency,' he said. 'When the soldiers came you could see that most of them didn't like the job. Except [for] one fella [who] was a bit nasty … I was very young but I still remember my mother very coolly placing a newspaper over one of my father's dress swords.'

Agnes endured 'more battles', physical, financial and emotional, in the years after her husband's execution. She was not a public figure like Kathleen Clarke or Áine Ceannt, and her sole priority was the maintenance and protection of her young family. Joseph explained:

> In the beginning we lived on the White Cross.[35] That kept us going but my mother was a very good manager [and] … we learned to live poorly with not much, but it was hard on her I know … [She was] fiercely independent of any favouritism from the government, [because she] felt that she would be letting the family down. [So] she made her own way [and] … had to work hard for it.

Under the provisions of the Army Pensions Act (1923), W. T. Cosgrave's Free State government provided an allowance for the widows of the men who died in 1916. Five years later Agnes was distressed to learn that the 'allowance to the widows of those who signed the Proclamation of 1916 [had] been substantially increased' under section 4 of the Army Pensions Act (1927). She appealed unsuccessfully to the Ministry of Pensions, reminding them that she was 'the only widow of one of the executed leaders' not to have benefited from the amendment.[36] Her distress was understandable considering that, in the preceding years, she had been forced to take on two jobs in order to support her family, and the work and the emotional strain had seriously undermined her health.[37] 'Dr Kathleen Lynn couldn't diagnose it,' her son explained, but he 'accidentally heard Surgeon Stokes say her breakdown in health was a direct result of 1916'.[38]

Agnes was diagnosed with tuberculosis of the spine in 1924 and 'that year, when my mother was in hospital, we lived with Mrs Pearse in St Enda's and I stayed on there for the rest of my studies'. Agnes never fully recovered and relapsed in the early 1930s. She was hospitalised again and thirteen-year-old Maura travelled every second day to the hospital in Dun Laoghaire. When it became clear she was dying, 'Seán Connolly's sister, Kathleen Barrett, organised that Agnes would be brought home' and her sister-in-law, Kate

Mallin, who lived 'not very far away in High Road, would come over every week'. Kate, incidentally, 'was my godmother, and a member of Cumann na mBan', Joseph added, and 'it was from her I learned certain things [about] where I came from'.

Seán Mallin, who was a Jesuit novice in St Stanislaus College in Tullabeg, County Offaly, came home to be with his mother in her final weeks, but Agnes did not see her eldest son before she died on 29 September 1932. Séamus, whom his father had directed to be a 'good, strong' man, had fought on the republican side in the Civil War. He was arrested in October 1922, narrowly escaping execution for his part in an armed attack on Free State troops in Dublin. The commutation of his death sentence to penal servitude was later attributed to the fact that he was the son of Michael Mallin. As Hughes observes, 'executing the son of a 1916 leader would have offered an opportunity for powerful anti-Free State propaganda'.[39] He served two and a half years in prison, during which time he engaged in a hunger strike, and finally left Ireland for Venezuela in the late 1920s. His obituary in *The Irish Press*, on 17 June 1982, suggested that his destiny was as directed by his father's legacy, as were those of his siblings. It proclaimed that he 'possessed all the sterling qualities and high-minded principles of his illustrious father' and that it was 'inevitable that … he would play a part in the national struggle'.

Joseph was sixteen and Maura just fourteen when Agnes Mallin died. Almost sixty years later, Maura Mallin said:

> My mother's life and death is the bit I feel saddest about … There were no hand-outs of any kind when we were children … I remember her as the most wonderful person in the world. I never remember her making our lives remotely unhappy. Not that she wasn't sad – she was.[40]

Her brother, Joseph, remembered 1932 as another year of 'displacement'. There were 'huge crowds in the park' for the Eucharistic Congress but, once again, 'we had no home':

> My eldest brother was travelling back from South America and we couldn't con-tact him. My second brother was in the Jesuits [and] Una was over in Spain [in an

enclosed Order] so we lived with Mrs [Austin] Stack who helped me more than I know. She was a wonderful lady all right.

Her home was a 'hide house for Republicans', where 'I met Seán Russell. I liked [him] very much. [He was] a very cool type of man, very friendly [and] he taught me how to play cards.'[41]

Seven years later, Joseph Mallin fulfilled his father's final request and joined the Jesuit order. 'It was a natural choice,' he explained, 'because of the Jesuit connection with 1916' when they 'looked after those who would otherwise have been forgotten'. Joseph expected to stay in Ireland, but 'was sent to Hong Kong [which] took four weeks by boat. Six of us went out and I was the oldest. They're all gone now. I'm the oldest Irish priest in the world.'[42]

Fr Joseph Mallin, the last surviving child of an executed leader of the Rising, has visited Kilmainham Gaol at least three times since it was opened to the public in 1966. His most recent visit was in 2009, when, at ninety-six years old, Joseph was too preoccupied with sadness about his mother's struggle to consider any valour or glory in his father's sacrifice. His thoughts were heavy with regret, even resentment: 'She had four children and another one coming. We were destitute. He'd brought his family to that.'

EDWARD DALY

Edward (Ned) Daly, commandant of the 1st Battalion in the Four Courts area of Dublin in 1916, was almost twenty years younger than Michael Mallin when he was executed on 4 May 1916. His nieces, Mairéad de hÓir and Laura O'Sullivan, and his nephew, Edward O'Sullivan, have an obvious admiration for their famous relative, but they are also invested with a distinct awareness of the family's legacy of grief and the ripples of influence on their lives and on those of their parents. Ned Daly's sister, Laura, married Ned's 'best friend' and fellow Volunteer, James O'Sullivan, and their son and daughter share a strong sense of their family inheritance. They also appear to have inherited their mother's sense of humour and their interviews are marked with lively and very human descriptions. Their first cousin, Mairéad de hÓir, is Nora Daly's daughter, and she remembers the indomitable Daly sisters with a fond admiration. Her father, Éamonn de hÓir [Dore], who fought with the GPO garrison in 1916, was also an important influence in her life. He was described in 1947 by Dan Mulcahy as 'a quiet, unassuming, yet loveable gentleman' whose home 'was a veritable museum of pictures and mementoes of days that were great and glorious for resurgent Ireland'.[43]

The Daly family of Limerick was steeped in the republican tradition. They were, in Laura O'Sullivan's words, 'born and bred and brought up in Fenianism and they didn't know anything else'. Her grandfather, Edward Daly, was arrested in 1866 at the age of seventeen for Fenian activity. He and his brother, John, took part in the ill-fated Fenian uprising of the following year, and in April 1883, the latter was arrested for treason and dynamite offences and sentenced to life imprisonment. Edward married Catherine O'Mara in January 1873, but the rigours of imprisonment in his youth had devastated his health and he died of a heart attack at forty-one, just six months before the birth of his ninth child and only son, John Edward (Ned) Daly. Catherine 'was only thirty-six years old when she was widowed' in 1890, Laura explained, and she 'never came out of black afterwards'.

The Daly sisters in the 1960s (*courtesy of Helen Litton*)

The infant Ned was fatherless but much loved by his eight older sisters: Eileen, Madge, Kathleen, Agnes, Caroline (Carrie), Laura, Annie and Nora.[44] Their home in Limerick was a hive of female activity; Catherine and her nine children shared No. 15 Barrington Street with her husband's mother and her sister-in-law Lollie. 'I don't know how they all fitted,' Mairéad laughed. Five years later they made room for their uncle, John Daly, who joined the family soon after his release from Chatham Prison in 1896.[45] He provided an occasionally antagonistic but unequivocally republican male influence. 'I always felt sorry for John Daly,' Laura O'Sullivan smiled. 'He got out of jail after fourteen hideous years and came back to a family of girls.' Her brother's impression is that John was 'a kind of a solemn man [with] terribly old-fashioned ideas. If a girl went out to a dance it was nearly a sin.' That didn't suit Laura Daly, 'who loved to go out dancing', at all. 'So she went out the window.'

An influential figure both inside and outside the Daly home, their uncle established a successful bakery business with premises at William Street and Sarsfield Street, and held the mayoral office in Limerick three times between 1899 and 1902. John Daly was also heavily involved in the formation and maintenance of the Lord Edward Fitzgerald Sluagh of Na Fianna in Limerick, and Catherine's house in Barrington Street became a refuge and base for those working in the cause of Irish independence before and after the Rising.[46] In fact, said Mairéad, the family was often 'harassed before 1916 because Tom Clarke used to visit'.

The Daly family first met Clarke after his release from prison in 1898, when he travelled to Limerick to visit his old prison-mate and fellow Fenian John Daly. 'Even though people think of Tom Clarke as an old, thin man with a moustache,' Laura said, he was actually 'great fun; he would have to be to come into a family of eight girls [and] they all loved him'. It was during this period that Kathleen fell for their house guest, who was twenty years her senior. Her mother 'was dead against it because she felt that he was somebody with nothing, an old man', but the Daly sisters thought that Tom Clarke was the 'greatest'. To Kathleen, who had been brought up in the nursery of Fenianism, he was the embodiment of patriotic sacrifice, having served fifteen years' penal servitude for treason. They were married in 1901, when Kathleen was twenty-three years old.

The couple lived in America until 1907, when they returned to Dublin and Tom Clarke became actively involved in rebuilding the IRB. They opened a tobacconist's shop at 55 Amiens Street and shortly afterwards opened a second

Nora, Laura and Carrie Daly in Gaelic costume (*courtesy of Helen Litton*)

alike' and offered his assistance in navigating the unfamiliar streets of the city. It was an offer that Mairéad feels her mother and aunt willingly accepted, because 'medical students seemed [to have] a bit of charm'. They arrived in Dublin and Laura was shaken at the sight of the 'dead horses on the streets'. 'That was what she remembered,' her daughter said, 'not the dead bodies, but the horses, it always got her down.'

Dore delivered his charges safely to Kathleen Clarke's home in Fairview, where they exchanged news with their sister and had supper by candlelight, before setting off for the GPO.[51] 'Laura got a message to [take] to Limerick,' Mairéad explained, and Nora was chosen to deliver a verbal message to Terence MacSwiney, 'because the Dalys were familiar to the Cork leadership'. According to Nora's witness statement, the message was: 'Tell Terry McSweeney [*sic*] we are in action and we know he will follow us.'[52]

The sisters left the GPO once more 'under the guidance of Éamonn Dore' and spent a restless night in Fairview. The next morning, Dore led them through the British lines to Kingsbridge, where a train was waiting to evacuate refugees from the besieged city. Having discharged his duty, Dore made his way back to the GPO:

> All I can remember is running, crawling under wire with things whizzing past, and trying to pray … I got a slight flesh wound in the leg and fell into the arms of the sentry who opened the gates to my kicking … I could feel things whizzing behind my back and thudding into the jambs … Having got in I reported to Tom Clarke and Seán Mac Diarmada and the latter said 'Didn't I tell you not to come back'. I told them that the messengers had got away all right … [53]

Éamonn's daughter is very matter-of-fact about her father's participation in the Rising: 'they were young [and] pretty hot on the subject … my mother's family, all of them were involved in it … [But] he wasn't anything special, he was there.'

While Mairéad's father took up arms in the GPO, her mother made her way 'on to Cork and disappointment'.[54] 'She didn't get much of a reception' from Volunteer leaders Terence MacSwiney and Tomás MacCurtain, 'because she was trying to tell them that they should rise and fight and they weren't going to do that. [The authorities] were watching for her at the railway station and the Dalys were that well known to them, [so] they dressed her up as an old woman to get her back to Limerick.' Before she left Cork on the Thursday of Easter Week, Nora learned that the Volunteers had 'actually handed' their arms over to the Bishop of Cork.[55]

Laura delivered the appeal from Volunteer headquarters to the Limerick Volunteers to relieve the pressure on Dublin, and she and Nora were reunited in Limerick city in the latter part of the week. Meanwhile, their brother Ned held command in one of the most fiercely contested battlegrounds of the Rising. The 1st Battalion occupied the area around the Four Courts on the north side of the Liffey, and Volunteers in Church Street and North King Street came under heavy fire for most of the week, until Daly received news of the surrender on Saturday. His second-in-command, Piaras Béaslaí, recorded:

> Daly showed [me the order to surrender] … and his eyes filled with tears. He had borne himself like a gallant soldier through the week of fighting. Again he rose to this fresh test of soldiership. He checked the murmurings of those who objected to surrender by an appeal to discipline … [and] impressed the English officers with his dignity.[56]

Éamonn Dore also remembered his brother-in-law in his submission to the Bureau of Military History:

> … while we [the GPO garrison] still stood prisoners in O'Connell Street … Into the street from Abbey Street came the old First Battalion with their loved Commandant, Ned Daly, leading. Still the same quiet, calm, self-possessed Ned, unconquered and unconquerable as his men marching four deep behind him … He and

they had fought the good fight, held their positions intact and could have held out much longer, but, against his better judgement, he accepted the order of surrender.[57]

When news of the surrender reached Limerick, Laura and Madge travelled to Dublin to be with their sister Kathleen, 'who had three small boys' and was pregnant with her fourth child. Laura told her daughter:

> The minute she opened the door [to her sisters] she burst into tears and said, "Twas Our Lady sent you', because she prayed that somebody would come from Limerick. She told them that Tom [had been] shot that morning [3 April], and to be prepared, that Ned was next. He was their baby brother, so they were shocked and horrified, but at least they were there together.

A military lorry arrived in the early hours of 4 May to convey the sisters to Kilmainham for their last meeting with their brother. Madge later recalled that when their transport arrived they 'were trembling and could not keep back the tears'.[58] But she felt that their prayers for strength were heard because 'from the moment we passed the gate of Kilmainham and faced the soldiers, our pride in the sacrifices of our heroes gave us new strength. We walked in, heads erect, and told our names with pride'. As they passed through the entrance hall, a soldier called out 'Relatives of Daly, to be shot in the morning.'[59]

Kathleen was in possession of the only visitor's permit, but Madge's and Laura's vociferous protests forced the guards to capitulate and all three sisters entered the cell to find their brother asleep on the floor. Kathleen thought Ned 'looked about eighteen', but to Madge he appeared 'so strong and noble that it was hard to believe that he was a captive, doomed to be shot … he looked like a brave young knight who had won some victory. And so he had, of course, he and his comrades had saved the soul of Ireland. We rushed to him, entwined our arms around him.'[60] Laura's memory was less poetic, but somehow more real. In her daughter's words:

> It was a tiny cell [and] there was only an old bit of a rug on the floor. They said goodbye, which was very short [and] a soldier [was] standing in the cell with them so they couldn't talk about a whole lot. Of course it was awful but at least Kathleen

had somebody with her … She had already lost her husband and she never told Tom she was pregnant … of course, she lost the baby afterwards.

During their short time together Ned reiterated points he had made at his court martial, insisting that 'all he did … was for Ireland, his own land' and that he had acted 'as he was bound to as a soldier of Ireland in all matters under the orders of his superior officers'.[61] He paid glowing tribute to the men who had fought beside him and spoke affectionately of Tom Clarke, Thomas MacDonagh and Patrick Pearse, who had been executed that morning. His sisters told him that they drew consolation from knowing that he would not have to serve long, hard years in prison as his brother-in-law had done, and before they left he gave them mementoes – buttons from his tunic, a small purse with a few coins in it and two pencils. Madge wrote, when 'a soldier called "Time up!" … we kissed and embraced our boy, once only and walked from the cell without a tear or a moan, heads held up. The cell door banged behind us and we walked down the endless stairs.'[62]

According to Catherine Daly's obituary in the *Irish Independent* in April 1937, when she heard the news of her only son's execution, she 'thanked God to have given her the honour of being the mother of such a noble Irishman'.[63] Mairéad's recollection, however, belies her grandmother's apparent steadfast patriotism. 'Their mother was shattered. There were eight girls and one boy. He was her only son.' Laura told her daughter that the sisters suffered terribly at the loss of their beloved brother and their brother-in-law. The family also mourned the loss of John Daly, who died on 30 June 1916, living just long enough to learn of the failure of the Rising and the execution of his only nephew.

Both James O'Sullivan and Éamonn Dore were arrested after the surrender. Mairéad's father was shipped to England, but James, as a captain in the 1st Battalion, was lodged in Kilmainham to await the verdict of his court martial. According to his daughter:

He and Tommy MacDonagh were in two separate cells side by side in Kilmainham, and [they] had an arrangement that they would bang on the wall as to what sentence they got. So anyway, Dad was sentenced to death but then the warder came back and told him that [it was commuted] to eight years penal servitude, he banged eight times on the wall. There was no answer from the other side, so he knew then that MacDonagh was going to be shot. That's my story told to me by my father.

From June 1916 Cumann na mBan, led by the Daly sisters, administered the Volunteer Dependants' Fund in Limerick; they held fund-raising events and commemorations, worked for prisoner welfare and contributed to the propaganda machine for the election and anti-conscription campaigns. They provided a cover behind which rebels who escaped arrest could begin to rebuild the Volunteers.[64] Madge, for example, gave jobs in the family bakery business to two Dublin men, Peadar Dunne and Peadar McMahon, on their release from 'all the best jails in England'. Her future brothers-in-law, James O'Sullivan and Éamonn Dore, also benefited from her patronage.

Edward explained that 'when my father was released in 1917 he came down [to Limerick]'. He was on the run and 'living in the Dalys' attic' in Barrington Street. He was referred to as 'Mary' when strangers were near, because there wasn't supposed to be a man in the house, and 'during that time he fell in love with my mother'. And so Ned Daly's closest friend married his 'dearest sister' in a romantic midnight ceremony in a Limerick chapel.[65] Edward, 'was born in 1919 in Barrington Street', where they stayed for a year after they married. It was a happy arrangement, Laura explained, because James and his mother-in-law, Catherine, shared a mutual affection, and Madge offered her new brother-in-law the role of manager of the bakehouse. It was 'a big concern and employed fifty people', but Jim was a capable manager. 'He trained originally as a grocer in Dublin' and was, in his son's words, a 'very good worker … always spick and span, a military type'.

Mairéad felt that her parents must have 'fallen in love at first sight' on the train to Dublin because, after being released from prison, Éamonn went to the Daly home in Limerick to reunite with Nora. However, his time in prison had permanently damaged both his health and his prospective medical career:

There were far too many of them in [prison] and lots of them got TB. He came out with one lung gone. He tried to return to medicine but just collapsed and was told he could never go back to study like that again. We had cousins out in the country and he went there for a year and seemed to recover a certain amount. My mother used to visit him and they got married in Kilcolman church out in the country in 1918.

After the Rising, the RIC followed Madge Daly's activities very closely, and Nora told her daughter that the family 'were always being watched'; they had a 'permanent RIC man outside the railing when they were in Barrington Street, taking down who went in and out, and all that was passed back to Dublin Castle. They were under surveillance always.' In addition, 'Limerick wasn't too pleased with the Dalys after 1916. They were kind of cold-shouldered a bit.' According to Laura, 'they found out who their friends were. Certain pro-British people [they] knew would cross over the street so they wouldn't have to talk to [them].'

The Daly home was also a target for military raids during the War of Independence. Madge recorded her memories of this fraught period in the family history: 'We were raided regularly, our business place was set on fire, and our furniture seized for unpaid fines imposed by court martial.'[66] Her nephew, Edward, who was an infant in 1920, felt they had a 'terrible time' and offered a family version of one particularly brutal raid: 'The Black and Tans entered the house ['Ardeevin' on the Ennis Road, to where the Daly family had moved in 1919] and took every bit of furniture out and burned it on the main pathway', while the girls struggled to help their elderly aunt, Lollie, down the stairs. 'Agnes was dragged out of the house … her hair shorn off and her hand cut with a razor.'[67] 'They cut it in half practically,' Edward exclaimed, but the element of the story that 'sticks in a boy's mind' is that a detective was seen coming out of the house with a chamber pot on his head. He also recalled being shown the burnt patch on the pavement, which remained as uncomfortable evidence of the event until the 1970s: 'They had to go into the George Hotel for a few nights before they distributed themselves out to members of the family.'

His first cousin picked up the story:

My aunt's arm was bleeding all night and … one of them [Carrie] had a bit of nursing knowledge and she managed to keep her from dying until the morning when they could get a doctor. [On] another occasion my grandmother got a blow of a rifle

79

and that turned into an ulcer. [It] never healed the rest of her life … It was touch and go. It was a bad time.

Despite the dangers it posed, the family business was central to the IRA communications network during the War of Independence. According to Mairéad:

Messages would be passed in to my father [through the bakery in William Street]. He'd keep them and they would call in for them, it wouldn't be as noticeable. One night he'd got messages and he had them in his pocket in his coat behind the door and the Black and Tans came to search the house. He was a tough man and he said he'd let in the officer but he wasn't going to let in the others. Funnily enough they agreed to that and then the officer went to put his hand into the pocket where the notes were and my father said, 'Oh, they are only letters from my mother; you wouldn't be interested.' He took out his hand.

Madge Daly features prominently in the cousins' memories of childhood. Edward smiled at the thought of his formidable aunt, who would 'walk down the street and buy a shop and sell it before she came home. She was fantastic.' Mairéad remembered her as a 'tough businesswoman' but 'very generous'. When she expanded the business she handed the proprietorship of the William Street Bakery to Éamonn, and Mairéad lived over the shop until she was eight, when the family moved to a home provided by Madge on the North Circular Road.

The cousins were also aware of the shadow of 1916 on their childhoods. Edward's father and Éamonn Dore 'shared a lot of 1916 talk', and, even though 'it would have been 1925 before [he] was catching on to anything', he had an early memory of hearing that Pearse was a 'rather distant' and 'austere' man. He also recalled his mother telling him that Tom Clarke was 'young in his mind' and 'loved sweet things after being in jail for so long'. Mairéad recorded that 'anyone who had anything to do with 1916 called into the [bakery] if they were in Limerick and [my father] promptly brought them out [to the house] for a meal'. She recalled one occasion in particular when she was preparing tea for some visitors. She went to tell them that the tea was ready, to which they replied: 'We're only at Tuesday yet. [You] are going to have some wait.'

Mairéad feels that men were more inclined to discuss the events of 1916 because, 'It [was] an adventure to them [but] my mother used to say it was heartbreak to her … Men are funny,' she observed. 'When they had the 50th anniversary they [invited] one of the British commanders that was there in 1916 … [he] and my father had a … long conversation and they both agreed that … war was war, military matters.'

Mairéad's mother didn't have the same pragmatism about her family tragedy:

> She was like me really in lots of ways. I don't know if you would call that strong-minded or not. She liked meeting people and talking to people but when they started on 1916 the tears dropped. All her life she was that sad for losing her brother and Tom Clarke.

Despite James O'Sullivan's personal sympathy with the republican cause, and Madge Daly's vigorous opposition to the Treaty, James was not actively involved in the Civil War. 'He got out of everything,' his daughter explained, and she and her brother agreed that his old association with Collins was central to his decision. 'My mother and father adored Michael Collins,' Laura smiled, 'he was gorgeous.' James furnished him with 'confidential reports during the War of Independence, and he was godfather to my brother John'. Edward added that his father was deeply impressed by Collins' 'sheer brain power and charisma. I don't think [he] liked de Valera.' They were in gaol together, 'but he used to say: "He has a Latin mind".' In other words, de Valera was a 'statesman and Collins was a soldier'.

Mairéad's father, on the other hand, was 'very friendly' with Éamon de Valera, and she recalled his long telephone conversations with the ageing president in the 1960s. 'You know de Valera's sight was so bad and if he was bored he would get the secretary to put him on to my father … I don't know what they used to talk about but he'd be half the night outside in the hall talking to him.' Éamonn was 'deadly against' the signing of the Treaty, said Mairéad, but the Civil War 'really upset my mother terribly'.

After the Civil War, the O'Sullivan family lived in O'Connell Street and Laura ran a small café. Edward's parents were 'total sympathisers' with the republicans, but there was a time, he says, between 1925 and 1932, 'when people wanted to get back to normality after the Civil War'. They had a young family and 'were trying to start a new business'.

Edward treasures the relics of his family's participation in the Rising, particularly his mother's Cumann na mBan medal, his 'father's cap badge' and 'the boots he wore in 1916', and admitted that his family heritage spurred him to join the IRA in 1939: 'My brother [Seán] and I were republicans and my mother was a steaming republican … and my father, of course, was [but] he didn't feel he had to be showing off … We probably felt we did.' Their tenure didn't last long and involved little more than 'a lot of drilling'. In fact, they 'retired out of it' when a local garda told James O'Sullivan that his sons should be minding their 'Ps and Qs'. 'Just as well, really,' Edward sighed, 'I think we were a bit disappointed in it anyway.'

CON COLBERT

Like Edward Daly, Con Colbert was one of the youngest rebel leaders to be executed in 1916. As captain of 'F' Company, 4th Battalion, the twenty-seven-year-old was in command at Jameson's Distillery when it was surrendered on Sunday 30 April. His sister, Catherine, and his brother, Jim, mourned the loss of a beloved brother when Colbert was executed on 8 May 1916.

Born twenty-two years apart, Catherine's daughter, Sr Íde (Honora) Woulfe, and Jim's son, Con, who spent most of his youth 'listening to the various stories about the family', are equally conscious of their uncle's legacy. His nephew believes that Colbert 'followed his heart and the heart said, "Ireland must be free" and he ended up giving his life for the cause'.

Catherine's daughter said that Cornelius Colbert, known as Con, was born on 19 October 1888 in Monalena, Castlemahon, Newcastlewest in Limerick. He was one of thirteen children born to Michael Colbert and Nora Josephine McDermott, who died aged thirty-seven in 1892. 'Their father wasn't very much of a manager,' Sr Íde explained, and 'they struggled to make ends meet', particularly after he moved his family to a small farm in nearby Athea. Their mother's family, the MacDermotts of Cooraclare, County Clare, helped with the education of the Colbert children, but after their father's death in 1907, the family scattered. 'Some emigrated,' said Jim's son, Con. 'Uncle John and Uncle Willie went to live in San Francisco and … another sister [Johane] went to

America and one went to England. Others stayed at home. Uncle Dan [for example] lived in Portlaois and was a jockey.'

At the start of the twentieth century, Catherine went to Dublin 'to make her living' as a dressmaker. She rented a house at 7 Clifton Terrace, Ranelagh Road, and once she was settled, she sent for her sixteen-year-old brother. 'My mother was the boss in the home,' Sr Íde smiled, but Con was 'particularly close to Lila' (Elizabeth), who worked as a typist in Lafayette's in Dublin. In her witness statement, Elizabeth affectionately recalled her brother's 'unbounded energy', and that he 'was always full of life and fun', but he also had an 'earnestness' which 'was applied to everything he did'.[68] She and Catherine hoped that Con's education at Skerries College would lead to a job in the British civil service, a prospect that did not appeal to the young nationalist, who had joined the Gaelic League and 'was enthusiastic about everything Irish'.[69] Instead, he secured work as a clerk in Kennedy's Bakery in Parnell Street in 1905.

Attracted by its emphasis on Irish culture and folklore, Colbert joined Na Fianna Éireann after it was established in Dublin in August 1909. He was a highly motivated member, becoming proficient in drill, marching, scouting, signalling, map-reading, first aid and the use of small firearms. His model membership led to his promotion to the captaincy of his branch, and eventually to the council. Bulmer Hobson, a key figure in the IRB, used his influence in the Fianna to recruit new members into the secret organisation; Colbert was among the first to be sworn into a circle of IRB members within the Fianna known as the John Mitchel Literary and Debating Society.[70]

Clad in kilts and dark-green double-breasted tunics, the boys of the Fianna shared a motto with St Enda's: 'Strength in our arms, truth on our lips, purity in our hearts', and Patrick Pearse found in Colbert an ideal candidate for the post of part-time drill instructor at the school. In the autumn of 1910 he was 'teaching drill and marching', his nephew explained, and 'when someone offered him payment he was quite adamant that he didn't want it. He was there to work for the cause and train the people for whatever was going to happen in the future. He had a gift for organising and … a certain kind of intuition about what might be the best way to proceed.'

In November 1913 Colbert replaced Hobson as head of the IRB circle and was elected to the Provisional Committee of the Irish Volunteers. As captain of 'F' Company in Éamonn Ceannt's 4th Battalion, he was actively involved in training the newly recruited Volunteers, with the Fianna's drill halls and equipment at their disposal. In early 1916 Con Colbert and Seán Heuston were among the senior Fianna officers taken into the confidence of the Military Council of the IRB.

'I understand that he kept it very quiet,' his niece said. Con 'knew that [his sisters] would be displeased that he was so involved in politics [and] the only thing that my mother knew [was] that he was involved with some young boys because he used to bring them to the garden to teach them Irish'. Catherine 'suffered a lot' when she discovered the level of his involvement. Elizabeth, it seems, had more insight into her brother's activities. Writing in 1953, she said: 'He was able to combine his work with his enthusiastic activities for Ireland … he was constantly telling us that there would surely be a fight but I don't think I ever took him seriously.'[71]

Madge Daly recalled her last meeting with Con Colbert, on O'Connell Street in Dublin a week before the Rising. He was convinced of 'the righteousness in their effort to win freedom … he believed that they would all go down in the fight but the sacrifice would be well worthwhile'.[72]

On Easter Monday 1916 Éamonn Ceannt directed Colbert's 'F' Company to one of the three strategic outposts around the rebel headquarters at the South Dublin Union, James's Street. He and his reduced company of fifteen men took Watkins' Brewery to the east, with orders to impede the progress of British forces from the south-west. Captain Séamus Murphy was assigned to Jameson's Distillery in Marrowbone Lane, and Captain Thomas McCarthy to Roe's Distillery in Thomas Street. Hostile local residents, inadequate cover and a paucity of ammunition and food forced McCarthy and his men to abandon their post on Tuesday. In the early hours of Wednesday morning, Colbert received a dispatch from James Connolly to relocate to Jameson's Distillery to reinforce Murphy's besieged garrison. 'Obviously,' his nephew smiled, 'as a strict teetotaller, he had no interest in what was produced in Jameson's.'

Colbert assumed command, and for the next three days he and his men were, in Robert Holland's words, 'locked in a battle royal' with enemy snipers.[73] On Sunday afternoon Thomas MacDonagh arrived to deliver the order to surrender, much to the surprise of the men, who believed they were holding their ground effectively. 'It came as a great shock,' wrote Holland, 'Colbert could hardly speak as he stood in the yard for a moment or two. He was completely stunned. The tears rolled down his cheeks.'[74]

Con Colbert was tried by court martial on 4 May and received the sentence of death in his cell in Kilmainham three days later. His niece, Sr Íde, who was born in 1915, knew that 'during his time of detention he did not allow any visits from his family'. However, he wrote 'no fewer than ten letters', including one to his sister in which he tried to explain that a visit would 'grieve us both too much'.[75] His other letters were to relatives and friends, bidding them farewell and asking them to pray for his soul.

His nephew Con thought that Colbert 'seemed to have possessed a certain amount of calm on the day of execution and just faced up to what he felt was inevitable'. His cousin noted that Colbert asked to see Mrs Séamus Murphy, who had visited her husband at Marrowbone Lane on Tuesday and remained 'in the distillery and cooked for the Volunteers' until the surrender.[76] She was being held in Kilmainham with members of Cumann na mBan, including Éamonn Ceannt's sister-in-law, Lily O'Brennan. They were 'very friendly', Sr Íde continued, and on the night before his execution he gave her three buttons from his Volunteer uniform and a prayer book as a keepsake for his sister, Lila. He told her that he considered himself 'one of the lucky ones' because 'a martyr's death is a noble one', and that he was 'proud to die for such a cause'.[77] In the early hours of Monday 8 May, Sheila Murphy and her cellmate heard the volleys in the stonebreaker's yard: 'We got up and we said the *De Profundis* three times for the men who were passing into eternity.'[78]

On 1 June 1916 the *Evening Herald* published a letter by Fr Augustine, who had attended Colbert in his last hours. The Capuchin priest felt he owed it to Colbert's memory to correct 'inaccurate and fanciful' reports in the press that he had 'died joking the men who were preparing him for death'. Con Colbert's nephew, who admitted to being deeply moved by the priest's sincerity, read the article aloud:

> What really happened was this. While my left arm linked in the prisoner's right, and while I was whispering something in his ear, a soldier approached to fix a piece of paper on his breast. While this was being done he looked down and then,

addressing the soldier in a cool and perfectly natural way, said: 'Wouldn't it be better to pin it up higher – nearer the heart?'

The soldier said something in reply and then added, 'Give me your hand now.' The prisoner seemed confused and extended his left hand. 'Not that,' said the soldier, 'but the right'. The right was accordingly extended, and having grasped and shaken it warmly, the kindly, human-hearted soldier proceeded to gently bind the prisoner's hands and afterwards blindfolded him.

Some minutes later, my arm still linked in his and accompanied by another priest, we entered the dark corridor leading to a yard and, his lips moving in prayer, the brave lad went forth to die.[79]

Catherine was unaware of her brother's execution until late on the evening of 8 May, when it was announced in the papers. Elizabeth's colleagues in Lafayette's had concealed the newspapers from her, and she received the news from Fr Albert at the Capuchin Friary in Church Street. Like her siblings, Elizabeth later received a letter in which her brother wrote: 'May God help us – me to die well, you to bear your sorrow.'[80]

Even though Catherine never spoke to her daughter about her sorrow, Sr Íde saw it manifest in that 'she used to play the piano and she never played the piano after he died. That was the one thing I knew about it. Oh, she felt it very much.' Con's father would speak 'in general' about his brother's execution, but betrayed little about his personal grief. However, Con suspects that Jim Colbert's subsequent involvement during the War of Independence speaks of his anger and sense of responsibility to his brother's memory: 'I suppose he felt impelled to carry on the fight.'

Sr Íde's father, Richard Woulfe, from Cratloe in West Limerick, 'was studying chemistry in Dublin when he met Catherine Colbert'. They married in 1913, 'but I understand that my father was very anxious that they would come back to Limerick', so they returned to Abbeyfeale before the Rising. His daughter's impression is that Richard had no involvement with the Volunteers, but she admits that she 'heard very little of the politics of those days. The only thing my father would have been involved in a bit would be the Black and Tan time', when he was an officer in the West Limerick Brigade IRA.

James Collins, of the Abbeyfeale Company of the Irish Volunteers, testified that he was an apprentice to Richard Woulfe in his chemist's shop in Abbeyfeale in 1914, and that the 'Woulfes were great supporters of the Irish independence movement. Their shop and house, from the earliest days of the movement, became a meeting place for men like Con Colbert, Captain Ned Daly and others who later figured prominently in the fight for freedom'.[81] After Easter Week, Richard Woulfe directed his young apprentice to go to Kerry, to take Captain Monteith, who had landed in Kerry with Roger Casement, to Limerick. During the War of Independence, the chemist's shop was used as a conduit to pass messages from headquarters in Dublin to the Volunteers in Kerry, and in 1919 Catherine identified a man claiming to be Peadar Clancy as a spy.[82]

Honora Woulfe was just six years old in 1920, but she situated her fragmented flashes of memory in stories of raids on the family home during the War of Independence, when her mother told her 'they were a marked family by the British forces'. On one occasion when she and her sister were on holiday with a grand-aunt in County Clare, their father narrowly avoided arrest, or worse:

> A policeman who was living next door seemingly gave some information about my father to the Black and Tans and one night they came along and wrecked the house … They had [my father] up against the wall outside and were going to shoot him … and had locked my mother and her babies (Con and Risteárd), into a room upstairs in the house they rented at the time. Catherine screamed [providing a distraction sufficient to allow her husband time to release his family]. They got out the door and down to the River Feale, which ran at the end of the garden.

The lady next door 'heard the pandemonium' and took in Catherine and the children, while Richard made his escape: 'The story is told that he walked such a way that he got to the convent and the nuns took him in and hid him behind the altar.' When the soldiers came to the convent the Reverend Mother met them, 'but I think she must have told them that they couldn't go into the chapel and they respected that. He escaped and … was on the run from then on until the Truce.'

While her husband Richard was evading arrest, Catherine and her sons stayed with her brother in Athea. She felt the separation from her daughters 'very much', because Honora and her sister remained with their father's family in County Clare: 'They told me that my father used to go there when he was on the run,' Sr Íde explained. He shaved off his moustache, thus rendering himself unrecognisable to his six-year-old daughter, who was told that he was 'her Uncle Jack'. The apparently cruel deception was to prevent her telling 'the girls at school, whose people were on the other side, that [her] father had been there'. The story assumed a deeper poignancy when Sr Íde described the eventual revelation:

> When the Truce came … they told me that this was my daddy and I went under the table and said, 'No! No! No! It was Uncle Jack.' I was crazy about Uncle Jack because, naturally, when he would come to the house he was everything to me … it took them quite a while to get it into my mind that this was my father.

The Woulfe family was reunited after the Truce in July 1921 and Richard built a house in what was appropriately called New Street in Abbeyfeale. During the Civil War, Woulfe's Pharmacy was boycotted because of the family's republican politics: 'The shop was kept open but [he had] very little business at that time and we were a family of five. It was very difficult for my parents.'

Despite the fact that Catherine 'had her own convictions about things', neither she nor Richard took an active part in the Civil War, and they told their children very little about the period: 'As a matter of fact, we were kept completely out of politics [and] weren't allowed to mix with people except for [the few] we were friendly with in the town at the time. There was a lot of discord,' Sr Íde recalled, 'families were very divided due to politics' and 'your friends were not your friends any longer'.

Richard Woulfe was arrested briefly during the Civil War, but released 'because of the family, I think', and when he died in 1937 his obituary in *The Irish Press* declared: 'Many people attributed his death indirectly to the heroic sacrifices which he made in the service of his country.'[83] His daughter agrees that his death from cancer at the age of fifty was 'due to the hardship during those times', but considers that her mother's sacrifices were just as significant. Despite the disruption in early childhood, 'we never had an unhappy life [and]

... we never felt insecure. Our parents sacrificed [so much] to give us the best they could and we never felt the difficulties that my mother and father underwent '

Sr Íde's uncle, Jim Colbert, had been a member of the Volunteers in Limerick in 1916, and 'was bitterly disappointed when the eagerly awaited orders to rise never arrived'.[84] He was active during the War of Independence and fought on the anti-Treaty side in the Civil War during which he was arrested and detained in the Curragh. 'I'm sure it was traumatic losing your brother and then ending up in prison yourself,' his son said, and he 'didn't like to talk about it very much'. Con learned about his father's experiences of participation and imprisonment from other members of the family, and 'it was all more or less word of mouth'. He heard, for example, about Jim Colbert's escape from 'No. 2, Tintown' in the Curragh via an underground tunnel in December 1923. Jim subsequently made his way to Limerick on board a canal barge and, evading capture, continued westwards.[85] 'They were on the run for quite some time,' Con said, 'and they ended up not too far away from Kill ... up in the hills.' The ceasefire marked the 'end of his involvement' in militant nationalism, but he organised a Sinn Féin Cumann in Athea and was later elected as Fianna Fáil TD for West Limerick.

Con's mother, Rose Ryan from Tuam, 'who was involved with the Cumann na mBan' was more forthcoming about her participation: 'She was a courier, cycling around the city of Dublin taking messages here and there. She also ended up in Kilmainham for a short period. So,' Con laughed, 'I have a family of jail birds.'

JOSEPH MARY PLUNKETT

Born in 1877 to George Noble Plunkett and Josephine Cranny, Joseph Mary Plunkett was a founding member of the Irish Volunteers and Director of Military Operations on the IRB Military Council.[86] He joined the other members of the Provisional Government in the GPO during Easter Week and was executed by firing squad on 4 May 1916. Plunkett's brothers, Jack and George, fought at his side in 1916; the latter had five children, the eldest of whom died suddenly in 1966. His second son, Count Eoghan Plunkett, born in 1927, just days 'after Kevin O'Higgins's assassination', was the oldest surviving member of his generation when he was interviewed in 2013. His brother Seoirse is four years younger and while he accepts that the siblings' versions of events do not always correspond, he and his brother are agreed on the complex nature of their family inheritance and share a certain resentment about what they consider to be the relegation of the Plunkett name to one of history's furthest corners.

Seoirse attributed the family's failing fortunes and bruised reputation to their anti-Treaty republicanism, which extended into the early 1940s. 'The effect on our family' of George and Jack's involvement in the anti-Treaty IRA was that they were 'on the wrong side of the political divide'. 'We had no access to any of the perks of those who had joined the Treaty forces. That was the principal effect that we noticed rather than any of the historical things you might think of.'

The Landlord and Tenant Act of 1923 'created havoc' and much of the family's substantial property portfolio was 'sold off for a pittance'. George and Jack were both at college but had to leave 'because they were more or less told that they weren't going to get any degrees'. 'Members of the family couldn't get

Count Plunkett
(*courtesy of the Plunkett family*)

good jobs,' Seoirse explained, and pointed in particular to his impression that his uncle Jack was 'blackballed' from the Electricity Supply Board (ESB). The Plunketts 'got raw deals' and were 'treated like dirt on occasion'.

Neglected too, Seoirse feels, is the work of his grandfather, Count Plunkett, whom he credits with planting the revolutionary seed and 'educating his children so that they went ahead and did all the things that they did'.[87] George Noble Plunkett was educated in Nice, where he had all the 'concepts of the French Revolution drummed into him', and latterly in Trinity College Dublin, where he socialised with Oscar Wilde. Eoghan added that, while in Italy, his grandfather studied Botticelli and became a world authority on the Renaissance artist. A founder of the *Irish Independent*, a poet, bibliophile, committed Parnellite, and later Sinn Féin TD for Roscommon, he was invested with a papal title in 1884 for his patronage of a house of Irish nuns in Rome. 'He was Count of the Holy Roman Empire, High Commander of the Holy Sepulchre, Knight of St Gregory and he was well in with the Popes,' Eoghan laughed. 'I inherited the title of count eventually because everyone died and I was left holding the bag even though I was never really ready for it.'

Seoirse feels that his uncle, Joseph Plunkett, was not only neglected but also misinterpreted. He pointed to historically contradictory depictions of his uncle, and mentioned, for example, 'the programmes produced by RTÉ for the 50th anniversary of the Rising', which depicted Plunkett as a 'fat, useless, namby-pamby person with a silk scarf flying in the wind and rings on his fingers'. The truth is slowly emerging that he was a 'real man … strong-willed, powerful, intelligent and a leader'. Seoirse insisted that people still 'don't seem to understand' Joseph Plunkett's role in engineering the plans for the Rising. He was the Volunteers' director of military operations and 'familiar with literature on the subject of war and the running of countries.' He was 'a competent man', said his nephew. In Geraldine Plunkett's words:

> [My brother] Joe was always engaged in keeping the efficiency of the organisation up to standard. He was never done reading history, in order to have the theoretical and technical knowledge necessary to avoid errors, and to take advantage of the conventional errors made by soldiers and governments. He made his plans always with an eye to the mistakes the enemy would make.[88]

According to his biographer and grand-niece, Honor Ó Brolcháin, Plunkett decided to take a defensive approach that would put the British forces at a disadvantage. He judged correctly where reinforcements would be brought in and could be stopped, but his planning was undermined by the confusion of the countermanding order and the failure of the country to rise.[89] 'He was [also] mathematically and mechanically quite clever,' Seoirse added. In 1913 'he made colour photographs using the Carbro process, he drove cars and they all rode motorcycles'. According to Eoghan, his uncle 'could make a Model T sit up and beg'!

He was also a 'wireless expert. He followed the Marconi experiments from the beginning', and from early on he realised the potential of radio to bypass the British censor and broadcast news of the Rising to the world.[90] On Easter Monday, Plunkett sent three Volunteers from the GPO to occupy the Atlantic School of Wireless in Reis's Chambers (now the Grand Central Bar) at the junction of Lower Abbey Street and O'Connell Street. From Tuesday into Wednesday, after which their position became untenable, the message that the Irish Republic had been declared was broadcast in Morse code at regular intervals.[91] Seoirse believes that his uncle's use of the radio system was a step that had never been taken before: 'Plenty of messages had been sent to a specific destination [but] this was broadcast to whoever would receive it. So it's different to email, it's more like Twitter.'

As well as mechanical expertise, Seoirse added, Joseph, who 'was quite a young man, … had produced plays, written poetry [and] had edited magazines, all before I had a degree to my name'. Like Thomas MacDonagh, his Irish tutor, fellow poet, friend and co-editor of *The Irish Review*, Plunkett had laid the foundation for a potentially successful literary career. His sister Fiona recalled that he 'spent much of his time writing poetry. He would often lock himself in his room for three days at a time, writing one poem'.[92]

Fiona Plunkett felt that the romanticised story of her brother's midnight marriage to Grace Gifford in Kilmainham Gaol, often compared to the doomed union of Robert Emmet and Sarah Curran, overwhelmed her brother's actual accomplishments during his short twenty-eight years. In the early 1970s she told a journalist for *The Irish Press* that her brother was 'the forgotten of the 1916 leaders. His genius, his courage, and his humour are not fully realised.

People speak of him as if he was a myth', but 'he was a wonderful, colourful man [and] … an extraordinary genius and could make everyone laugh'.[93]

The story of Grace Gifford's marriage to Joseph Plunkett on the night before his execution will eternally be associated with the 1916 Rising. A special correspondent for *Lloyd's News,* writing from Dublin on Friday 12 May 1916, described it as 'one of the most poignant of the many tragedies which stand out from the grim and sordid drama which in the last ten days has been enacted in Ireland'.[94]

Joseph Plunkett met Grace Gifford in late 1914 and they cultivated a deep friendship based on a shared religious devotion, which developed into a love affair and culminated in a hasty marriage in the prison chapel at 11.30 p.m. on 3 May 1916. Their wedding was, in reality, less romantic than nationalist history has assumed. Grace recalled:

> I was never left alone with him, even after the marriage ceremony. I was brought in; and was put in front of the altar; and he was brought down the steps; and the cuffs were taken off him; and the chaplain went on with the ceremony; then the cuffs were put on him again. I was not alone with him – not for a minute.[95]

Grace Gifford
(*courtesy of Mercier Archive*)

Whatever the reality of the circumstances of the union, the story of her midnight marriage to the fragile, tubercular Plunkett evoked widespread sympathy and contributed to the turning tide of public opinion.

Grace opposed the Treaty and during the Civil War found herself a prisoner in Kilmainham Gaol, where she had been married years before. While imprisoned, she composed a flattering character sketch of Plunkett:

> He was a rare mix of vivacity and repose. His conversation was full of lightning wit. He had great moral courage and friendship would never prevent his rebuking profanity or tolerating slackness in national work, and while being warm and kindly to all, he was at the same time reserved to an extraordinary degree.[96]

Elected to the Provisional Committee of the Irish Volunteers on its establishment in November 1913, Joseph Plunkett 'promoted the organisation in *The Irish Review*' and his intemperate language provoked the seizure of numerous copies of the publication. In 1914 he was appointed to an advisory committee of Irish Volunteer Leaders within the IRB to devise a military plan for the uprising. By 1915 he was secretly engaged to Grace Gifford, but almost all of his energies were focused on preparations for the Rising. When Plunkett was appointed director of military operations on the Military Council, Tom Dillon and Rory O'Connor were co-opted as 'advisors in chemistry and engineering', and his brothers, George and Jack Plunkett, were also on his staff. In April Plunkett travelled via Spain, Italy and Switzerland to Berlin, where he saw the imperial chancellor and made arrangements to send a cargo of arms and ammunition to Ireland at a date apparently then not fixed, in the spring of 1916.[97] In October he went to America to meet with Clan na Gael with the plans for arms importation. By the beginning of 1916 Plunkett's tuberculosis was at an advanced stage, but he 'spent the rest of the time till Easter, whether in bed or out of it, on military plans for the Rising'.[98]

His twenty-four-year-old sister, Geraldine Plunkett, who worked as his aide-de-camp between 1912 and 1916, had planned a double wedding for Easter Sunday 1916, but Grace Gifford's bridegroom was otherwise occupied. Geraldine went ahead with her wedding to Tom Dillon on Easter Sunday and the newlyweds enjoyed an unhindered view of the arrival at the GPO of 'about 100' Volunteers on Easter Monday from a vantage point at the window of the front sitting-room of the Imperial Hotel, where they spent their honeymoon:

> We recognised Pearse, Connolly, MacDermott, Willie Pearse and my brother Joe – George was with the Liverpool Lambs and I think they came later. ... [We watched as] the staff of the GPO began to run out, hysterical girls screaming ... The tri-

colour was run up at the south front corner of the building and the recruiting posters ripped off the pillars with the bayonets to the cheers of the crowd at the [Nelson's] Pillar.[99]

Joseph Plunkett, who was recovering from a major operation on the glands in his neck, joined the other members of the Provisional Government in the GPO, attended by his aide-de-camp, Michael Collins. Piaras Béaslaí remembered that he 'looked like a dying man' and 'felt that it was only by a tremendous exertion of will power that he kept on his feet'.[100] According to Brian Barton and Michael T. Foy, however, 'there were enough sightings of Plunkett in the GPO, animated and in good humour to confirm that he enjoyed periods of remission'.[101]

Joseph Plunkett struck an impressive figure in his 'high tan leather boots, spurs [and] pince-nez'.[102] London-born Joseph Good, of the Kimmage garrison, observed that 'Connolly looked drab beside him in a bottle green thin serge uniform. The form of dress of the two men impressed me as representing two different ideas of freedom.'[103] Good, who was so fascinated with Joseph Plunkett, had been among the men under George Plunkett's command at Count Plunkett's Larkfield Estate in south Dublin in the weeks before the Rising. Section Commander Séamus Robinson recalled that, on Easter Monday, George's preoccupied demeanour changed and 'he was wearing a broad, proud, confident smile and a sword'.[104] Sometime before noon he read a dispatch instructing the Kimmage garrison to parade at Liberty Hall. When the party arrived at the tramline at Harold's Cross, the men 'boarded one tram, George Plunkett paying our fares'.[105] He famously asked for 'fifty-two tuppenny tickets to the city centre', his son Eoghan smiled. 'We were a unique body of soldiers,' said John McGallogly from Glasgow, 'going into action on a tram.'[106]

The Kimmage garrison took up positions in O'Connell Street, and Seoirse was particularly proud when, 'as a youngster' he heard the 'nice story of [his father] rescuing a British soldier in the street alongside the GPO' after the evacuation on Friday. According to Volunteer Seán Nunan:

On the far side of Moore Street, a British soldier was lying, badly wounded in the stomach and calling for help. Despite the fact that the street was swept by machine

were given whistles 'to let my father know if there was anybody coming up the avenue who shouldn't be, so that he could make a run for it':

> There was a story about my elder brother when he was about seven. A man at the gate asked him 'Is your father at home?'
> 'No he's not.'
> 'Do you know where he is?'
> 'I do.'
> 'So where is he?'
> 'He's in his pants!' (laughs)
> So at the age of seven he knew what you didn't say to strangers.

The precaution was not surprising, considering that their house guests, like their parents, were all 'unrepentant republicans'. Conversation about politics was also 'strictly forbidden in school', said Seoirse, who was educated by the Christian Brothers in Dundalk: 'I would have been at school with the sons of policemen, Fianna Fáil TDs, Fine Gael TDs and the like. You knew when to keep your mouth shut.' They were silent, for example, about their father's role as one of the seven signatories of the IRA's Declaration of War on the United Kingdom to liberate Northern Ireland in January 1939. It led to the S-Plan bombing campaign of England which, Eoghan insisted, his father voted against, because as far as he was concerned 'the civilian population … should be protected'. He recalled:

> When we were children going to school in the car we heard that war had been declared some months before the rest of the world heard that war had been de-clared. But we admired him thoroughly as a person so anything he did was right; it was simple. My mother [supported him] even though it was causing considerable hardship to the family … They felt it was their duty to continue the fight they had begun.

Eoghan agreed and added, 'they were revolutionaries' and 'I was proud of them … The men of 1916 did that; the Rising made them want to see the thing through.'

Seoirse knows little about his father's various incarcerations, other than the fact that he 'was on the run in the 1940s when I was old enough to see these things'. He was captured, and then he was let out on parole, which he hated 'because he couldn't do what he had promised not to do. It drove him crazy.' His last incarceration was in the Curragh Camp, or 'Kildare University', as Seoirse called it: 'They didn't have a very bad time there other than the fact

George Plunkett, photographed by Jack Plunkett at 'Owenstown' in 1942 (*courtesy of the Plunkett family*)

that they couldn't get on with their life's work, which was fighting the British.'

On 21 January 1944 George Plunkett, who Ernie O'Malley called a 'rock of gentle determination', died in Louth Infirmary from head injuries received when he was thrown from a pony cart.[112] According to his son, 'he had just been in to see the superintendent who told him that he was released on parole … So he died a free man.' Eoghan's version of the story is that, once released, his father 'got up on the cart [and] the horse bolted up the road. George stood up to try and stop it and it ran into the iron railings outside the old jail. He was thrown against the railings and crushed his skull.'

George Plunkett's funeral was held on 24 January, his coffin draped in a tricolour, and in attendance were J. J. O'Kelly, Frank Aiken, Seán McEntee, the widows of Cathal Brugha and Austin Stack, and members of the 1916 Kimmage Garrison. Éamon de Valera, whom the Plunketts regarded as 'a turncoat', sent a telegram of condolence, and Seoirse remembered that it was opened in the kitchen in Ballymascanlon House and was regarded with derision: 'If he loved him so much, why was he in jail?'

'My grandfather, Count Plunkett, could never stand de Valera,' Eoghan said, 'and I was introduced to him on the anniversary of *The Irish Press* – I worked in advertising – and when he heard my name he said: "Oh, that's a very good name. I hope you are living up to it". I didn't bother answering him.'

Seoirse was just ten years old when George died, so he received little first-hand information of his father's experiences:

> I presume he thought he'd live forever, like the rest of us, and that by the time he was an old man he would be able to tell us the stories. Either that or he assumed we already knew, but there was nobody to tell us what we didn't already know. The same applies to Jack.

After their father's death, Jack Plunkett assumed a paternal role in the brothers' lives. 'He tried to help,' remembered Eoghan, '[but] he had been on hunger strike [and] it wrecked him. He was only in his forties when he came to live with us in 1936 but ... he was a hopeless man.' Seoirse remembered his uncle as being 'extremely kind but rather rigid, a true Victorian ... He was a quieter, more straight-laced version of my father, but you could use him to guess what my father would have thought about something.'

The Plunkett brothers have been left with few material reference points for their family's integral involvement in the 1916 Rising. Eoghan admits that he was 'never really interested in the paraphernalia of it because we didn't talk about it, you know'. His brother, however, was more concerned with the artefacts of their family history and regrets that there are so few images of his uncle: 'All possible photographs [of Joseph] were destroyed to prevent him from being identified by British intelligence. ... Some did creep through the net but they have mostly been published.' George and Jack Plunkett 'didn't get medals; they were on the wrong side. They didn't sneer at people who took them because they weren't given to sneering, but they just wouldn't take medals from ... people who had not stuck to the line.'

ÉAMONN CEANNT

On Easter Monday morning, Áine Ceannt and her son Rónán watched as the tall, lean figure of Éamonn Ceannt, clad in Volunteer green, left their home at 2 Dolphin Terrace, a house that had played host to many clandestine IRB assemblies before the Rising. As commandant of the 4th Battalion, Ceannt told the 120 men assembled at Emerald Square in Dolphin's Barn that their objective was to occupy and hold the strategically important South Dublin Union, a workhouse complex covering over fifty-two acres in close proximity to Kingsbridge Station and the British Army barracks at Richmond and Islandbridge.

Cathal Brugha's section seized the James's Street entrance of the complex, while Ceannt took control of the Rialto entrance and directed companies to occupy the three strategic outposts at Roe's Distillery, Jameson's Distillery and Watkins' Brewery. The fighting began immediately, when the Volunteers fired on a company of British soldiers en route to Dublin Castle; they responded with an attack on the Rialto gate, and Volunteer positions were hit by machine-gun fire from the Royal Hospital. Forced back into the centre of the complex, the Volunteers suffered heavy casualties during the first day of the Rising. The following two days were quieter, but on Thursday military forces launched a major assault on Ceannt's headquarters, the Night Nurses' Home, during which Brugha was badly wounded by shrapnel from a grenade.[113] The troops attacked in short rushes, advancing then dropping to return fire, and forward again. The gunfire seemed to be coming from all directions and ripped through the timber, plaster, walls and ceilings. Eventually, the attack subsided and the British withdrew to the Royal Hospital. Quietness returned as darkness fell over the Union, but away towards the city the night sky had turned bright crimson.[114]

On Sunday morning, a temporary ceasefire allowed Thomas MacDonagh, accompanied by two priests, to go to the South Dublin Union and discuss the surrender terms with Ceannt. Resigned to the capitulation, he marched with forty-three surviving Volunteers to the surrender point at St Patrick's Park, where he ordered his men to pile up their arms before the rebels were removed to Richmond Barracks. Ceannt was identified as a leader on Monday morning and on Wednesday he was sentenced to death. Late on Friday 5 May he was transferred to Kilmainham.

Áine was permitted to see her husband in his cell in Kilmainham on Saturday, but the presence of a sergeant at the door meant that they 'could say very little'.[115] She left with his promise that he would send for her 'no matter what happened'.[116] On Sunday, Áine and her brothers-in-law, Richard and Michael Kent, were escorted to Kilmainham, where she spent 'about fifteen minutes' with her husband before they parted for the last time. The next day she visited Fr Augustine at Church Street and he gently related the details of her husband's execution.[117] Holding a crucifix, pressed into his hand by the Capuchin priest, Ceannt had been marched to the stonebreaker's yard as dawn was breaking. He was blindfolded, and Fr Augustine watched as the twelve-man firing squad took aim and fired. When the priest had finished his description, he produced Éamonn Ceannt's last letters: one for Áine, one for his son and one for the Irish nation.[118] To his wife he wrote:

> Dearest, silly little Fanny! My poor little sweetheart of − how many − years ago. Ever my comforter, God comfort you now. What can I say? I die a noble death for Ireland's freedom. Men and women will vie with one another to shake your dear hand. Be proud of me as I am and ever was of you. My cold exterior was but a mask. It has served me in these last days.
>
> You have a duty to me and to Rónán, that is to live. My dying wishes are that you remember your state of health. Work only as much as may be necessary and freely accept the little attentions, which in due course will be showered upon you. You will be, you are, the wife of one of the leaders of the Revolution. Sweeter still, you are my little child, my dearest pet, my sweetheart of the hawthorn hedges and Summer's eves. I remember all and I banish all so that I may die bravely.[119]

To his ten-year-old son he wrote:

> To my poor little son Rónán, from his father who is about to die tomorrow for the sake of Ireland. Goodbye and blessings …
>
> P.S. Take good care of your little mother. May God help you both and give you both a long and fulfilled life. May God free Ireland.[120]

Rónán followed his father's last instruction and remained with his mother throughout her life, but he was imbued with a tragic sense of his comparatively unheroic life. Writing in the *Irish Examiner* on the ninety-seventh anniversary of Éamonn Ceannt's death, Dave Kenny described how, when 'rustling' through his grand-aunt's (Máire nic Shiubhlaigh's) papers, he discovered a letter 'from a man who had lost his mother'. Kenny realised it was Éamonn Ceannt's son, who wrote with such 'tragic modesty':

Máire, from time to time, for years past, I have wondered if Mamy [*sic*] was, in a way, disappointed in me for not having shown myself to have been as fine a man as my father was. I never had the courage to ask Mamy [*sic*] and she never gave me any special reason for my idea, but, yet, she may, deep down, have felt I was a bit of a failure. I'd rather know the answer to that question than be kept in ignorance, so if Mamy [*sic*] ever spoke of the matter, will you please tell me what she said, even if it's hard to hear.[121]

Deeply touched by the letter, Kenny tried to imagine being a ten-year-old, 'knowing your father is about to be shot', and then 'living in the shadow of a colossus you could never hope to emulate. Ceannt's death was not a sterile *blood sacrifice*,' he wrote, 'it was a tragedy for his family. He was not an icon, he was a man.'[122]

Mary Gallagher has often tried to imagine the man who was her grand-uncle. As Michael Kent's granddaughter, she knew 'embarrassingly little' about the details of Éamonn's story when she was growing up because hers was a very 'apolitical family' and 'certainly didn't discuss Irish history over the dinner table'. Her mother, Nora, 'would have talked about her parents but very little about her uncle. She was certainly proud of him', but 'she was only two years old in 1916 and had very little knowledge about that period'. Mary was vaguely aware that her grand-uncle and his wife played 'an important part in the history of modern Ireland' and even though her family attended the annual memorial service at the military cemetery in Arbour Hill, where fourteen of the executed leaders are buried, it was 'more a day out than having any historical significance' for Ceannt's young grand-niece.

In adulthood, Mary has made a detailed study of 'one of the more capable military leaders' of the Rising, who 'held out with a very small troop against very significant odds in terms of the British Army … and one of the last to surrender'. She was motivated to embark on her research in the late 1990s after William Henry, 'who was writing the first biography of Éamonn', made contact with the family:

Unfortunately, by that time, my mother Nora, her sister Joan and their brother Éamonn, who were the nieces and nephew respectively of Éamonn Ceannt, had all died and we had asked them very little about the family history, so my sister and I found ourselves scrabbling round to try and put together the pieces … With hindsight I realise we probably gave William Henry far less than he would have liked because we simply didn't know ourselves.

The sisters relied on Áine Ceannt's witness testimony to the Bureau of Military History, which Mary admits 'was very illuminating for me in my ignorance', and the only 'other source of information we had at the time was my grandfather's diaries. I call them diaries, but they were really the story of the Kent family, of himself and his wife and their children. They started around 1911 on the day his oldest child was born' and the first diary is called 'Joan's Story by her Daddy'. He continued writing until the 1930s and 'the diaries became not just Joan's story but also the story of the family'.

Joan Kent 'treasured these diaries' and 'kept them wrapped up in brown paper up on top of a wardrobe … She never really allowed anybody to read them' but 'to be fair,' Mary smiled, 'we never looked for them either'. In fact, 'our eyes glazed over when grandfather's diaries were mentioned'. When her aunt died, Mary took responsibility for the diaries, but 'only took them out and started to read them' when 'we started looking for information for the biography'. They were 'a real eye-opener':

> They are charming [and] … a wonderful history of our family, but in the middle of all of this you suddenly find yourself in Easter Week 1916 reading about how your grandfather went along on Easter Sunday morning to his brother's house: their sister-in-law [Liz Kent] had died shortly after childbirth down in Wicklow and Michael went to Éamonn's house to see who would go to the family funeral. It was typical family stuff you know. The front of the house covered in bicycles and all these people coming and going from the house – complete *rí rá* and *ruaile buaile* (noise and activity) … [Michael thought] that this was another of Éamonn's enthusiasms and hopefully he would grow out of it.

Mary read from a letter from Éamonn Ceannt that she found pasted into her grandfather's dairy. It is dated Sunday 22 April 1916:

To Master Michael and family with best Easter wishes. All well here – on the defensive. If the friends of the small nationalities should decide on interfering with our Inspections tomorrow, I would advise you to make yourself scarce. Your own house is the safest place from 4 p.m., our hour of assembly, until such time as the danger of an attack is passed which would be about 7. Come what may, we are ready.

On the next page is a photograph of Éamonn Ceannt that Mary feels was put in at a later date 'because it was obviously produced as one of the postcards of the Irish rebellion'. Her grandfather also carefully pasted into his diary a piece of paper on which is inscribed: 'Dublin Metropolitan Police Permanent Pass. Please pass Michael Kent of 111 Phibsboro Road through the streets of the city and DMP area.' This, said Mary, 'was obviously produced to allow people to actually go to work during the 1916 week':

> [There is also] some extremely touching material about being brought to Kilmainham Gaol at 4 o'clock in the morning with Éamonn's wife Áine and their brother Dick to see Éamonn for the last time. The first time I read this I was sitting with tears flowing because it was just so immediate and so touching to read about, and to imagine yourself into that position. I had never thought about [it] before.

She turned to the pages dated Friday 5 May and Sunday 7 May 1916 and was clearly moved as she read the entry. Her grandfather's words evoked in her a strong affective response, mediated not through recollection but through imaginative recreation:

> He received us and shook hands quite calmly and, after a word or two, he put his arm around Áine, bent down with a sweet smile and kissed her lovingly. They were lovers again – he wanted those few minutes – and seeing them wrapped in one another, we turned away and conversed near the two sentries at the door (who stayed all the time), while Éamonn and Áine sat on the edge of the low plank bed at the corner, and had their last quarter of an hour on earth together …
>
> After we left the cell, and before the sentry shut the door, I looked back at poor Ned and that picture I shall bear with me till the end. He stood sideways, right side

towards me, the candles showing him up clearly from the exterior darkness, looking down at the little table where he had been writing, wrapped in thought, silent, a pucker at the base of the forehead, just at the nose. My heart welled up with infinite pity for the poor, poor lad that I had brought to school, but, controlling myself, I said out loudly, almost fiercely, '*Beannacht Dé leat*' [God's blessings on you] and back he answered at once, in his old calm, quiet way as if he was saying good night, '*Go soirbhidh Dia duit*' [May God favour you] …

[That night] I prayed on [*sic*] as I never prayed before, bringing down my Sacred Heart statue and altar lamp to the dining room … Keeping a glass of water near me to moisten my lips, sometimes kneeling, occasionally sitting and every hour or so going out to the parlour to look out between the blades of the venetian blinds at the coming dawn. Poor Éamonn's last earthly dawn … I pulled out my watch, seven minutes to four. I felt I knew then definitely that all was over with poor Éamonn. I put out the lights and as I went upstairs into bed I cried bitterly from the depths of my heart, but God's will be done.

Mary paused to point out that her grandfather's handwriting is 'very tiny' on that page. Michael had obviously left the page blank, intending to return and record the event when he 'could bring himself to write about it'. He was to find that in the act of recording his memories of that seminal night, he would be limited by the confines of a page.

Michael Kent recorded other 'extraordinary events' such as his sadness at the death of his older brother. William Kent, a company sergeant major in the Royal Dublin Fusiliers, was killed in action during the Battle of Arras, in France, on 24 April 1917; a year to the day after the Rising broke out in Dublin. According to his grand-niece, William represented the people in Ireland who saw the British Army as a career in the absence of many other options:

He was the oldest of the family and probably wouldn't have had very many more options, whereas Éamonn was more educated. He came up at a time when Ireland had changed significantly; there were more opportunities and I suppose in a sense they both applied the same capabilities militarily but on two different sides of the fence.

My grandfather recognised those [deaths] equally, he didn't differentiate …

> These were his brothers [and] he was as upset about the death of his brother Bill in 1917 as he was about the death of his brother Éamonn in 1916.

Michael Kent's diaries motivated his granddaughter to embark on 'a journey of discovery' during which she learned about Ceannt's early life and his induction into extreme nationalist circles. 'His military expertise,' she explained, was partly attributable to 'the military tradition in the family'. Éamonn's father, James Kent, was an RIC head constable and his older brother had served with the British Army in the Boer War, in Malta and in Egypt.

When James Kent retired in 1892, the family moved to Dublin and, like Seán Heuston and Con Colbert, the Kent brothers were educated at the Christian Brothers' O'Connell School, North Richmond Street. 'Éamonn would have been a very bright student,' Mary said, but his schoolboy diaries, housed in the Allen Library, are typically adolescent 'at a time when adolescence hadn't been invented'.

On leaving school, the brothers secured employment with the Dublin Corporation 'almost simultaneously'. Éamonn 'was a bookkeeper' in the City Treasurer's Office and Michael was a clerk. Éamonn 'refused to do the civil service exam because he didn't want to be paid directly by the British treasury, whereas he was happy to work in Dublin Corporation, where he was being paid by the citizens of Dublin'. Mary feels that her grandfather's 'political sensibilities' were not quite so strong: 'Dublin Corporation was a good, secure, pensionable [job], bearing in mind they were both sons of an RIC man and the major attraction of the RIC was the pension.'

'What I have learned about him suggests that Éamonn Ceannt was a very enthusiastic person [and] once he became enthusiastic about something [he would] learn about it in depth [and] follow it through in great detail and with great devotion.' For example, 'when he decided to learn piping, he was going to learn everything there was to know about the pipes'. He joined the Catholic Young Men's Society and 'went on pilgrimage to Rome in [September] 1908 [where] he played the Uilleann pipes for Pope Pius X'.

Éamonn displayed similar enthusiasm in his involvement with the Irish language movement. He joined the Gaelic League in 1899 and 'became an excellent Irish language teacher'. In fact, 'he taught Irish to the woman who would become his wife, Frances (Áine) O'Brennan'. He frequently begins his letters to Áine in Irish and their marriage ceremony in 1905 was one of the first for years to be celebrated entirely in Irish. Mary also discovered, in her grand-uncle's papers, his 'various attempts to come up with an Irish name for Kent'. He finally settled on Ceannt and 'was most insistent in all official correspondence' that the name would be used. His son Rónán, born in 1906, was baptised and registered in Irish, and in 1909 Frances changed her name to Áine B. É. Ceannt.

The Gaelic League also provided an introduction to 'the people in the whole Irish-Ireland tradition'. In 1908 Ceannt joined the Dublin Central Branch of Sinn Féin, and four years later Seán MacDermott swore him in to the IRB. He was a founder member of the Irish Volunteers, and Áine and her sister, Lily O'Brennan, joined Cumann na mBan on its formation.[123] In May 1915 Ceannt was appointed to the IRB Military Council and became commandant of the 4th Battalion of Volunteers.

'It sounds paradoxical,' his grand-niece Mary smiled, '[but] I think, as a family, they come across as very gentle individuals.' Michael's diary suggests that he was an 'immensely soft and gentle person', and Éamonn's 'romanticism [and] gentleness comes through if you go back to the letters [he wrote] to his wife.[124] So, for somebody who found himself in this extraordinary situation his personality was very religious [and] very romantic but he was also intensely capable and efficient.'

Mary 'just missed' her 'Auntie Fanny' (Áine) who 'died almost nine months exactly before [she] was born', but Éamonn's letters reveal that he saw her 'very much as the little woman who needs to be protected'. After his death, however, Áine had 'a fascinating career'. She quickly assumed a public role after 1916 and 'was very involved in the Irish National Aid Association and Volunteer Dependants' Fund, set up to support the widows and orphans of people who had been killed in the Rising'. Later she became secretary of the Children's Relief Association (Orphans' Fund).[125] In 1917 she was elected vice-president of Cumann na mBan and, in 1918, vice-president of the Rathmines Urban District Council. She was a district justice in the republican courts in 1920–21 and a member of the Executive Committee of Sinn Féin. When Countess Markievicz, Minister for Labour in the First Dáil, set up a Labour Court, Áine

Ceannt was one of the first members. 'All of which,' added Mary, 'was done simultaneously to being there for Rónán as he was growing up.'

Like the other 1916 widows, Áine Ceannt was subject to harassment by the Black and Tans during the War of Independence, when she provided refuge for Michael Collins and Robert Barton at the house she and her son shared with Lily and Elizabeth O'Brennan in Ranelagh. In November 1920, in the immediate aftermath of Bloody Sunday, it was raided by 'nine lorry loads of Black and Tans'.[126]

Áine and her sister Lily, who had been a secretary to the Treaty delegation in 1921, opposed the final document, which 'achieved too limited a degree of independence and was a betrayal of all that for which Éamonn had died'.[127] They were raided frequently by Free State troops, and in a letter to her sister in Kilmainham Gaol in April 1923, Áine described how 'men with blackened faces' invaded her house. They smashed windows, ate the food, and the etchings of the seven signatories were torn down and ripped to pieces.[128] Áine mourned the loss of a little gold brooch Éamonn had brought her from Paris. 'However,' she wrote, 'we are still alive.'[129]

Áine Ceannt retired from politics at the end of the Civil War and devoted the remainder of her life to her role as a member of the Central Council of the White Cross, which her grand-niece feels reflects her 'maternal concerns'. *The Irish Press* of November 1933 proclaimed that Mrs Ceannt is 'one of the most capable women in Ireland … travelling to all parts of the nation and presiding like a particularly loving godmother over the destiny of the children whose fathers fell or were disabled in the seven years of struggle'.[130] She was 'an amazing woman', Mary said, 'and a story still to be written to be perfectly honest.'

THOMAS MACDONAGH

Like the other widows of the 1916 leaders, Muriel MacDonagh was afforded the bittersweet consolation of a last letter written in a cell in Kilmainham:

> I am to die at dawn 3.30 a.m. 3rd May. I am ready to die … for myself I have no regret. The one bitterness that death has for me is the separation it brings from my beloved wife, Muriel, and my beloved children, Donagh and Barbara … it breaks my heart to think that I shall never see my children again, but I have not wept or

mourned. I counted the cost of this, and am ready to pay it … my dearest love, Muriel thank you a million times for all you have been to me. I have only one trouble in leaving life – leaving you so. Be brave, darling, … but for your suffering this would be all joy and glory. Goodbye.

Barbara MacDonagh was only eighteen months old when her father was executed, and her mother Muriel Gifford died in a drowning accident just over a year later. Speaking to a journalist in 1969, on the fifty-second anniversary of her mother's death, she said: 'I can't really remember what [my mother] looked like … my only memory of her is of a soft hand that used to come down to comfort me.'[131] Acrimony followed swiftly on the heels of tragedy, when she and her brother Donagh became the subject of a bitter custody battle between the Gifford and MacDonagh families. Understandably, Barbara spoke little to her daughter, Lucille Redmond, about this rootless period in her young life. Like many people who had 'a difficult childhood, she would speak about it – but she wouldn't speak about it'.

Donagh, slightly older than his sister Barbara, had clearer recollections of May 1916, but they were distinctively the memories of a child. In Lucille's words:

> He was playing in a rockery and a boogie man in a long black dress arrived with terrible news [of his father's execution] and then soldiers came and started shouting and flinging stuff around. His mother put my mother in the pram and [took him] by the hand and they went outside. He wanted to walk along the backs of the soldiers who were lying there with their guns fixed on the house, but she wouldn't let him.

In adulthood, Donagh described what he considered the nobility of his father's sacrifice:

> A poet, a scholar, a musician, and a dramatist, he was, as Yeats said, 'coming into his own'. Like his friends and fellow-poets, Pearse and Plunkett, he balanced all the future and its promise against the needs of the country and threw his own future into the country's scale. He was my father and he was executed on May 3rd 1916.[132]

Thomas and Muriel MacDonagh
(*courtesy of the National Library of Ireland*)

Thomas MacDonagh was born in Cloughjordan, County Tipperary, on 1 February 1878 and received his early education from his parents, Joseph and Mary, who were national schoolteachers. They imbued in him a passion for music and literature and a strong Catholic ethos. 'When he was fourteen or perhaps fifteen, the Holy Ghost fathers recruited him into Rockwell College' in Cashel, County Tipperary, where he taught and studied for the priesthood, but he 'realised that he really didn't have any great belief in organised religion' and was released in 1901.[133] His granddaughter said:

> On the way from the seminary he met Plunkett on the train and a red-headed lady, Molly Colum (née Maguire), who was his sweetheart for a time. These two meetings on the train led him to a lifelong love of the revolutionary movements and of red-headed ladies![134]

MacDonagh taught for a year at St Kieran's Secondary School in Kilkenny, where he cultivated a friendship with pacifist and social reformer Francis

Sheehy-Skeffington, began experimenting with poetry and discovered a love for the Irish language, having gone to 'a Gaelic League meeting for a lark'. He tendered his resignation from his teaching post in June 1903, 'finding the environment at St Kieran's incompatible with his newfound nationalism', and subsequently secured a position at St Coleman's Monastery School in Fermoy, County Cork.[135] During this period he travelled to the Aran Islands, off the west coast of Ireland, to further immerse himself in the language. There he met Patrick Pearse, who was 'starting up his school [St Enda's] at the time'. Pearse hired MacDonagh as a teacher and, because he had been a teacher at Rockwell 'and had a very good reputation', he was a 'big attraction for the new school'. He acted as assistant headmaster at St Enda's, and his home in Oakley Road, Ranelagh, became a meeting place for many of Dublin's literati, including James Stephens and Padraic Colum. Its proximity to the school meant that 'the boys of St Enda's used to find one of their greatest sources of amusement in discussing MacDonagh's latest love affairs'.[136]

Lucille thinks that Thomas met her grandmother, Muriel Gifford, 'a tall, willowy redhead', around 1908, because a letter exists from that year in which she invited him to tea. Muriel was one of five daughters born to Frederick Gifford, who 'is said to have been the great-grandson of Lord Edward Fitzgerald'. He had set up in practice as a solicitor and 'the Yeats family, for instance, were his clients'. Lucille has inherited a painting of her grandmother by John Yeats and is inclined to identify another of her maternal relatives in Frederick Burton's famous watercolour *Meeting on the Turret Stairs* (1864). 'I've often wondered if the model was my great-grandmother, Isabella. She was red-headed and she would have been sixteen when it was painted.' This is a distinct possibility, because Isabella Gifford's maiden name was Burton. Her father, Robert Nathaniel Burton, rector of Clonagoose Parish in County Carlow, died of 'famine fever' in 1850, and his widow and her eight children were taken in by her brother-in-law, Frederick Burton, 'who brought them up in Corofin, County Clare'.

The clandestine meeting depicted in the painting foreshadowed Isabella Burton's subsequent rebellion, which was 'unthinkable for a rector's daughter: she ran off with my great-grandfather, who was a Catholic, and they married and had twelve children'. Muriel, according to her granddaughter, was 'the prettiest of the Gifford girls'. Lucille's understanding is that her grandfather 'was introduced to a bunch of the [Gifford] sisters in St Enda's' by the suffragette and journalist, Nannie (Nora) Dryhurst, who told him: "I think you should marry one of these girls". I think he put his eye on my grandmother fairly fast.'

'They courted for a time', and in September 1910, having studied in Paris for some months, MacDonagh began to study for an MA at University College Dublin (UCD) under Professor Robert Donovan. 'His best friend in UCD was Eoin MacNeill,' Lucille added. 'The two of them were always together talking Irish.' They would walk 'along, having these animated discussions together. Everybody, if they saw one they would expect to see the other.'

Despite the disapproval of her Protestant mother, Muriel Gifford married Thomas MacDonagh on 3 January 1912, by which time he had secured a position as a tutor and an examiner with the National University: 'Between 1911 and 1913 his interests seem to have been almost completely literary.' He was 'bringing out books of poetry' and working on his first academic book, *Literature in Ireland: Studies in Irish and Anglo-Irish* (1916) and co-editing *The Irish Review*. He was also writing plays and was among a group that broke away from the Abbey Theatre in 1906 and formed the Irish Theatre Company (also called the Theatre of Ireland). The group, which included Pearse, Markievicz and Plunkett, maintained close links with the Abbey, but theirs was often 'a more forcefully revolutionary' programme. In May 1908 the Irish Theatre staged MacDonagh's *When the Dawn has Come* and in April 1912 produced his *Metempsychosis*. In Lucille's opinion, the Irish Theatre was 'the opposite to the Abbey' and 'the drama of the Celtic Twilight'. Its intention was to showcase 'more gritty and urban modern Irish drama'. 'If he had survived,' she said, 'Irish literature might have been quite different … my grandfather was just beginning to develop as a poet when he was executed. He had a turn of phrase and kindness about humans that might have made him a major writer.'[137]

On the formation of the Volunteers in 1913, MacDonagh was appointed captain of 'C' Company, 2nd Battalion, and made a thorough study of arms, drilling and street fighting. His granddaughter's impression is that 'he wouldn't have been a radical nationalist in the way that Pearse would have been … his ideas would have been socialist and humanist', but Thomas MacDonagh was also a skilled tactician. This first became evident during the Howth gun-running of 26 July 1914, when 'he and Darrell Figgis managed to bamboozle the British so that everybody could get away with their guns through the fields'.

By 1915 Thomas and Muriel had two children, and Thomas, now a member of the IRB and the Volunteers' director of training, was working as a full-time lecturer in English at the National University. One of his students, Austin Clarke, observed that in the early months of 1916 MacDonagh 'looked worried and for moments during lectures he would appear abstracted'.[138]

In April MacDonagh was appointed to the Military Council of the IRB and was among the signatories of the Proclamation on Easter Sunday. On Easter Monday, he marched to Jacob's Biscuit Factory in Camden Street and with 150 Volunteers seized the building as his headquarters. His granddaughter's understanding is that MacDonagh 'was marching with them along Grafton Street where he passed Captain Richard McCormick with his Citizen Army troops and [he] called across the street – I haven't got the exact phrasing – "There must be as little bloodshed as possible".'[139]

Jacob's occupied a large area between Bishop Street and Peter Street, and was surrounded by a warren of densely populated residential streets. It was chosen for its position between Portobello Barracks and the city centre, and its 'two immense towers give a bird's eye view of a large portion of the Bridge Street end, which enabled the snipers to cover Portobello Bridge, the roof of Ship Street Barracks and Dublin Castle'.[140] The main body of Volunteers took the factory at midday on Easter Monday and set up outposts in Fumbally Lane, Camden Street, Wexford Street and Aungier Street, as the largely pro-British local community shouted abuse at them. MacDonagh's men barricaded themselves into the factory, piling sacks of flour against windows and doors.

The military assault envisioned by the rebels never materialised and they had little taste of battle. The only engagement occurred on Easter Monday, when some of the military from Portobello Barracks, on their way to relieve Dublin Castle, moved into Camden Street towards MacDonagh's position. MacDonagh ordered his men, who were itching for action, not to fire until the party was well within range. However, they fired too soon and the military escaped with slight casualties. Except for the occasional exchange with snipers or small British patrol parties, the garrison 'enjoyed a very quiet week' and the men from the outposts were recalled to Jacob's.[141]

As the days wore on, the rebels under the command of MacDonagh, John MacBride and Michael O'Hanrahan waited, increasingly impatient for action. They were taunted by the sounds of gunfire from the city and 'the glow of fire in the skies'.[112] They were also deprived of sleep, but their commander's indomitable confidence served to maintain morale. Seosamh de Brun described how 'the spirit of officers and men was redolent of comradeship and cheeriness. Although the responsibilities of the situation were heavy on Commandant McDonagh [sic], no sign of this appeared in his demeanour.'[143] Lucille remembers her grandfather 'through research and family stories – less for the militarism than for the human qualities he showed ... He was very gallant, very old-fashioned. He treated his British prisoners very well and his men respected him for that.'[144]

At 3.45 p.m. on Saturday 29 April, Pearse signed an unconditional surrender on behalf of the Provisional Government. The next day Elizabeth O'Farrell carried the order to Jacob's, but MacDonagh, convinced that it was signed under duress, refused to surrender. Fr Augustine organised an interview with General Lowe, after which MacDonagh, in consultation with Éamonn Ceannt, accepted the surrender. According to de Brun's statement, his commandant told the assembled ranks that the senior officers, in conference at staff headquarters, had concluded that 'a splendid assertion of Irish Independence had been gallantly made' but 'Commandant General Pearse was convinced that further sacrifice of life would be futile' and had 'decided to cease hostilities'. MacDonagh 'broke down and sobbed bitterly'. There were loud cries of dissent among the men but 'the Senior Officers ... were silent. They were resigned to the inevitability of surrender.'[145]

Lucille picked up her grandfather's story in Richmond Barracks, where, apparently, 'he made demands for the rights of the prisoners being held there' and 'was [among] the first to be court-martialled'. He was transferred to Kilmainham Gaol on 2 May and at midnight word arrived that he would be shot at dawn. His wife had not heard from him since Easter Sunday, when he told her, "I may or may not see you tomorrow." ... He did not say anything about the revolution.' She only learned of his arrest when it was reported in the evening newspapers.[146] Muriel MacDonagh was the only one of the 1916 widows denied the consolation of seeing her husband even briefly before he died. Geraldine Plunkett recorded: 'The night before Tomás McDonagh [*sic*] was shot, Muriel got a message brought by a private soldier, that it was thought her husband was to be shot. She tried to get a 'phone message to the Castle to ask permission to see him [but] … the only one working was at Du Cros' [house] and they refused to let her use it.'[147]

In fact, 'there are a couple of different accounts of what happened next,' Lucille said. The British claimed that they sent a staff car to collect Muriel in Ranelagh but it 'couldn't get through the sniping remains after the Rising' so they sent it to Basin Lane to collect his sister Mary [Sr Francesca], who was a Sister of Charity there. Other accounts suggest that Muriel was given permission to see her husband, but the soldier neglected to give her a permit enabling her to travel through the city.[148] But the 'family story' is that Muriel 'made her way to Kilmainham where she was refused entry because MacDonagh had already had a visit from his sister [and] prisoners were only allowed one visit. So I don't know what's true.'

When Mary MacDonagh was taken to see her brother, she learned that he had already received confession and communion, and had written to his wife. She gave Thomas rosary beads that had belonged to their mother, and on the morning of 3 May MacDonagh was marched to his death. 'Their bodies were put into a field ambulance and carried off to Arbour Hill,' Lucille said, 'and then a British soldier scratched their names on stones so their burial place would be remembered, and put a stone at the head of each grave, which shows the kind of kindness and reverence for life that somebody could have from the other side.'

'Muriel brought the children to her mother's house but Isabella [was] very angered by it.' Her husband had recently suffered a stroke and her sons were fighting at the Front, 'so she probably wasn't in her best form'. She 'scolded my grandmother and then tried to give her money [but Muriel] walked out and left there and that was it.' And so Thomas MacDonagh's widow, who was prone to ill-health and bouts of depression, was left to care for two young children without any means of support. She was forced to leave her home in Oakley Road and stayed first with the Plunketts and later with her brother-in-law, Joseph MacDonagh.[149]

A newspaper cutting from 1917 described Muriel as 'tall and slim with a pale complexion, vivid blue eyes and copper-coloured hair', a sympathetic beauty, which perhaps provoked General Maxwell to send her a command to appear in public as little as possible.[150] Maxwell could not have realised how tragic a figure Muriel MacDonagh was to become. In early 1917 her four-year-old son, Donagh, was badly injured in a fall on the marble steps in Switzers Department Store in Grafton Street. During his slow convalescence, Muriel was persuaded to take her two-year-old daughter and join the other widows of executed leaders on a retreat to Skerries organised by the National Aid Association for the widows and orphans.

'What happened at Skerries has been the subject of rumour, conjecture and exaggeration,' wrote Lucille. On Monday 9 July 1917 Muriel and her sister Grace took Barbara to the beach. 'An abstracted Muriel put seashells into a cosmetic box for the child, who prattled to her mother. In the afternoon Muriel told her daughter "Be a good girl now, Babbily, and I'll be back soon", and stepped into the water.' She swam out, the tide pulling her out fast. Grace became concerned when she lost sight of her sister and Ina Connolly took the shrieking Barbara inside. All of Skerries, including the teenaged Seán Lemass and Jimmy O'Dea, turned out to search. The next morning, 'IRB man Rory O'Connor' found Muriel's body a quarter of a mile away. Contrary to romantic speculation that the grief-stricken widow had taken her own life, 'the post mortem found that, aged just thirty-two, Muriel had suffered a fatal heart attack'.[151]

On 12 July Donagh watched as his mother's mile-long funeral cortège passed the window of the children's hospital. Thousands of mourners followed the horse-drawn hearse with Muriel's coffin 'covered by the Tricolour she had sewn'.[152] 'My mother kept the collection of shells in a cosmetic box,' Lucille said, 'and after she died I took out a few for myself and then I gave my sister Muriel the remainder with the box.'

Mary MacDonagh was informed of Muriel's drowning by Noel Lemass and Rory O'Connor, and wrote about how saddened she was at the loss of her sister-in-law, who was 'a gentle creature and never put on side'.[153] Her brother, John MacDonagh, took charge of the orphaned children. In Barbara's words: 'The idea was to keep us from the influence of our Protestant grandmother, yet we were made to visit her once a week.'[154] Lucille is inclined to agree with

Sinéad McCoole, who observed that, 'Donagh and Barbara were true victims of the 1916 Rising.'[155]

The MacDonagh family lost another member when Joseph MacDonagh died of peritonitis on Christmas Day 1922. His appendix burst while he was on hunger strike in Mountjoy. 'Joe was our standby,' his sister, Mary, wrote, 'and when he went everything went.'[156]

Despite her family heritage, Lucille does not recall her mother having any 'time for divisions'. In fact, one of Barbara's childhood recollections of the Civil War epitomised her later neutrality:

> When she was a little girl she would be sitting on the lap of Michael Collins and somebody would come running in and say, 'Quick, quick, Rory's coming [Rory O'Connor].' Michael Collins would give her a kiss on the cheek and run out the back and Rory would come in and she would be sitting on his knee. She would be warned not to tell Rory that Michael was there, or Mick that Rory was there … I think she thought that the Civil War was the worst thing that could have happened … it tore the country apart.

Barbara didn't believe in imposing on her children the legacy of a bitter civil war, the details of her tragic childhood or the burden of a martyred grandfather. Nonetheless, it is difficult to shake off the heavy mantle of such an iconic forebear. Donagh MacDonagh, a district court justice in Dublin and a successful poet in his own right, lived in the shadow of his father, who was 'a stranger to [him] in all but blood'.[157] The weight of his father's legacy is highlighted in a comment by sculptor Oisín Kelly, whose preliminary study for a bronze head of MacDonagh included sketching the profile of his son. The artist said that it helped him 'to appreciate the affinities, spiritual and physical', between the two poets, and observed that Donagh inherited his father's 'heroic quality … Don too was proud and fearless and had he been tested as his father had been tested he would not have failed'.[158]

Lucille has also felt that pressure. In 1978, on the centenary of her grandfather's birth, she told the *Sunday Independent*: 'It's revolting being a direct descendant of a 1916 signatory. I feel like an approved relic, a piece of St Valentine or St Patrick.'[159]

PATRICK PEARSE

Patrick Pearse, the commander-in-chief of a rebel army, seemed, in life, somewhat unsure of his own identity. Posthumously, he has become variously the embodiment of noble sacrifice, a youthful idealist and a dangerous ultra-religious fanatic. In 1932 the subject of Louis N. Le Roux's biography was 'possessed of all the qualities which go into the making of a saint'[160] and in 1966 David Thornley observed, 'It would be almost blasphemous to discern a human being of flesh and blood.'[161] His memory was appropriated as a touchstone for Irish republicanism and, as such, his reputation was subject to vigorous revisionism in the 1970s, when his legacy was reduced to a 'triumph of failure'.[162] He has emerged in more recent decades as a progressive educationalist and a national hero. It is no wonder, then, that his grand-nephews are at odds about the significance of their family inheritance.

Patrick Pearse's father, James, was a stone carver and sculptor, born in Middlesex in 1839. Attracted by a 'boom in church building' he moved to Ireland in the mid-1850s, where he married Emily Susanna Fox and they had four children: Emily, Agnes, Amy and James Vincent.[163] Agnes and Amy both died at a young age, but Emily and James Vincent survived to adulthood and both married. James Vincent Pearse was Noel Scarlett's grandfather, and Alf MacLochlainn is Emily Pearse's grandson. Both men are, as Scarlett explained, 'grand-nephews of Patrick Pearse', and because none of the children from James Pearse's second marriage had children, the cousins have carried the family legacy into the twenty-first century.

'The earlier Pearse family,' Noel Scarlett's son, Kieran, said, 'is kind of written out of history [and] ... when you say you are related, people don't believe you.' His father, who has been an active participant in 1916 commemorative events since the 1950s, always encouraged Kieran to embrace the association with Pearse and 'to get involved', because the Rising 'should never be forgotten'.

James Pearse's first wife, Emily, died in 1876, and he married twenty-year-old Margaret Brady in October 1877. The couple went to live at 27 Great Brunswick Street, where Pearse established a successful monumental stone-carving business.[164] Their daughter, Margaret Mary, was born in 1878 and in the following year their son Patrick Henry was born. Their second son, William, was born 1881 and Mary Brigid arrived seven years later.

men in the country on Sunday next will be Mr Henry Noel Scarlett … a grandnephew of Pádraig Pearse [who] has been selected as a member of the Presidential Guard of Honour at the GPO.' 'It was a proud day,' smiled Noel. The guard was provided by the 'Pearse Unit' of the Forsa Cosanta Aitiuil (FCA) – otherwise known as 'D' Company, 20th Battalion. Scarlett's comrades in the FCA understood his connection to Pearse and 'thought it was very prestigious', but 'everybody wanted to get on the guard of honour', so 'there was fierce competition'.

Noel's second cousin, Alf MacLochlainn, writer and former director of the National Library of Ireland, had a less visible role in the proceedings: 'I was on one of the commemoration committees in 1966 with Frank Burke and various [past pupils of] St Enda's.' His brother, Piaras, author of *Last Words, Letters & Statements of the Leaders Executed after the Rising* (1971), was also involved as 'Secretary of the Commemoration Committee'. Their maternal uncle, Seán Dowling, a senior IRA officer during the War of Independence and the Civil War, shared the committee table with his nephew, and as active members of the Kilmainham Gaol Restoration Committee, both men were present when the prison was opened as a national monument in the same year.[174]

Despite his heavy involvement in the Golden Jubilee and his academic understanding of his grand-uncle's life, Alf MacLochlainn is disinclined to use the word 'proud'. His feelings about Pearse, he said, are 'quite neutral: no pride or shame':

> The whole thing was ten years over by the time I was born … and my views on what happened then are irrelevant. My views on what happened are in no way improved or made more relevant by the fact that I am related to Patrick Pearse. Whatever else the men of 1916 were doing, they were not founding a family dynasty.[175]

He still maintains that 'there is no wisdom attached to being connected to famous people', and resents people 'appointing themselves representatives of those who happen to be their uncles and aunts, sisters and cousins. They have no special role in advising what is to be done about commemoration'. He is concerned, however, about the 'hijacking of the commemorations' by 'spoiled Provos', who reveal themselves as such by referring to his grand-uncle as 'Pádraig Pearse'. Alf insisted that his grand-uncle never used that name: 'He was Pádraig Mac Piarais or Patrick Pearse but never Pádraig Pearse.'

His second cousin, Noel Scarlett, has no such reservations about declaring that he is 'very proud' of his connection with the Pearse family, and is 'reminded very forcefully of that connection every Easter'. In fact, when a new exhibition opened in the Pearse Museum in The Hermitage at Rathfarnham in 2004, he felt compelled to write to *The Irish Times* to correct an erroneous comment that the display included information about the 'discovery of two extra daughters by [James Pearse's] first wife'.[176]

Noel's mother, Florence, daughter of Patrick Pearse's half-brother, James, married William Scarlett from Enniskillen, County Fermanagh, in 1915. Almost immediately after their wedding, he left for the trenches of the First World War with the Royal Dublin Fusiliers and fought at the Somme. Noel, who feels a strong connection with both traditions, is adamant that 'the men [who] died in the trenches should be respected as well as the men who fought in 1916':

> When I was growing up the feeling towards them was actually hostile in parts of Dublin. If you wore a poppy or an emblem like that, you would be looking for trouble in some areas. I think they should have been respected, the same as the other people. They were somebody's sons.

William Scarlett later took up a position as sergeant in the Irish Army, and was an instructor in the Curragh Camp when his son, Noel, was born in 1928. Noel feels that his father found the transition to the Irish Army difficult, but nonetheless he served until after the Second World War: 'That was his life.' He was a 'strict disciplinarian but a wonderful man'.

When the Scarlett family relocated to Dublin in 1932, Patrick Pearse's sister was instrumental in securing accommodation for them in Cabra. Noel recalled that Senator Margaret Pearse was 'very kind to the family in general and in particular to my Mam and me'. She was also an indulgent godmother: 'The toys were bought in Lawrence's, a large toyshop in Dublin on the corner of Abbey Street, and as I grew older I got tickets for the opera because she knew I was very fond of music.' His brothers, William and Vincent, attended

St Enda's, and Margaret extended 'an open invitation every summer' to spend the holidays there. Noel has 'wonderful memories' of The Hermitage with its 'very spacious grounds, extensive orchard and cultivated gardens'.

After a visit to Margaret Pearse in Rathfarnham in 1932, Fr P. J. Carroll described his impressions of The Hermitage as Noel would have known it in childhood:

> Within the entrance hall are hung two pictures of Pádraig Pearse and his brother William. Pearse's last letter to his mother, in which he tells her to be brave in spite of all the harsh things she will hear spoken about himself and his comrades, hangs near the pictures [and] little memories of the Easter Rebellion are seen within the cases. Not numerous or prominent memories, however. The block on which Robert Emmet was executed is shown in the hallway.[177]

When Noel Scarlett married Mary Barrett, daughter of 1916 veteran William Barrett, in the 1950s, Margaret Pearse bestowed her patronage on her godson. The site of the original St Enda's in Cullenswood House, 'had been converted into apartments', Kieran Scarlett said, 'and we lived there for a number of years' in the late fifties. He has 'vivid' memories of his early years there: 'Up and down the stairs, all the rambling gardens. It was a fabulous place to have an early childhood.' The school in Rathfarnham had closed in 1935, but Margaret Pearse remained in the enormous, dilapidated house for many years, before she died in 1968. Kieran recalled Sunday visits to The Hermitage in the 1960s, when it was 'more or less in rack and ruin', and admitted that it had 'a very big influence on myself and my family growing up'.

Patrick Pearse's half-sister, Emily, also found a home in the grounds of St Enda's. Her grandson, Alf, remembers her as a 'cross little old woman when I knew her. She was bent in the way that I am now.' Her 'crossness' is understandable, perhaps, when one considers her fortunes. Emily lost her mother in 1876 when she was twelve years old. Six years later she married Alfred McGloughlin, architect and son of her father's friend.[178] Patrick Pearse later wrote of his half-sister's 'magnificent wedding', when 'my sister was her little bridesmaid, and I was her little page. I held up her train as she walked from the carriage into the church'.[179]

The couple was content for a time and Emily gave birth to three children while her husband gained a reputation in Dublin for his impressive High Victorian architectural style, but he left her 'in disgrace' in early 1900, after he had a liaison with a domestic servant.[100] When their parents' marriage collapsed, the McGloughlin children were sent to different homes. Alf said that Emily, who 'was a nurse and midwife by profession' went first to Donegal, but [in 1930] returned to Dublin, where she lived in Emmet's Fort, 'a folly at the corner of St Enda's'. It was 'a kind of picnic house for the big house. [It was] three rooms joined together and she lived in a kind of lean-to shack, of which you can still see the remains.' Alf, who was born in 1926, remembers visiting his grandmother there and, like his cousin, enjoyed the expanse of the grounds and playing in the woods.

Alf's father, Alfred Vincent MacLochlainn, who was active with the Volunteers in 1916 and fought on the republican side in the Civil War, died when Alf was very young. He has clear memories, however, of how his mother, Marcella Dowling, struggled to provide for her eight children in the 1930s:

> There was a [White Cross] fund for those who were involved in 1916 and that would have helped her a small bit. [In fact] there is a famous portrait of Patrick and Emily Pearse sitting on the side of a gateway that was in all the books. My father, who was a keen photographer, apparently took that photograph and my mother gave the copyright to the White Cross and it was sold widely as a keepsake.

Marcella revealed nothing about their father's activism, and Alf thinks that perhaps she 'shared more confidences' with his sister Charlotte, the only girl in the family and therefore 'closer to my mother than the seven boys': Jimmy, Pierce, Fergus, Michael, Alfred, Gerard and John. The two eldest, Jimmy and Pierce, were members of Fianna Éireann, which 'was really a training ground for the IRA but they never went ahead with it'. Alf's own politics are staunchly 'left wing' and he is 'an active member of the Labour Party'. His political preference, he says, 'seemed logical': 'I don't see why society should be organised for the benefit of the wealthy few who drag along behind them some of the poor below them.'

Alf was working in the National Library as Assistant Keeper of Manuscripts in 1966 when his grand-uncle's 1916 experiences were made more tangible. He was visited by descendants of Pat Plunkett, the owner of No. 16 Moore Street, the building in which the Provisional Government made the decision to surrender on Saturday 29 April 1916. They told him that when the Plunkett family returned to their home after Easter Week, they discovered that 'the bed was all sodden with blood and it was Connolly's blood'. They also brought into the library for examination 'a document [written] in the hand of Pearse':

> It was composed on a rectangle of cardboard with an 'X' in the corner which told me that it was taken out of the back of a picture frame … and I knew, being a librarian, that it was the draft of the surrender in 1916. It was different from the usually received version of the surrender document [and said] 'The members of the Provisional Government have decided by *a majority* to surrender' … So this means that there was a vote. You will have to work out for yourself who you think constituted a majority because you know who was present.

The National Library eventually purchased this important historical document for an agreed price. 'It's in the Library still, of course,' said Alf, who is aware that he was privileged to be in 'a position where [he] saw first-hand these items coming in' and, in a way, 'it instilled in [him] a deeper understanding' of the events a century ago.[181]

JAMES CONNOLLY

James Connolly's long shadow wrapped itself protectively and with suffocating inescapability around the lives of his wife and daughters. One of the seven signatories of the Proclamation, and one of three to sign the surrender, Connolly was a self-taught intellectual whose philosophy of national revolution was grounded in authentic compassion for the 'underdog' and 'practical experience rather than theoretical analysis of oppression and exploitation'.[182] His great-grandson, James Connolly Heron, commented:

> There was always that burning sense within him to change things. He talked about the notion of Irishness and being proud of Ireland, but if you could pass through

the streets and witness the degradation and shame that was there without burning to end it, then you weren't an Irish person at all … The basic principle [was] to create a full, free and happy life for all or for none.

Connolly Heron is three generations removed from the events of Easter 1916, yet his great-grandfather's spirit is a palpable presence in his life and he feels an unequivocal pride at 'being connected to somebody who is obviously revered in the country. [His] portrait was always on the wall, and his books [and] writings were always available in the house.' However, his central role in the history of modern Ireland was 'never rammed down our throats … we were allowed to discover him [for] ourselves'.

James Connolly was born in Edinburgh in 1868 to Irish immigrant parents: 'The family lived in poverty in the slums [and] it is quite an extraordinary story that … somebody of [such] great talent and ability would emerge from that kind of a background and become the great writer that he was.' There was 'always a connection, an association to Ireland', and after he enlisted in the British Army at fourteen, he was stationed in Cork and Dublin, and later in the Curragh in County Kildare: 'It's said he guarded a Fenian prisoner overnight before the prisoner's execution and that radicalised his position on Ireland.'

'He met his wife, Lillie Reynolds, while he was stationed here in Ireland.' She was from a 'Protestant background' and worked as a servant to a family called Wilson 'in one of the grand houses' in Fitzwilliam Square in Dublin. They met 'at a tram stop' and 'forged this relationship'. The couple were married in Perth in Scotland in 1890 and settled in Edinburgh, where Connolly worked as a Corporation employee and became increasingly immersed in the two creeds that would dominate his life, socialism and nationalism.[183] Lillie 'was an extraordinary character in her own way,' her great-grandson smiled. 'She would help Connolly with his writing [and] he would always refer his work to her.' Nora Connolly later claimed: 'Without her, my father could never have done the things he did.'[184]

The family moved to Dublin in 1896 and Connolly founded the Irish Socialist Republican Party. In the same year, he celebrated the birth of his daughter, Ina. She was the first of his seven children to be born in Ireland and he affectionately called her his 'Irish Molly'.[185] In the early years of the twentieth

Ina Connolly (*courtesy of James Connolly Heron*)

century, Connolly spent much of his time in America, where he served as national organiser for the Socialist Party of America and founded the Irish Socialist Federation. His wife endured a nomadic lifestyle, an absent husband, extreme poverty and the horrific loss of her eldest daughter, Mona, in a domestic accident in August 1904. Of her mother, Ina Connolly said: 'The world would be richer by far if there were more like my mother here today. She had a heart of kindness and sympathy and understanding.' She told her children, '"Bread I may not be able to give you … [but] mother's love no one can deprive me of giving to you", and this she gave most generously.'[186]

James Connolly returned to Ireland in 1910 to join James Larkin in the campaign for workers' rights, and moved his family to Belfast, where he assumed his role as organiser for the Irish Transport and General Workers' Union (ITGWU). 'They led an extraordinary life, really,' his great-grandson said. 'They travelled more than some of us do today. My grandmother [Ina] remembered the endless crates of books … She [was] always being moved from place to place.'

Connolly co-founded the Labour Party in 1912 and was instrumental in organising the 1913 strike in Dublin and in the establishment of the ICA in the same year to protect the striking workers. His great-grandson is understandably conscious of the long-term legacy of the trade union movement, and feels that the strike in 1913 was a 'fantastic achievement' at a time when 'we had the worst slums in Europe. [But] out of this terrible poverty came this great movement that we benefit from today.' His grandmother's recollections of 1913 were based more on the fear that she and her family felt when they learned of her father's arrest and hunger strike in Mountjoy:

He was the first man in Ireland or the British Isles who adopted this method of fighting for his rights and free speech. 'What was good enough for the suffragettes to use,' he said, 'is good enough for us' … This was terrible news for the family. We were so far away [in Belfast] and knew so little.

The concern for their father's safety was born out of filial duty, but also out of a genuine affection and deep respect. According to Ina's grandson:

The relationship within the family circle was very interesting, in that he was held in such amazingly high esteem by his daughters, despite the fact that he wasn't around in the normal sense of the family. He wasn't there as head of the household because of the political work he was engaged in. [Nonetheless] listening to my grandmother or Nora talking about him, they obviously held him in amazingly high esteem.

James Connolly succeeded James Larkin as general secretary of the ITGWU in 1914 and launched a vigorous anti-recruitment campaign at the outbreak of the First World War. In 1916 he was co-opted into the IRB Military Council and committed his ICA force to a joint insurrection against imperial rule. His great-grandson's conclusion is that Connolly was 'intent on going ahead with or without the nationalist side':

Pearse and the other leaders were becoming increasingly worried about the danger of Connolly going on his own with the Citizen Army, so he was putting pressure, if you like, on the nationalists to act … [Of course] there were differences between James Connolly and the other leaders (largely the nationalist disapproval of Connolly's socialism) and I suppose there was a lack of trust in ways, but by the time of the Rising itself … [there] was the great coming together of national, social and cultural movements all joining this magical moment in our history, a coming together of that golden generation of people.

Both Ina and Nora Connolly were part of that 'golden generation'. They were founding members of the first and only girls' branch of Fianna Éireann, which they named after Betsy Gray, the heroine of the 1798 Rebellion.[187] Ina's grandson feels that 'they were the feminists of their time, along with many other great women of that period, largely written out of history'. James Connolly, who 'referred to women as the slaves of the slave [had] great time for the Women's Movement and saw them in many ways as being a lot more principled than a lot of the men he was involved with at the time'. In 1927 Countess Markievicz wrote that, for Connolly, women were never 'classed for work as a sex, but taken individually and considered, just as every man considers men, and then allotted any work we could do'.[188] In an interview with Donncha Ó Dúlaing in 1963, ICA Council member Helena Molony elaborated:

> I was a member of the Citizen Army whose idea of freedom was of the widest and most comprehensive kind: The abolition of the domination of nation over nation, class over class and sex over sex. We women therefore had, as part of our military duty, to knit and darn and march and shoot, to obey orders in common with our brothers in arms.[189]

ICA member Brigid Davis told her daughter, Mary Dawson, that Connolly 'was the only man who had any time for women. In those days women were put down very much – you had to stay at home and be quiet. But my mother told me that Connolly said: "If they gave me an army of women Ireland would be free tomorrow".'

Connolly Heron identifies his great-grandfather's contribution to the Proclamation of the Irish Republic in the familiar, progressive language 'of equal rights and equal opportunities'. But there were other contributors, he said, and the document represents 'a magical' conjunction of ideologies.

As well as contributing to what would be regarded as the foundation document of the independent state, 'Connolly and Plunkett planned the military side of the Rising' and, as commandant general of the Dublin Division of the Army of the Irish Republic, 'Connolly directed the military action' from the GPO during Easter Week. According to witness statements, he executed his leadership admirably. The Volunteers under his command testified to his 'remarkable coolness' and his high energy. He was 'always on the move'. He could identify many of the men by name and never asked them to take chances he was not willing to take. Some recalled that he 'personally led them to their outposts, inspected their positions and solved any crises that arose'.[190] Foy and Barton observed:

> [Connolly's] performance during Easter Week established indisputably that he was a born leader of men. It was a role for which, in a sense, he had been preparing himself for years, gradually shedding his earlier persona as a trade organiser and agitator in favour of that as a charismatic military boss and theorist. By 1916 he was no longer referred to as Mr Connolly but routinely addressed as 'commandant', and an aura of remote authority surrounded him.[191]

On Thursday of Easter Week, Connolly was wounded twice, 'once in the arm and once in the ankle, [and] the ankle was the more serious wound'. He was shot on his return from establishing two outposts in Liffey Street, though he had managed to drag himself into Prince's Street, where he was collected by a stretcher party. 'Arguably, as commandant general he should never have put himself in such jeopardy at a crucial time, but Connolly reviled those First World War generals who, safely ensconced in chateaux behind the front line, dispatched countless soldiers to their deaths.'[192] In the GPO he was treated by a British Army doctor and anaesthetised with chloroform while his wounds were dressed. 'He was lying on a stretcher in the middle of the GPO, still issuing orders,' his great-grandson said, and 'he was still in command up until the time they entered the first house in what we refer to as the "1916 Terrace" [in Moore Street].'

Connolly was 'on the first council of war after the evacuation', after which he passed his command to Seán McLoughlin, a young Fianna Volunteer who had impressed the commandant by taking control in the laneways around Moore Street during the chaos and 'panic' of the evacuation.[193] McLoughlin, who had been in the Mendicity Institution with Seán Heuston and acted as courier to the GPO, was appointed commandant general of the Dublin Division of the Army of the Republic in the last hours of the Rising: 'It was [said] afterwards that de Valera was the last surviving commandant; in actual fact this young Volunteer outranked de Valera. It is quite an extraordinary story.'[194]

Once the council of war had agreed to seek surrender terms, James Connolly beckoned to Seán McLoughlin from his bed and said, 'you must not take it so hardly [*sic*] … we have done our best; it was better than we hoped. It has

Nora Connolly inherited an immense sense of duty to her father's legacy. In her grand-nephew's words:

> She was a very seriously committed republican all her life. Right at the very end she was concerned about the hunger strikers in the north. She appeared on platforms at that time as well. I imagine because she was so closely identified with her father that his shadow was in the background. He was on her shoulder so she remained always committed to the republican ideal, the thirty-two-county workers' republic.[200] She was active during the Civil War on the republican side [and] ended up being imprisoned in Kilmainham Gaol. [It] ... was extraordinary that she was imprisoned in the very place that her father had been executed and was there, I think, on an anniversary of his execution [in 1923] ...
>
> Later on in life she emerged as an active member of the Restoration Committee, involved in the restoration of Kilmainham Gaol ... That tradition is carried on today by [me]. I am involved in the ongoing campaign to save Moore Street from demolition, along with other relatives of other signatories, I hasten to add.

James Connolly Heron is in proud possession of his grandmother's Fianna medal, and 'a medal that was presented to [James Connolly] by the trade union movement after the 1913 Lockout'. Ina and Nora retrieved just a 'watch and a pocketbook' from General Maxwell, and 'I have his letter of proposal to Lillie [and] ... a lock of his hair that was cut the night of his execution' and smuggled by a nurse out of Kilmainham at Lillie's request. Other than that, 'there was surprisingly little left; you would assume that the families of the signatories would have a lot of memorabilia, but there actually wasn't afterwards'. Because he never knew his great-grandfather, the material mementoes mean less to Connolly Heron than they did to his grandmother, for whom they represented a tangible connection to the father she had loved and lost. For her grandson, it is a grief twice removed and a loss that he can rationalise.

'No Hero Stories'

⟶ The GPO Garrison ⟵

As Diarmuid Lynch's niece, Dolores Lynch, has pointed out, claims to membership of the GPO garrison in 1916 often prompted the 'cynical or sarcastic ones in the pub' to say: 'Oh! He was in the GPO as well was he? It must have been a huge building for all the people that were in it.'

It is unsurprising, perhaps, that the claimants have been so numerous, as the General Post Office in Dublin's O'Connell Street has a deep symbolic resonance in the national imagination. The grand, neo-classical structure, a physical expression of the imperial presence, became the headquarters of an idealistic revolution and emerged from the rubble as a national icon. For the children of the combatants in the GPO in Easter Week, the building is part of a shared family narrative, and for their fathers it was a focal point for memory.

The interviewees from the second generation traced their relatives' different paths to the GPO and offered an insight into the distinct political and personal after-lives of those who shared a place at centre stage in the theatre of revolution.

ÉAMONN BULFIN AND FRANK BURKE

Éamonn Bulfin, the Volunteer lieutenant who hoisted the green flag bearing the words 'Irish Republic' over the GPO on Easter Monday, was twenty-four years old in 1916. His daughter, Jeanne Bulfin, has inherited his 'passionate interest in history' and his 'black sense of humour', but very few stories about the Rising. Like many of the interviewees from the second generation, she tends to attribute her father's relative silence about Easter Week to its inextricability from the subsequent violence of the 1922–23 period. The Civil War 'literally

Studio portrait of Éamonn Bulfin
(*courtesy of Jeanne Bulfin*)

traumatised him' and affected his willingness to discuss his experiences beyond select anecdotes. Furthermore, she said, 'he never wished to be thought of as a hero'.

Éamonn and his sisters, Mary, Anita, Aileen and Catalina, were born in Argentina. Their father, William Bulfin, and their uncle Peter had left Derrinlough, County Offaly for South America in 1884. 'The family story is that Peter was a wild boy and had been capering around with [the] ladies ... so my great-grandfather considered it a good idea if [he] left the country.' They carried letters of introduction from their uncle, Fr Vincent Grogan, to the Passionist Fathers in Buenos Aires, and found work among the Irish diaspora already settled there. Twenty-one-year-old William, who was 'into horses' and could 'ride extremely effectively', began work on John Dowling's ranch as a 'capataz or gang boss'. Soon afterwards, he was introduced to his future wife, Annie O'Rourke, a 'charming lady' who had 'left Westmeath to work as a tutor to the Dowling children'. She was impressed by both the charisma and the writing talent of the young Offaly man, and encouraged him to make contributions to various magazines in the United States. His work was also published in the *Southern Cross*, the Argentinian newspaper of which he was subsequently proprietor and editor. In 1902 Bulfin wrote *Rambles in Eirinn*, a sensually descriptive account of his travels around Ireland by bicycle, in which he implicitly bemoans the Anglicisation of Ireland and rails against the old colonial order. The work, which was initially serialised in Arthur Griffith's *United Irishman*, became a favourite in nationalist circles.[1] A strong proponent of cultural nationalism, Bulfin also founded the Buenos Aires Hurling Club and 'as far as I know he also had a small printing business. Altogether [he] did quite well for himself', so much so that Patrick J. Little dubbed Bulfin 'the most eminent Irishman in the Argentine'.[2]

Despite his success in South America, William Bulfin was 'passionately in love with Ireland' and in 1902 he sent his five children to Offaly so that they could receive an Irish education. His sixteen-year-old son, Éamonn, 'was the second student' enrolled in St Enda's College after it opened in Cullenswood House in Ranelagh in September 1908. Jeanne suggested that her father's ardent nationalism was the result of the combined influences of 'Pearse's considerable charisma' and 'the politics in the family'. Éamonn's uncles, Frank and Joe Bulfin, 'were old IRB'. They were 'Land War people and very active but they were not romantics; they were very angry humanitarians'. As far as his daughter is concerned, Bulfin inherited their 'instinct to fight', but his 'desire to prevent an event like the Famine ever recurring [was] … more of a motive [for him] than the romantic fight by poets. Underneath the romantic sacrificing yourself for your country element was a very hard core of practical humanity – that's the best I can tell you.'

It wasn't long, his daughter said, before 'Éamonn became a favourite pupil of Pearse's'. He was 'far less of an ebullient personality than his father, [but he] was handsome and charming'. He was also 'a born-again feminist so he was extremely well liked by women because they would instantly detect his respect and affection'. That is why he was 'a particular favourite of Mrs Pearse and Margaret Pearse'.

Catalina, Mary, Aileen and Anita Bulfin (*courtesy of Jeanne Bulfin***)**

Like Éamonn Bulfin, Frank Burke was one of the early cohort of students in St Enda's, and according to his son, Éanna de Búrca, 'Pearse himself was quite fond of Da'. Frank Burke was a native of Carbury, County Kildare, whose lifelong dedication to sport began in national school, where his teacher, 'a man by the name of Horan from Offaly', imbued in him a love of hurling. In 1908 he was sent as a boarder to Knockbeg College in County Carlow, but, according to his son, was disappointed when he had to explain to his fellow boarders what a hurley stick was:

Frank Burke
(*courtesy of Éanna de Búrca*)

[During the summer holidays] his mother returned from a trip to Dublin bringing with her a copy of *An Macaomh (The Youth)*. It was about this new school that was founded in Cullenswood House by a man called Pearse. He [had] never heard of him but he read the magazine and was enthralled by the idea that the pupils of the school, as well as the teachers, actually contributed to this magazine and everything Irish was put first and foremost. [They] played Irish games, spoke the Irish language and it was completely different to what he was used to in Knockbeg. So he persuaded his parents to send him to this new school [and] he was enrolled on 6 September 1909.[3]

Frank Burke, or Feargus as he was known to the 'St Enda's family', 'talked about Pearse [as] a most noble individual. He was up there on a pedestal and the greatest Irishman that ever existed, to my father.' Frank, like all of the St Enda's boys, was subject to Pearse's distinct educational vision, which diverged from the 'filthy', utilitarian British education system, the 'murder machine' that took its raw material and remoulded it or ejected it, 'with all the likeness of its former self crushed from it'.[4] His educational philosophy was student-centric and grounded in the promotion of a national religious spirit, a love of ideas and books, and with a specific focus on the heroism radiating from the Irish mythological stories. His early ambition was to 'recreate and perpetuate in Ireland the knightly tradition of Cúchulainn', the 'Christ-like tradition of Colmcille' and 'the stories of Wolfe Tone and Robert Emmet'.[5] For his students, Pearse's success as a teacher was the result of a combination of his personality and the use of pageant, athletics and 'modern methods of language teaching'.[6] Éamonn Bulfin recorded that 'In his talks to his students, [Pearse] always stressed the fact that every generation of Irishmen should have a rising in arms. He stressed it in such a way that you felt impelled to believe that he did actually believe that there should be some attempt'.[7]

Like Jeanne Bulfin, Éanna de Búrca claims that his father had a special relationship with Patrick Pearse, who 'employed him to help him in managing the financial end of St Enda's. He would run messages when he was a student in the school' and after he started 'going to the university in 1912', Pearse guaranteed that 'Frank would have a job as a teacher' after he graduated. Éamonn Bulfin was also attending university, having embarked upon a science degree in UCD in 1911; in the summer of 1912 he was sworn into the IRB 'on Wolfe Tone's grave in Bodenstown' by Art O'Connor.[8] Con Colbert organised a company of the Fianna in St Enda's and, as one of its members, Frank Burke had the 'honour of being' a steward at the inaugural meeting of the Volunteers in the Rotunda in November 1913. Like the other ex-pupils of St Enda's in residence at the college, the two men joined 'E' (Rathfarnham) Company of the 4th (Pearse's Own) Battalion of the Irish Volunteers, and Éamonn Bulfin was appointed 2nd lieutenant.

In the months before the Rising, both men were among the group of St Enda's past pupils engaged in the production of shotgun ammunition and grenades, using Willie Pearse's moulds: 'You see, that's where the Science [degree] came in,' his daughter smiled, 'he knew enough to make explosives.' Under the direction of St Enda's science master, Peadar Slattery, better known as 'Sla', the boys continued making munitions up to and during Easter Week 1916.[9] Frank Burke recalled:

> During this period of feverish activity (in the 'University Room') we managed to procure as much equipment as possible. Each Volunteer had to provide himself with a bandolier, haversack and knapsack.

> I had a lovely, long Lee-Enfield rifle which I had got from the hands of P. H. Pearse himself some months before. It was, to me, a lovely weapon and perfectly new and I took great pride in keeping it well-oiled and free from rust. We kept our rifles at the head of our beds.[10]

Fifty years later, Pearse's sister, Margaret, recalled that during that period there was an outbreak of measles in the school and 'Willie proceeded to disinfect each bullet on its completion. "We don't mind giving the English bullets", he said to me laughingly, "but we don't want to give them germs as well".'[11] The clandestine activity was not without danger and, according to Desmond Ryan, when raids became more frequent, 'Pearse made us all carry around several hundred rounds of .303 concealed on our persons, on trams, on the streets, everywhere until the alarm died down.'[12]

The air hummed with excitement on the afternoon of Easter Saturday, 1916. John Kilgallon 'who was an American and happened to have a camera', seized an opportunity to capture the moment on film. He marshalled the nine members of 'E' Company in St Enda's to a position in the quadrangle and 'took a snapshot of our group in "full kit"'.[13] Éamonn Bulfin stood proudly in the back row with Conor McGinley, Frank Connolly and Desmond Ryan, and kneeling in front were Brian Joyce, Frank Burke, Eunan McGinley, Joe Sweeney and Fintan Murphy. Their young faces smile at the camera, eager and optimistic about 'the morrow's fray'.[14] They were 'Pearse's Own Battalion', 'soldiers in the battles spiritual and temporal of their country'.[15] Fifty years later, Fintan Murphy, veteran of 'E' Company, proposed a re-enactment of the occasion. 'They were all still alive,' Éanna explained, '[but] it was not an exact reproduction as not all of them turned up' and 'they were not able to get into the courtyard because it was so overgrown, [so] they took the photograph on the steps of St Enda's standing in [almost] exactly the same positions'. That was fitting, perhaps, because 'it's sometimes said that it was on the steps of St Enda's that the dismantling of the British Empire began'.

The Pearse brothers spent Easter Saturday night in the city, and on Easter Sunday morning, Bulfin attended mass at Rathfarnham with Margaret Pearse and the St Enda's boys, 'to make a good Confession' and receive 'the Blessed Sacrament'.[16] As they left the chapel, Eoin MacNeill approached the Volunteer

Members of 'E' Company in 1966
Standing (left to right): Éamonn Bulfin, Dick Humphreys (nephew of The O'Rahilly
and past pupil of St Enda's, who took Conor McGinley's place), Desmond Ryan
and Fintan Murphy
Kneeling: Brian Joyce, Frank Burke and Joe Sweeney
(*courtesy of Éanna de Burca*)

lieutenant and asked him to carry a dispatch. Bulfin refused, concluding that it 'was a part of the calling off of the manoeuvres', and excused himself after what Fintan Murphy called a 'spirited conversation'.[17] 'E' Company received orders from Pearse 'to stand to and await further instructions', and Frank obtained permission from his lieutenant to go to his sister in Glen Tolka to inform her 'of the tidings'.[18] Aoife (Eva) Burke was a nurse and lived with their aunt in Drumcondra. 'Her sympathies were with Cumann na mBan,' Éanna explained, '[but] she was never an active member.' Her brother had submitted her name 'as one that would give assistance when the need for it would arise'.[19]

On Monday, Bulfin received a 'fresh mobilisation order' from his commanding officer. In 'full staff officer's uniform', he paraded the reduced company of twenty men, including Frank Burke, Desmond Ryan and John Kilgallon, outside the church at Rathfarnham, and they made their way on board a tram to Liberty Hall.[20] According to Éanna:

> [Aoife] was nursing a colonel in Malahide when she heard rumours on the Easter Monday [that] the Rising had started in Dublin, so she got up on her bicycle and cycled in. When she found it was [true] she returned to Malahide and told her patient that she couldn't stay with him any longer and the next morning she cycled back into Dublin, made her way into the GPO, and reported to Pearse as a nurse.[21]

Her brother and the Rathfarnham Company arrived in the city to find 'Ireland in arms'. A 'momentary spasm of sickness', was followed for Desmond Ryan by 'wild exaltation or sheer wonder'.[22] 'E' Company followed their lieutenant to O'Connell Street, where they were greeted with 'confusion and noise' as the mounted troops of the 6th Reserve Cavalry Regiment were fired on from Volunteer positions on O'Connell Street. The Volunteers negotiated their way past the fallen cavalrymen, and Bulfin 'hooched' his men through a broken window on the Prince's Street side of the GPO. They tumbled into Volunteer headquarters, where 'wild confusion [reigned] … Noise and excitement, desolation without, disorder within …'[23] 'E' Company reported to Pearse, who ordered the St Enda's boys to take up positions on the roof. 'They probably put him up there because he really was a crack shot,' Bulfin's daughter suggested. 'We all knew it because he went out shooting [with] three cartridges and he came home with three dead birds or rabbits.'

One of Éamonn Bulfin's shared memories involves what has been inaccurately described as the 'Charge of the Lancers' down O'Connell Street, during which three of the thirty cavalrymen dispatched to investigate disturbances in the city centre were killed and another fatally wounded: 'One horse was also killed and its putrefying body lay in O'Connell Street until the end of the Rising.'[24] The image of the 'dead horse', which so affected Laura Daly, was more shocking to Jeanne Bulfin in childhood than any of the other elements of her father's handpicked anecdotes.[25] 'I said, "Pop, did you aim at them?" and was consoled when he said, "I didn't shoot at the horses".' He was more evasive when his daughter asked him, '"Did you shoot at the men?" … He sort of hummed and hawed and said that he shot over their heads.' This version of the truth was accepted by his daughter, who insists that the father whom she 'loved very much' was not a violent man: 'I would say that the likelihood is that he did shoot over their heads, but I don't know.' As with so many of the interviewees, this version of heroic endeavour is more comfortable for the daughter of a revolutionary than the reality of what insurrection entails.

While Bulfin was reticent about sharing any of the details of combat with his children, he was proud to have been the man who hoisted 'the Green Flag' over the GPO: 'As far as I know there were two flags put up. One was a green flag and the other was a Tricolour.' Fintan Murphy recalled seeing 'Eamon [*sic*] Bulfin and Willie Pearse together at the flag-post', and in 1966 Éamonn Bulfin confirmed that he 'hauled up the green flag on a pole over the Prince's Street corner … and written across the flag in white paint were the words "Irish Republic". I gave the other flag – the tricolour – to one of the Kimmage "Exile Unit from Britain".'[26] The first thing that Aoife Burke noticed when she arrived at the GPO on Monday was the flag 'proudly floating from one end of the building'.[27]

Aoife was dispatched almost immediately to Captain Tom Weafer's outpost in Reis's at O'Connell Bridge, where she joined eight members of Cumann na mBan on the upper floors of the building. 'Some were quite young,' she remembered, '[but] I never met a braver or more intelligent lot of girls; they were ready for any duty, no matter how dangerous. Some of them even carried dispatches under fire, or took the places of wounded Volunteers.'[28] Her mind was on Frank, however, and 'every shot' she heard, she 'beheld in [her] imagination the dead or wounded body of my loved young brother who was in the Great Adventure'.[29] She grasped the first opportunity on Tuesday to 'race across to the GPO' to see him, and was delighted to find him 'in such good spirits'. Frank entrusted her with 'all kinds of messages for our mother in case he should fall in the conflict', but he told his sister that he was '"perfectly resigned to die if such should be my fate, and proud and happy to fight in such a cause." He gave me great hope and courage,' she said, 'and I could not feel sad while speaking to him.'[30]

Jeanne Bulfin offered a 'lovely story' about the early part of Easter Week in the GPO, which testifies to her father's 'respect' for the opposite sex. Someone said that 'there were some women outside, wanting to talk to someone in the GPO'. Éamonn, who was 'a lieutenant at that stage', was dispatched down to talk to these Dublin ladies. 'He said, "You know it's very dangerous for you to be here", to which they replied, "We brought some of the Citizen Army

Drumcondra [and] … was actually assisted by one of the British soldiers to get through'. She was 'terrible laid back … Her attitude was, "Sure, what would they shoot me for?"'

The floors in the GPO began to give way, and thick clouds of smoke enveloped the Volunteers as debris crashed around them. A hastily convened council of war determined that The O'Rahilly would lead a front guard from the GPO, after which the rest of the garrison would evacuate in batches. Fintan Murphy and Frank Burke were among those involved in the 'bustling activity to collect what stores we could take with us', and Bulfin recorded that a 'chap standing beside me was wounded in the foot when his shotgun went off'.[42] Éamonn Dore was put in charge of the Henry Street entrance to the GPO, 'the only exit not on fire':

> After some time, O'Rahilly and a group of men filed out and I asked one, John R. Reynolds, RIP, where they were going. In a most cynical voice he said, 'We are going to clear the British out of Moore St., fight our way to Williams & Woods Jam factory in Parnell St. and then try to connect up with Ned Daly in the Four Courts'. … With me at the door was a man called Paddy Murray. I turned to him and said, 'Will you come with them Paddy?' To which he agreed and in less than a quarter of an hour he was lying very badly wounded in Moore St. and O'Rahilly with many others were dead.[43]

When no dispatch arrived from The O'Rahilly, Pearse made his final speech to the GPO garrison, paid tribute to their gallantry and ordered the evacuation from the Henry Street entrance. As Fintan Murphy dashed from the building, he had his 'last glimpse' of his schoolmaster and military commander, who 'looked weary … but not defeated – still the same quiet voice which had inspired us on so many occasions'.[44] They went through the door in ones and twos, across the 'flame lit and bullet swept street', bending low to avoid the rifle fire.[45] 'There was no cohesion' during the evacuation, said Bulfin, 'nobody seemed to be in charge … It was every man for himself' as they crossed Henry Street under heavy fire.[46] They rushed forward into Moore Lane, and Fintan Murphy 'was horrified' when he saw Lieutenant Bulfin trip and fall in front of the barricade just as a 'burst of firing swept down the lane, but the trip saved him and he scrambled up and on unharmed'.[47] They managed to break into a store at the entrance of Moore Lane and the exhausted St Enda's boys took 'turns at wall-boring and window-barricading'.[48]

On Saturday came the order to surrender. Seán McLoughlin paraded the GPO garrison in Moore Street. The image of 'waxen' corpses of British soldiers, Volunteers and civilians, 'strangely still and quiet', was seared on Desmond Ryan's memory.[49] As they turned into O'Connell Street and lined up in front of the Gresham Hotel, Ryan looked upwards towards the republican flags that flew defiantly 'over the ruined Post Office and the huge shell of the Imperial Hotel'.[50] Once their names were taken and their arms abandoned, the garrison was 'herded to the Rotunda Gardens', and Bulfin, who was quite near to Collins and Joe Plunkett, remembered 'a British officer threatening to shoot the whole lot of us'.[51] That night, they remained under armed guard 'higgledy-piggledy' on the grass on the front of the Rotunda and on Sunday the garrison was marched to Richmond Barracks.

Despite her personal tragedy, Margaret Pearse felt compelled on 4 May to contact the Argentine representative at his office in Molesworth Street, to request that he declare Éamonn Bulfin an Argentine subject. 'He made the necessary representations' and Bulfin joined the Volunteers, including Frank Burke, in Stafford Prison in England for three weeks before being transferred to Frongoch Camp in North Wales.[52] His daughter has no recollection of her father speaking about his time in Frongoch, except to tell her that 'he became very friendly with Michael Collins'.

Frank Burke sometimes spoke about Stafford Prison, where they were 'treated as absolute criminals'. The people at the station 'spat at them' and 'he was put in solitary confinement for three weeks' until they were given 'prisoner-of-war status'. Similar to many of the second-generation interviewees, Éanna de Búrca's impression of Frongoch is that 'it wasn't that hard'. There were 'lots of people sending parcels of goodies in to them so they would have parties in different cells. It must have been a marvellous time there when they got over the initial shock.' They played football. Dick Fitzgerald, the Kerry selector, was in Frongoch too and they organised great games: 'I think Michael Collins was unbeatable in the 100 yards and I know Dad won the three-legged race with John Kilgallon.' After 'a rising of teachers' they also had 'plenty of classes' in

Frongoch: 'They learned not alone Irish, but European languages too, [and] they got in books on military tactics. They planned what they were going to do when they got out.'

Like Jeanne Bulfin, who was described by her father's friends as *clusa fada* (long ears), Éanna often eavesdropped on conversations between his father and Éamonn Dore, whose stories about internment 'were absolutely hilarious'. Young Éanna would 'get down on the floor behind them' and listen to 'how they used to taunt Michael Collins because of his short temper'. They had to parade in silence in the exercise yard in Stafford Prison and a few of the 'bright sparks' would 'get behind Collins and pass some nasty remark about him and of course Collins would blow up ... they'd just do it for a few laughs'.

Frank Burke and Éamonn Bulfin were released 'on the day before Christmas Eve 1916'.[53] Frank got the train from Dublin down to Enfield Station in Kildare, where his brother Jack met him with his pony and trap:

> There was great excitement at the station because a contingent going down to Galway was having a great sing-song on the train. Jack and Frank joined in ... and when he came out the pony and trap [which Jack had neglected to secure properly] was gone. It transpired that the newly purchased pony went back home to Kilcock, three miles down the road.

When the brothers eventually reached the family home 'in the heart of the country ... every window was lit with candles to welcome him home. That was the father's doing.' Frank Burke was summoned to all of the local houses that Christmas to give his own dramatic version of the Rising. 'He said he had it off by heart by the time he was finished,' his son smiled.

After his release from Frongoch, Éamonn Bulfin canvassed with Michael Collins in the Cavan-Monaghan election and was appointed vice-commandant of the Offaly Brigade of the Irish Volunteers. In July 1918 he was arrested with his uncle, Jeanne's godfather, Frank Bulfin, TD, during the 'German Plot' and imprisoned for a term in Durham in England, before being deported to Argentina in May 1919 under the provisions of the Aliens Restriction Act (1914).[54] In his own words, Éamonn was 'fired on to the first ship, and three years passed before I saw Ireland again'.[55] His Uncle Frank had the unfortunate task of breaking the news to his sister-in-law that he was '[coming] home without her son'.

Éamon de Valera appointed Éamonn Bulfin as the first representative of the Irish Republic to the Argentine government. 'De Valera was a practical man,' Jeanne said, '[and] he found it convenient [that] he had this man there who had all the right connections and the right education, [and] who spoke Spanish.' The aims of his mission were to inaugurate direct trade between Ireland and the Argentine Republic, to influence Irish opinion in Argentina and to bring it into line with the Irish demand for a republic. Bulfin established a contact network with government officials

Éamonn Bulfin and his sister Anita, *c.* 1920
(courtesy of Jeanne Bulfin)

and Irish–Argentine leaders, launched the Republican Bond drive and negotiated shipments of munitions from Argentina to the Irish Republican Army.[56] Notwithstanding his impressive title, Bulfin received insufficient funds to support himself and he supplemented his income by working for a Jewish firm of tailors in Buenos Aires, 'the Paris of the south'. The tailors dressed their handsome bookkeeper 'in the smartest [suits]. He was six foot two inches tall and good-looking, so they had a model and he got the clothes as well as the wages.'

While Bulfin worked for the republican cause in South America, Frank Burke returned to St Enda's. The school had reopened in Cullenswood House after January 1917, with Thomas MacDonagh's brother Joseph as headmaster. He 'didn't stay long', Éanna explained, and Peadar Slattery succeeded him as headmaster. They 'got back to The Hermitage just before Easter 1919', and when Slattery left at the end of the academic year, 'Da was asked to take over and remained as headmaster until 1935.' It was 'a labour of love,' he added, 'because he loved the job and he loved the Pearse family … and tried to follow Pádraig Pearse's example as best he could.'

Despite being party to the playful taunts in Frongoch, Frank Burke had 'enormous respect for Collins' and was one of the original members of his Squad. But, his son said, 'He just did not like the idea of going into a house and shooting a person in bed … so he resigned and his place was taken by Frank Coughlan who lived in Ballyboden.' He continued:

> He kept friendly with Collins up to the time of the split [but] he could not forgive him for signing the Treaty. His allegiance was to Pearse and to the thirty-two-county Republic [and] anything else less than that was reneging on Pearse, reneging on the sixteen that were executed in 1916, [and] reneging on all his companions.

Frank Burke did not become involved in the Civil War, despite his personal convictions and admiration for Éamon de Valera, 'who came nearer to Pearse than anyone else. He just could not take up arms against his former colleagues and he wouldn't do it.' Furthermore, at that time he was a headmaster, he was about to get married [to Angela Curran] and he was very much involved with football and hurling.[57] However, 'St Enda's came first and he couldn't give up that'.

His old comrade Éamonn Bulfin's latent sympathies lay with the Free State, but he similarly had no involvement in the Civil War. He told the Military Pensions Board that when the Treaty was signed the members of the mission 'were dissatisfied and disgusted' with the instructions received from the Provisional Government and 'decided to close down the Legation'.[58] He returned to Dublin in July 1922, in the midst of the Civil War. 'He said he walked down Grafton Street and he didn't know who to salute. He was absolutely horrified that his friends from the old days [were fighting] one another and he could not bring himself to side with either … so he stayed strictly out.' In terms of the Treaty, 'he felt that this was the best deal we [could have] got from the Brits, and we had to stick with that. He would have been pragmatic.' Bulfin guarded his neutrality to the point that the family was known in Offaly as 'that crowd of gravestones'. It was common knowledge that 'you'll get nothing out of them'.

In 1923 Éamonn Bulfin inherited the family farm, 'but the only stock on the farm when he got the place [was] twenty-four unsaleable polo ponies'. In order to 'maintain a standard of living, he got a job as [a] rate collector; a job which, after four years of uncollected taxes, could only be done by a "local hero"', his daughter laughed. Four years later he married Nora Brick, a young woman from a prosperous farming family in Caherbreagh, Tralee, County Kerry. She 'was much too young to [have been] actively engaged in the Rising', but in 1921 'she went to work as a secretary to Austin Stack, when he was Minister for Home Affairs'. She met Éamonn's sister Catalina (who later married Seán MacBride) in Stack's office and they became 'very friendly', so much so that, in 1922 Catalina invited Nora to the Bulfin home for Christmas and it was there 'she met my father who had just come home'. They married in 1927, and Maud Gonne MacBride and Grace Plunkett were among those who attended.[59] 'They were a very happy couple,' Jeanne smiled. 'His pet name for her was "Fairybird".' She was 'beautiful' and 'very charming' with a 'wonderful laugh' and 'she was a lovely person as well. God! She'd give you the coat off her back.' The only thing that 'shocked and horrified' her four children was the fact that Nora continued to vote for Fianna Fáil.

Jeanne is convinced that her mother helped her father to recover from the horror of the Civil War. The 'shooting of Michael Collins just switched him off' and the idea 'that all their dreams had ended in people at one another's throats, really wrecked him emotionally for years'. About ten days before he died, on 12 November 1976, Éamonn Bulfin offered his daughter his final word on revolution: 'Violence solves no problems.'

Frank and Angela Burke's youngest child and only son, Éanna, was born in 1930. He and his two sisters grew up in one of the 'bungalows on Whitechurch Road' that Mrs Pearse had had built in the early 1920s 'for the headmaster and the assistant head of St Enda's'. Brian Joyce lived in the other house, and his son, Piaras, a year younger than Éanna, was his childhood playmate. Frank's enduring love of Gaelic games was a significant feature of his son's childhood: 'We never had a Sunday lunch, we had that on a Saturday … Sunday started off at 9 o'clock mass, [then] home, breakfast [and] off somewhere to a match.'

Senator Margaret Pearse also loomed large in Éanna's childhood. He does not remember his godmother, Mrs Pearse, who died in 1932, but has fond memories of her daughter, who 'continued the very onerous task of looking after my spiritual welfare as godmothers are supposed to do. ... Everywhere she went she would send me a postcard or bring [me] a souvenir ... They are only little trinkets but they are from Margaret Pearse in memory of her mother [and] you can't put a value on these things.'

Like Jeanne Bulfin, Éanna de Búrca 'always looked up to [his] father'. He was 'a very upright sort of a person,' Éanna said, 'but at times I felt that he could have asserted himself a bit more.' He was 'too gentle in his own sweet way'. Frank Burke died on 28 December 1988 at ninety-three years of age, and 'he never wavered in his ideas'. At school, 'he was very much under the influence of Pearse and he lived up to those principles all his life'.

THOMAS MCEVOY

Concepta Butler is proud of the fact that her father, Thomas McEvoy, 'was one of the original 150 men who marched from Liberty Hall to the GPO on Easter Monday 1916. Various groups joined during the week ... but I think there were only 150 in the original group.' He attended 'the Easter parade every single year' and he 'was always accepted as one of the GPO. ... It's actually inscribed on his headstone' in Kenure cemetery in Rush.

Thomas McEvoy was 'one of the youngest volunteers in the GPO in 1916' but, like most of the second generation, his daughter is unclear about the details of his activities because 'he didn't talk about it an awful lot'. Her patchwork account is stitched together with the threads of overheard conversations and personal research.

Thomas McEvoy and his seven siblings were brought up at No. 2 Sampson's Lane, off Moore Street, barely a hundred yards from the GPO. It was a [three-storey] tenement house and the McEvoy family 'had only two rooms on the middle floor'. Thomas' father, Andrew McEvoy, 'had been in the Boer War' (1899–1902) and 'he joined up again in 1914' and served in the 5th Leinster Regiment. 'He wasn't in combat,' Concepta explained, 'he was a cook in Northampton but still, that would have meant that my grandmother, Annie, was home alone with her children.' Thomas, who had left school at fourteen, 'was the man of the house' and 'by degrees [he was] influenced by ... the Celtic Dawn of Irish literature, the Irish Revivals and all the rest of it'. The fact that

Thomas McEvoy in his Fianna Éireann uniform (*courtesy of Concepta Butler*)

his father was injured in the baton charge in O'Connell Street during the 1913 strike and Lockout 'may have influenced him too'.

Thomas joined Na Fianna Éireann as a young teenager and was 'out at Belcamp House with Countess Markievicz'. Among his daughter's most treasured keepsakes is a photograph of an earnest Thomas in his Fianna Éireann uniform, and a copy of a reference from the grocer's shop in Henry Street where he was working as a junior clerk in February 1916: 'It said he was a very industrious boy.' He was at the same time industriously drilling and training with 'G' Company, 1st Battalion of the Irish Volunteers.

Patrick O'Neill of 'C' Company remembered seventeen-year-old Thomas McEvoy when he described for Max Caulfield the scene outside Liberty Hall at 12 o'clock on Monday 24 April 1916:

Plunkett, his chief of staff and the mercurial brain behind the military planning and the strategy of the rebellion, dramatically unsheathed a sabre and took up his position [beside Pearse]. Then Connolly, having satisfied himself that all was in readiness, placed himself between Pearse and Plunkett, and behind the three commandant generals, as they had ranked themselves, came the rest of the column in orthodox fours. Captain Brennan-Whitmore took the extreme left and next to him stood Plunkett's ADC Michael Collins ... Further back stood ... young Thomas McEvoy age 17, a grocer's assistant, who marched into insurrection blindly believing that he was taking part in an ordinary route march.[60]

Like Éamonn Bulfin and Frank Burke, McEvoy was stationed on the roof of the GPO. He fired on the Lancers on Easter Monday, and on Tuesday he surveyed the frenzied looting in the streets below: 'Men, women and children swarmed about, carrying off furniture, silks, satins, pushing baby carriages filled with sheets, stockings, garters, curtains. Trails, winding and twisting, showed what they had discarded.'[61] According to his daughter, Thomas 'always maintained that James Connolly [told] them to shoot at the people looting the shops, not over their heads, he said to shoot at them'. A short distance away in Sampson's Lane, his younger sister, Rosie McEvoy, watched as the 'tattered bare-footed kids gorged on sweets, pelted one another with packets of tea and sugar, footballing tins of preserves into the roadway to the delight of grinning, shawled "auld ones"'.[62] She later recorded the opportunism of a neighbour who held up looters with a toy gun, took the stuff and kept it for himself.[63]

McEvoy was sent out 'several times as a runner with messages', and his daughter is confident that his familiarity with the warren of back lanes in the city centre meant that he was an obvious choice to act as an escort for Hanna Sheehy-Skeffington when she carried dispatches and food to the College of Surgeons.[64] He also carried messages to Edward Daly in the Four Courts and 'over to Brunswick Street'. Later in the week, he was sent on reconnaissance 'to the Williams and Woods factory ... to see if they could escape and regroup there and also to count how many British there were in what is now Parnell Street. He was in and out of the GPO several times during the week and just survived.'

After the GPO garrison evacuated to Moore Street on Friday, James Connolly told McEvoy: 'Go home to your mother, son', and he 'just slipped quietly across the road from No. 16 ... down into Sampson's Lane and home'. Thomas returned to find the family home had been badly damaged during the offensive, his young sister Rosie sobbing and his mother distraught. She had heard nothing from her son since the previous Monday, when he had left in uniform for what she presumed was a route march. She was also desperately worried about her brother, Joe, who was a junior sacristan in the Pro-Cathedral, which was 'being licked by flames from O'Connell Street'.[65] Rosie later said that 'we had housemaid's knees from continually saying the Rosary and while on our knees the window was blown in, which made us scurry down to our tiny backyard'.[66]

Their neighbour, Séamus Scully, was also traumatised in childhood when the British military erected a barricade within a few feet of his father's butcher's shop in 1916:

> Every shot ... rattled our old unsteady windows and the thunderous flashing shells from the 18-pounder shook the three-storeyed house as they whizzed past. Sniper bullets had already riddled our top back room window. The military had taken possession of our back yard. The arrogant officer had haughtily demanded us to prepare for evacuation as it was their intention to level whatever houses were necessary to 'root out the Sinn Feiners'.[67]

The military moved Annie McEvoy and her children from their uninhabitable tenement 'over to O'Connor's two-roomed house at No. 30 Moore Street.' They were subsequently 'transferred to No. 40 or 41 Parnell Street', and when the repairs were complete they returned to Sampson's Lane, where they lived for years before finally moving into a bigger house at 56 Moore Street. It was here that Concepta visited her grandmother when she was a child.

After the Rising, Thomas 'was still involved' as a member of 'C' Company 3rd Battalion. 'They met every week and they drilled,' his daughter explained, 'but there was nothing much going on until the people were released from Frongoch and came home at the Christmas that year [and] the whole thing was revitalised again.' Thomas participated in drilling, company patrols and armed raids, and the campaign against conscription.[68] In April 1918 he was transferred to No. 3 Company, 5th Battalion (Engineers), Dublin Brigade and 'was a bomber'. His pension application testifies to his part in a raid on the *Irish Independent* newspaper offices in 1919, his involvement in the destruction of Stepaside RIC Barracks in 1920 and in a raid for arms at Dalkey Castle in the same year. He was 'outside the jail the morning [Kevin Barry] was executed [1 November 1920] ... they had had a plan to try and get him out but it didn't work. But he was involved right up along for a number of years anyway.'

Annie McEvoy 'hid weapons in the house' during the War of Independence: 'She was properly supporting her son.' Concepta clearly recalled the day her grandmother showed her how the top could be lifted off 'a round table and two revolvers concealed in the square beneath – one facing each way'. Annie also hid guns and ammunition in the concealed pockets she had sewn into the curtains framing the fireplace. She once told her granddaughter about a raid on the house in 1919, when a British Army officer, searching for evidence of republican activity, 'saw the grandfather's [British Army] pension book and said: "Oh, Mam, you're firing with both guns"'.

In 1919 Annie lost a son. Concepta's 'family used to say that [Christopher] got a kick from a Black and Tan', but her research revealed that her uncle was involved in a 'skirmish at the edge of Prince's Street where a contingent of the British [Army] was dragging the Tricolour flag. [He] and the Fianna boys were marching in O'Connell Street and he was told to go and rescue the flag. Anyway, he got a kick in the stomach and two months later he died of peritonitis at the age of eighteen.'

Concepta said that trips into the Dublin Mountains with her father on a Sunday gave her the opportunity to learn some of the details of his experiences in 'the troubles'. Father and daughter walked from Tallaght to a little cottage in the mountains, where they visited an 'old lady with only one eye' who had provided 'a safe house' for the Volunteers during the War of Independence. Concepta also has fond memories of summer days on Tom Cotter's farm in Celbridge, County Kildare, where the family would visit her father's old comrade. The city children plucked apples from his orchard while the men reminisced about 'bringing in arms under the cover of darkness to Dublin Bay'.

Thomas McEvoy took the anti-Treaty side during the Civil War, during which he served as an engineer in the Dublin Brigade and was active in Dublin, Louth and Kildare: 'I think they thought that after all the trouble … they had come away without the full republic and it ended up rather bitterly.' McEvoy was active with the anti-Treaty forces in O'Connell Street during the occupation of the Four Courts in June 1922, and Concepta learned:

> At one stage my father escaped from the Hammond Hotel … The Free State Army came and, in trying to get the insurgents out, set the place on fire. They say Dev came out dressed as a woman in the fire tender and got away. Cathal Brugha came out the back way on to Cathedral Lane and was shot by a sniper from the roof of Findlaters. My father tunnelled through the basement, escaped through the back of the Pro-Cathedral on to Marlboro Street and away.

In the guerrilla stage of the Civil War, the IRA targeted communications and transport, and Thomas McEvoy was involved in blowing up railway bridges in Celbridge and Julianstown. Looking at it with hindsight, his daughter said, 'I don't think he was correct. The people had voted … and I think they should have accepted it.' Thomas was arrested in Prosperous, County Kildare, on 2 November 1922 and imprisoned in Newbridge Internment Camp until Christmas week 1923, 'which was good [because] he didn't kill too many of his own countrymen'.[69] While her father rarely spoke about the difficult reality of internment, he did share an anecdote about how he sang for the jailers 'to earn eggs for breakfast for his companions'. Concepta also remembers being told:

> They wouldn't wear the prison uniform while they were there [in a protest for prisoner-of-war status] so they were dressed in sacks and rags. At one stage his mother arrived down to see him. They had executed some of them you see and [when] he was called out he thought that was it, but it was his mother. She berated the officer for the way he was dressed and kicked up murder about the condition they were in. She didn't realise that it was of their own making.

Thomas McEvoy's involvement in militant republicanism ended with his release in December 1923. He left the IRA in 1927 and the following year married Concepta's mother, Elizabeth Ryan. The couple met at a meeting of the Gaelic League in Parnell Square 'after the whole thing was over and I don't think she was involved. But, by coincidence, the petrol for the burning of the Custom House [in which he was involved] was stored in a shed at the back of No. 11 Emerald Street in Dublin, owned by my mother's aunt, Ellen Downs.' To 'cap it all off,' Concepta laughed, 'my mother was in the Free State civil service. She was on the opposite side.'

Concepta's overriding impression is that her father was a 'very kind man and he worked hard'. From 1926 until he retired, he was employed as a grocer's assistant in John Shields in Moore Street. 'He was on the bacon counter and people … always went into Tommy McEvoy for the rashers in those days.' Various old comrades used to come in and visit him, including Dr Kathleen Lynn and Máire Comerford, and numerous people called to the house at different times 'to chat about the old days', but he didn't get involved any further. When he died in 1970 'the Irish Army came and played the *Last Post* and they fired the volley of shots over his grave'.

DIARMUID LYNCH

Diarmuid Lynch and Frank Henderson were the last to leave the GPO on Friday 28 April 1916. Their destinies seemed entwined, as Henderson helped

Diarmuid Lynch
(*courtesy of Mercier Archive*)

Lynch to orchestrate his clandestine wedding to Kathleen (Kit) Quinn in Dundalk Gaol on 24 April 1918 – two years exactly after the Rising began. Henderson later described his comrade in arms as 'a splendid type of Irishman, upright, honest, determined, unsparing in his efforts to advance the cause, of good personality, devoted to the "Gaelic and Free" conception of Ireland and somewhat stubborn'.[70]

For both his niece, Dolores Lynch, and his biographer, Eileen McGough, Diarmuid Lynch is a 'forgotten patriot', neglected in the annals of Irish revolutionary history. As one of the eleven members of the Supreme Council of the IRB, Lynch was at the heart of the plans for insurrection and Connolly's aide-de-camp in the GPO. A member of the Sinn Féin Executive, Lynch was arrested in 1918 and deported to America, where he was elected in absentia as TD for the constituency of Cork South-East in December that year. His efforts as national secretary for the Friends of Irish Freedom (FOIF) in America swelled the membership and the coffers of the organisation, but brought him into public conflict with Éamon de Valera in 1919. After his repatriation to Ireland in 1932, Lynch began an active programme of contacting, interviewing and recording statements from veterans of the GPO garrison, and after his retirement to his native Tracton in County Cork in 1938, he continued to chronicle various aspects of the 1916 Rising. It is his biographer's opinion that this first persistent and painstaking researcher of the Rising deserves recognition.

Dolores Lynch went to live with her Uncle Diarmuid and his wife, Kit, in 1946, and readily admits that she 'is very proud of him … He was not the kind of fella you'd go in and throw your arms around. He wasn't into that stuff. He was austere and I would think he was extraordinarily disciplined. He was strict but very gracious … and I was very fond of him.'

Diarmuid Lynch grew up in Granig, Tracton. His mother, Hanna Dunlea, died of bronchial pneumonia when he was only six months old, and his father Timothy 'quickly' remarried. He and his new wife, Margaret Murphy, had a daughter and four sons, the youngest of whom was Dolores' father, Michael Lynch. Dolores never knew her grandfather, who died of pneumonia six months before the birth of his son in 1890, but remembers her grandmother, Margaret, as 'a great, great woman' who raised six children alone. 'They used to say I look very like her [though] not as ample.'

As the eldest son, Diarmuid felt a strong sense of responsibility and left school at the age of twelve to help on the family's 200-acre farm. At eighteen, he passed the state examination for the British civil service and spent some months in London, working as a boy clerk in the Mount Pleasant sorting office at fourteen shillings a week.[71] 'He wasn't liking it,' Dolores said, and in 1896 he seized an opportunity presented by his uncle, Cornelius Dunlea, a manufacturer of farm machinery in New York, to emigrate to America. In Lynch's words: 'I can say that on my first sight of the Statue of Liberty I felt myself to be a good American.'[72] He became an American citizen 'early on' and spent eleven years in commercial employment, during which time he assumed the presidency of the New York State Gaelic League and the Philo-Celtic Society. He was extremely active in Irish nationalist activities and, his niece claimed, 'was very, very enthusiastic' about the Irish language: 'Apart from his country, that was his great love [and] he spoke beautiful, sort of idiomatic Irish.'

In March 1907 Diarmuid Lynch served formal notice to his employer and sailed again for Ireland. In the following year he was initiated into the Bartholomew Teeling Circle of the IRB, and in 1910 relocated to County Cork, where he was 'selected as Divisional Centre for Munster on the [IRB] Supreme Council'.[73] Under his brother's direction, Dolores' father Michael formed 'a strong company of Volunteers' in Tracton. In January 1914 Thomas Ashe and Diarmuid Lynch travelled to the United States 'to raise money for the Gaelic League', and returned after the outbreak of the First World War with a draft of US $2,000 from Clan na Gael to arm the Volunteers.[74] In May 1915 Lynch assumed the position of secretary of the IRB in place of the imprisoned Seán MacDermott, and at a meeting of the IRB Executive he proposed a motion for the appointment of Pearse, Plunkett and Ceannt to the Military Council. In late autumn he travelled to Kerry to identify a suitable landing place for the German arms promised by John Devoy: 'Pearse had Ventry in mind, but Lynch found that the Kerry IRB officers favoured Fenit and he so reported to Pearse.'[75] 'It would have made a terrible difference if that ship had landed,' Dolores said, 'but when that went down that was the end of it.'

In the same year, British authorities identified Diarmuid Lynch as 'a naturalised American citizen engaging in national activities' and 'consorting with men of extreme views'. He was compelled by a British court to register as a 'friendly alien' so that they could 'keep closer track of [his] movements'.[76] He was confined to within a five-mile radius of Dublin, which he regarded as preferable to deportation, and the restriction didn't hamper his activities in preparation for the planned insurrection. Lynch was among the ten members of the IRB Supreme Council gathered for a meeting in Clontarf Town Hall in January 1916, when the resolution to 'fight at the earliest possible date' was endorsed.[77] In early April 1916 he was assigned by MacDermott to work with Richard Mulcahy, in his capacity as an engineer in the Post Office, in making preparations for the proposed demolition of communications at the start of the rebellion.[78]

On Easter Monday Lynch was aide-de-camp to James Connolly in the GPO, and he and George Plunkett commanded a bodyguard squad for Pearse as he read the Proclamation of the Republic to the bemused citizens of Dublin outside the GPO.[79] That afternoon Lynch joined Thomas Clarke in looking through the letters 'which had been sorted into the pigeonhole marked RIC Headquarters'. Reports on 'the strength, armament and activity' of the Volunteers in the previous week made 'interesting reading' and they 'chuckled at the fact that all their spying was now in vain'.[80] On Wednesday, on Connolly's orders, Lynch and a squad of men began tunnelling through the south wall of the GPO to meet Frank Henderson's squad, who were tunnelling from the Coliseum Theatre on Henry Street.

Henderson and Lynch worked together again on Friday, when the fires raged out of control and evacuation became inevitable. On MacDermott's orders, the two men moved the unstable, improvised armaments from the basement of the GPO to the Prince's Street side of the building. Lynch recorded:

> Myriads of live sparks fell through the open shaft to the immediate vicinity of the Henry Street basement room in which the gelignite powder and bombs had been placed for safety; a possible explosion of those just then might have had serious consequences, not alone in casualties but in blocking the intended exit for retreat.[81]

'They were being bombarded from every angle,' said his niece, who was keen to emphasise that 'he got the prisoners out' of the basement. However, the 'great talking point in pubs', she smiled, is the question of 'who was the last fella to leave the GPO'. Lynch recorded that the garrison was evacuated while he 'was engaged in the task of averting the danger of a premature explosion' and most historians accept that he was the last to leave the burning building.[82]

Following the surrender, Diarmuid Lynch was tried and sentenced to death. He told them that 'he was an American citizen, but they disregarded that, so he was in his cell waiting for the dawn and he could hear his friends being shot dead out in the yard of the prison'. Neither her father nor her uncle spoke to Dolores about these things: 'I would hear more when people came to visit Diarmuid.'

Denis Lynch acted swiftly on his brother's behalf and telegraphed news of the death sentence to Lynch's American friends, Dick Dalton and Justice Daniel Cohalan. They succeeded, through a complicated line of communication, in prompting a cable from President Woodrow Wilson's office to the British Foreign Office, requesting the deferral of Lynch's execution pending investigation by the American government. He learned on 20 May that his sentence had been commuted to ten years' penal servitude. 'Denis really was responsible for getting that arranged ... but the whole family were involved at that stage ... I think he was in about six jails all together ... They moved him from place to place but he was never in Frongoch.'

Released in 1917, Lynch was one of the few surviving members of the Supreme Council of the IRB and was appointed director of supplies (food) at the Sinn Féin Ard-Fheis in October 1917. In accordance with Sinn Féin's intention to bypass the British government in Ireland, he began a campaign to keep Irish food at home at a time when 'the people of Ireland [were] half starving'. He took it a step further on 21 February 1918, when, in his own words, he undertook 'a protest against the policy of the usurping government in denuding Ireland of bacon and other foods contrary to the needs of the people'.[83] He 'kidnapped' a consignment of pigs being driven from the market at North Circular Road to the North Wall for export, Dolores explained. 'He had a whole lot of Volunteers', including Leo Henderson, and they 'unloaded the pigs from the lorries ... [and] drove them down into a depot' belonging to the Corporation Cleansing Department. 'I don't suppose the corporation were that impressed ... The butchers [were] all standing by when the pigs came in and bang, bang, the people all got meat for nothing. There were queues of them from all over.' Sinn Féin later compensated the pig farmers, Mr Bowe of Glasnevin and Mr Byrne of 61 Parnell Street.

Diarmuid Lynch was promptly arrested and charged with 'taking part in a conspiracy to seize pigs and other animals and prevent their export and taking part in an unlawful assembly'.[84] Kevin O'Sheil later commented that this extreme action 'drew forth strong and indignant protests from the Unionist press and the Castle people who designated it "an unparalleled outrage", but it certainly greatly enhanced the prestige of Sinn Féin, demonstrating to the country that it was what it claimed to be, the party of action and not of talk, prepared to act drastically when the national need demanded it'.[85] Lynch was sentenced to two months in prison and taken to Mountjoy, where his brother Denis and his fiancée Kit visited him. In March he was moved to Dundalk Gaol but soon after his arrival he received notification that he was being deported to America as 'an undesirable American citizen'.[86] Fellow prisoner Ernest Blythe remembered 'the principal item of interest during the period' was the marriage of Diarmuid Lynch:

> He made application to the Castle for leave to get married in the prison just before the end of his sentence. He got back from the Castle a rather nasty letter asking what special reasons he could give in support of his application. This annoyed him very much, and I think it was at least partly in consequence of the tone of the official letter that he determined to outwit the authorities.[87]

Nora Thornton and Muriel MacSwiney were regular visitors to the prison and acted as couriers between Dublin and Dundalk. The women made the necessary arrangements for Diarmuid's wedding to Kathleen Quinn.[88] Michael Brennan, witness to the wedding, wrote: 'If she were married to Diarmuid Lynch she automatically acquired citizenship – hence the urgency. If the marriage did not take place it would be years before they even met.'[89]

Dolores heard the story from her mother, Carmel Quinn, who acted as bridesmaid for her half-sister Kit. 'My mother was a good bit younger and she wasn't married at that time. I think she was only eighteen.' They came up 'from Dublin on the train' with the Capuchin priest, Fr Aloysius Travers, who 'was dressed in civvies … When they arrived at the prison they asked to see three prisoners, one of them to be best man.' Ernest Blythe recalled:

> The rule then was that the prisoners went behind a rail held by a trestle which stretched along one side of the room and the visitors stood behind another rail on the opposite side of the room. The priest stooped under the rail and brought the girl with him, saying, 'I want to talk to you two.' The warder did not like to object to the priest doing this and stood by. … The priest put his arm round the necks of Diarmuid Lynch and the girl and pretended to be carrying on a whispered conversation with them.[90]

Michael Brennan chatted 'brightly and loudly' with Carmel 'about everything and anything', and Frank Henderson put his 'back against the door of the visiting room' with instructions that 'if the warder … attempted to convey to the Governor what was taking place, to prevent him by force from doing so'.[91] After the hurried ceremony, Michael and Carmel signed the document produced by the priest 'certifying that [they] had witnessed the marriage'.[92]

Brennan delighted in the fact that there 'was, of course, a storm in official circles but the country had another good laugh at how the Government had been outwitted'.[93] Arrangements were made to expedite Lynch's deportation and Kit met her new husband at Amiens Street Station in May 1918. A police escort bundled the couple into the back of a 'Black Maria'. Michael Collins and Harry Boland 'insisted on getting in' and drove with them as far as Arbour Hill.[94] In his pension application, Lynch claimed that he and Michael Collins 'were enabled to hold a private conversation during which … we discussed methods of communication between America and Ireland'. Diarmuid Lynch, director of communications on the Volunteer headquarters staff and treasurer of the Supreme Council of the IRB, spent a week in the detention barracks before he was deported.

A week after his arrival in the United States, Lynch was elected national secretary of the Irish-American organisation Friends of Irish Freedom (FOIF), 'a nationwide organisation devoted to securing the permanent establishment and international recognition of the Irish Republic proclaimed in Easter Week'.[95] Kit joined her husband in June, and in December he was elected unopposed in his absence as TD for South-East Cork. For the next year, Lynch sent Collins numerous cables 'couched in prearranged camouflaged terms' from New York.[96]

In May 1919 Harry Boland arrived in the United States as special representative from Ireland, followed in June by Éamon de Valera. *The Freeman's Journal* reported that de Valera 'burst upon the American scene like a thunderclap. All of the strands of his earlier career, American birth … rebel commandant, escapee from British jails, president of Dáil Éireann combined to make him a fascinating celebrity in the American public eye.'[97] 'There was a clash of personalities right from the beginning,' Dolores said:

Dev came over and decided that he was in charge of everything even though he was totally a raw recruit to the US ... [and] didn't have a clue in Hades. Diarmuid had been there from the late 1890s and they had set up all these organisations ... Dev decided that he would take over the lot ... He was staying in the Waldorf Astoria, [while] Diarmuid would be going back to his wife to a flat in the Bronx. [They] did themselves powerfully well ...

They raised an enormous amount of money that time. They put on plays in Irish on Broadway for God's sake ... and second and third generation [Irish] came from all parts of America to see it. They had *feiseanna* (Irish dancing), *aeriocht* (outdoor music and dancing events) and all these sorts of things to raise money. Diarmuid was very active [and] as a matter of fact he almost lost his health that time ... and then Dev took the credit for all the fundraising which he didn't do at all ... He could never have got that money together ever, ever, only for their American counterparts over there.

Differences arose between de Valera and the leaders of the American organisation 'as to the proper conduct of the campaign in America for the recognition of the Irish Republic' and how to spend the money.[98] Bitter attacks against John Devoy, leader of Clan na Gael and founding member of the FOIF, were printed in both American and Irish newspapers. Dolores also points to what she considers to be de Valera's lack of respect for her uncle's old associate, Devoy: 'He had no time at all for the Fenian ... He just looked on him as an old man who was seeing Ireland through different glasses. [Dev] saw it as modern Ireland.'

Éamon Ó Cuív, on the other hand, feels that his grandfather's time in America, during which he launched a 'huge diplomatic offensive', proved invaluable to the cause of the Irish independence. Éamon de Valera had three aims: 'to ask for official recognition of the Irish Republic; to obtain a loan to finance the work of the new government; and to secure the support of the American people for the Republic'. The tour lasted until December 1920 and raised US $6 million:

They got down as far south as Louisiana and Alabama, visited democratic conventions [and] they actually got a motion to the floor of the democratic convention in Chicago … which was a hell of an achievement considering the power of British diplomacy. I think we were probably the first nation that sought to fight its independence battle on so many fronts at the one time: diplomatic; undermining the administration at home by setting up a parallel administration; and by a military campaign, the military campaign only being one leg of a three-legged stool.

Ó Cuív credits his grandfather's efforts in America as being enormously influential in 'forcing the British to [try] to make a settlement'. He also implicitly addresses his grandfather's critics, who claim that de Valera avoided the worst of the struggle for independence during 1919–21: 'I think it probably was the best thing he could have done in the circumstances, because being hidden away in Ireland and not being able to appear publicly anywhere wouldn't have achieved much, but being president of Ireland in America he was creating the reality of the Republic, openly canvassing' and collecting what would in 'today's money' be 'literally millions of euros'.

After a public clash, Lynch felt obliged to resign his membership of the Dáil, of which de Valera was president. On 2 August 1920 *The Freeman's Journal* printed a public letter from Lynch to his constituents in South-East Cork:

> No matter what vicissitudes the future may have in store for me, I shall always cherish with pride the part which I had the honour to fulfil in the councils of those who made Easter Week possible and solidified the foundations of the Irish Republic … I feel more free to continue my efforts here for the recognition of the Irish Republic on the lines which long and practical experience in America have shown me to be for the best interest of the Irish cause.

While his brother was in America, Michael Lynch remained active with the IRA Volunteers in Tracton. He also maintained his 'great friendship' with Michael Collins, with whom he had been interned in Frongoch after 1916. Dolores' father 'would wrestle with Collins' when he stayed overnight in the farmhouse in Granig,[99] and Michael Lynch always claimed to have been one of the last people to see the commander-in-chief alive when he stopped at Teddy Quinn's Eldon Hotel in Skibbereen on the morning of 22 August

1922. Despite his sorrow when his friend fell to a sniper's bullet in West Cork, Lynch's sympathies were with the anti-Treaty side during the Civil War. It was 'terrible', Dolores said, and the fraternal conflict had a bitter legacy in Tracton. The Lynchs and the Coveneys were the 'two big families in the parish and there was no way the Lynches ever spoke to the Coveneys because they were Blueshirts as we called them'. Dolores' brother, Diarmuid Óg, didn't relish the prospect of having to tell his father, 'who was quite ill', about his proposed marriage to Mary Coveney in 1957.

Michael Lynch was, in his daughter's words, 'a man well before his time'. In 1927 he got 'the great notion' that he would introduce Irish bloodstock to America. He bought brood mares and boarded a liner from Cobh with his pregnant wife. They lost their stock to storms in the Atlantic, and after the Wall Street Crash 'they stayed with Uncle Diarmuid and his wife. ... My brother, Diarmuid Óg, was born in America, [but] eventually they packed up and came back to the homestead in Granig, with nothing.' Michael Lynch 'needed a livelihood for his family' so he got a job in the Land Commission.[100]

Even though Dolores feels that her uncle was the 'driving force in America' and 'got on very well over there', she knows that he was 'always homesick', which is why he returned to Ireland in 1932. He stayed with his brother's family 'for a long time until he got a house of his own in Mallow'. His niece maintains that he felt 'let down by Fianna Fáil' after his repatriation: 'Dev was totally in charge [and] he wanted no part of that at all.' He 'applied for a pension' and was 'very lucky to get [one] at all after all the millions he raised for them ... and it's not like he was a rich man'.

In 1935 Diarmuid Lynch set about collecting testimonies from veterans of the Rising. He was concerned with ''16 and Dublin, the GPO in particular', his niece explained, so he 'devised a simple record sheet and dispatched it to hundreds of the known and traceable survivors'.[101] Clair Wills describes his concern with precision: 'He spent months, and in some cases years, verifying details, writing back to participants asking them to draw the precise shape of a sloping roof, the exact location of outposts and the exact routes taken in and out of the building.'[102] His niece added: 'There were so many accounts that were incorrect and so many mistakes that were made ... and he would not put up with that.' He had 'wonderful integrity' and was 'extraordinarily honest

Brunswick Street. Father Mathew Hall, a large red-brick building at the junction of Church Street and Nicholas Avenue, was commandeered by the Volunteers as a supply post and a field hospital. Captain Denis O'Callaghan's 'A' Company took over tenement houses on North King Street, while 'B' Company, under James O'Sullivan, erected barricades on the northern flank. Frank Fahy's 'C' Company gained entry to the Four Courts through Chancery Place and occupied the building, and Fionán Lynch's 'F' Company began to erect barricades in the area of Church Street. A public house at the junction of North King Street and Church Street, later known as 'Reilly's Fort', was occupied by twenty Volunteers under Jack Shouldice, while his younger brother, Frank, took his position as a sniper on Jameson's Malthouse Tower on Beresford Street, overlooking North King Street. 'D' Company, under Seán Heuston, occupied the Mendicity Institution as an outpost on the south side of the River Liffey, about half a mile to the west of the Four Courts. His orders were to cover the route from the Royal Barracks (Collins Barracks) to the Four Courts for a few hours, giving Daly's garrison time to establish its defences. Nicholas Laffan's 'G' Company occupied buildings on North King Street and Brunswick Street, connecting Daly's command north and south of the battalion area.

Jack Shouldice told his son that 'the first shock' occurred on Monday afternoon, when the Volunteers at a barricade at Church Street Bridge fired on a detachment of fifty Lancers escorting ammunition trucks from the docks at North Wall to the Magazine Fort in Phoenix Park. For the rest of the week, the Volunteers in Church Street came under fire from British positions across the river, a machine gun on the roof of Jervis Street Hospital and snipers in Dublin Castle, Power's Distillery tower and the bell tower of Christ Church Cathedral. On Wednesday Daly's men captured the Linenhall Barracks, but on Thursday their fortunes began to turn. The British planned to encircle the city, isolating the Volunteer headquarters, and this meant pushing the cordon down North King Street, cutting through the rebel area. A battle of ferocious proportions between the Volunteers and the South Staffordshire and Sherwood Forest Regiments lasted from Friday until news of Pearse's surrender reached the Four Courts on Saturday afternoon.

JOHN AND THOMAS O'CONNOR, JACK AND FRANK SHOULDICE

Eileen Butterly's father, John O'Connor, and her uncle, Tommy O'Connor, were members of Fionán Lynch's 'F' Company in the North King Street and Church Street areas during Easter Week. Born in 1936, Eileen was the fifth of John's six children and grew up in Howth Road, Clontarf, where from a 'young age' the children heard 'all about the rebellion in 1916'.

Eileen is unreservedly proud of her father's involvement in the Rising. 'I felt always very republican,' she said. 'We used to write "Bad Britain" in our schoolbooks … so he instilled that into us somehow from an early age.' Reminded of school in the 1940s, she frowned at the memory of there being a mere paragraph in her history book about the Rising: 'I was absolutely disgusted with that because, to me, that was a really important event.' Her brother, Johnny, is similarly proud to be able to say that his father fought in 1916: 'When I hear the national anthem being played, I stand to attention because my father was out fighting for that national anthem.'

The O'Connor family came originally from Limerick. In the late 1880s Eileen's grandfather, Thomas O'Connor, an 'upholsterer' and 'a Fenian', emigrated to England, where he met and married Ellen Maher. Their first child, Florrie, was born in London in 1888, after which the family returned to Limerick, where Tommy, John, Frank, Gertrude, Jessica and Margaret were born. 'I think there is a question mark about why they left London,' Eileen said. 'There may have been some republican activity but we have no back-up for that.' Thomas eventually moved his family to Dublin and they settled in Lower Sherrard Street: 'Seán T. O'Kelly, I think, was a near neighbour, and there was a lot of [nationalist] activity.'

The O'Connor girls worked in Dublin: Jessie 'made hats and Auntie Gertie, I think, was a typist'. John was studying law and Tommy 'went to sea'. He travelled on 'a series of different ships', but the most famous was the *Carpathia*, on which he sailed from New York to Liverpool in April 1912. 'They went off course to rescue [the *Titanic* survivors] and he was one of the people who helped to bring people on board … [The rescued passengers] were obviously very traumatised and very grateful to the people on the *Carpathia*, and Tommy later received a medal for his actions that night. His son Eugene,' Eileen added, 'is very proud of that medal.'

John and Tommy O'Connor in
Volunteer uniform
(*courtesy of the O'Connor family*)

By the time the O'Connor brothers joined the Volunteers in early February 1914, John was a promising law student and Tommy had an apprenticeship at Lynch and Deering Solicitors in Lower Ormond Quay. Both brothers took part in the Howth gun-running five months later. 'We thought it was a marvellous thing to get the guns,' John O'Connor told WNAC Radio Boston in 1966, but 'afterwards, when we got to know something about a rifle, we realised that the Howth rifle was not the beauty that we thought it was.'[1] He told his daughter that on the return journey from Howth, the Volunteers encountered British soldiers on the Malahide Road, and 'my father was knocked out when he was hit on the head with the butt of a rifle'. His rifle was confiscated and, on 22 August, 'he had the nerve to write to the Dublin Metropolitan Police looking for his gun back'. He received a curt acknowledgement of his letter, which Eileen proudly proffered for inspection: 'That was typical of him.'

At the outbreak of war in 1914, the British War Office imposed strict postal, cable and wireless censorship.[2] Thomas Clarke and Seán MacDermott, 'with whom [Tommy] was intimately acquainted, requested that [he] leave [his] employment and obtain a position of some kind on an Atlantic liner travelling between Liverpool and New York' in order to establish a regular and reliable communication with Clan na Gael.[3] Between November 1915 and April 1916, 'working in any position available on the ships', Eileen's uncle crossed the Atlantic at least six times, 'bringing messages from the headquarters here over to John Devoy in New York'. 'There were collections made there and he [brought] money back to Ireland for the cause'.[4]

Tommy's niece is particularly proud of the fact that he carried 'the message about the Rising itself'. In 1952 vice-commandant of the 1st Battalion and IRB member Piaras Béaslaí identified Tommy O'Connor as 'the bearer of a message to Germany which first fixed the date of the rising for 23 April 1916'.[5] Using his diaries for corroboration, Béaslaí explained that, in January 1916, Seán MacDermott entrusted him with an encoded message requesting that 'the German allies' add to their planned shipment of arms to Ireland 'a number of machine guns and some officers who could give instructions on their use'.[6] On board a mail boat bound for his native Liverpool, Béaslaí 'decoded part of the message which gave the date of the Rising as 23 April'.[7] He handed the communication to Tommy O'Connor at his lodgings in Liverpool, and

Michael J. Kehoe, a member of the Irish Brigade in Germany, recalled Tommy's arrival there in January 1916.[8] He had a meeting with Roger Casement before departing for America to meet representatives of Clan na Gael. During March 1916 he carried further enciphered messages between John Devoy in America and the Military Council in Ireland relating to the arrival of arms in Fenit.[9]

Kathleen Clarke was among the referees for Tommy O'Connor's application for a military service pension in 1937. She wrote:

> On several occasions I remember my late husband paying glowing tributes to his courage and integrity. Also I know the danger of his work. With the Great War on, had he been caught England's fury would have made short work of him.[10]

Tommy left Liverpool for Dublin on Tuesday 18 April 1916, but on the eve of the uprising he was asked to return to his work on the liners. According to his nephew, 'He said no. He wanted to be part of the action.' Clarke and MacDermott 'reluctantly gave [him] permission to remain in Dublin'.[11] He joined his brother in 'F' Company under Fionán Lynch, who recalled that tensions were 'at fever height' in the days before the planned uprising. In response to rumours that the leaders would be rounded up, Tom Clarke stayed with the O'Connors of Sherrard Street, and Seán MacDermott stayed with Lynch at 44 Mountjoy Street.[12] This is why his niece is convinced that, despite the countermanding order on Easter Sunday, Tommy 'knew that it was definitely happening on the Monday. He was very close to Tom Clarke.'[13]

On Easter Monday morning the 'attenuated 1st Battalion' mobilised in Blackhall Street. After Daly surprised his battalion by revealing that 'soon their leaders would proclaim an Irish Republic that he expected them to defend with their lives', he offered everyone the opportunity to go home with honour.[14] Only two men withdrew, one of whom was captain of 'G' Company; he left the hall with a declaration 'that the whole thing was lunacy', but the other officers, including Fionán Lynch, led their men to their pre-allocated positions.[15] Tommy O'Connor and his brother John were on active service in North King Street, Church Street and the Four Courts for the duration of Easter Week. 'John was just nineteen years old,' Eileen said, 'and Tommy was two years older. They took a terrible risk … [It was] very foolhardy in a way, but they felt very strongly.' Johnny reminded his sister that there 'was another brother, Frank O'Connor, who didn't take part in the Rising … He wanted to go out but the family agreed that he shouldn't because it would be bad enough if two boys were killed, but [not] three boys … That's why in most cases one boy stayed at home.'

Piaras Béaslaí testified that 'on the Saturday, 29 April, Commandant Daly and I sent [Tommy] out from the Four Courts on a very difficult and dangerous mission – to try and get in touch with GHQ, as a result of which he was, I believe, captured and subsequently interned'.[16] Tommy was detained in Knutsford and Frongoch until Christmas 1916. In January 1917, at the request of the Supreme Council that he resume his work in communications, he travelled to Liverpool and secured passage to America under the name 'Thomas Welsh'. His work continued until his eventual arrest in November 1917 by a British agent 'at the docks in New York'. He was charged with a violation of the Trading with the Enemy Act (1914) and sentenced to a year's imprisonment. Released pending an appeal, Tommy continued in the service of the IRB and the GHQ of the Irish Volunteers and IRA.

Tommy later said: 'One of my most pleasurable tasks in this period was making arrangements in connection with the secret visit of President de Valera.' He was also active in obtaining subscriptions for the 'Bond Drive' and 'arranging for the shipment of arms to Ireland'.[17] A fellow IRB member, Edmond O'Brien, attested to Tommy's involvement in the packing of the arms and ammunition, including 'a small supply of Thompson sub-machine guns', into 'convenient parcels' for transportation from New York to Ireland in 1920.[18]

After his appeal was dismissed in the Supreme Court in December 1920, Tommy began his prison sentence in Atlanta, Georgia. He was released in December 1921 and in March of the following year he escorted Countess Markievicz and Kathleen Barry on a tour of the United States 'to collect funds for the Republic'. Tommy returned to Dublin in December, but was arrested during a raid on his house by the Free State army and imprisoned in Mountjoy for three months.[19] Eileen expressed her regret that she was not able to question her uncle more closely about his dramatic experiences during the revolutionary period because, 'after the Civil War' he 'got a bit sick of things here', and once President John Calvin Coolidge had granted him 'an unconditional pardon' in December 1927, he went to America and became an accountant in New York.[20] 'My father used to go over and visit him,' Eileen said. 'He went over in 1934 and again in 1938', but the brothers, 'who were always very close', didn't see each other during the Second World War. Tommy finally returned to Ireland in 1953 to attend the *An Tostal* celebrations and to 'meet all the old friends from 1916'.[21]

His nephew, Johnny, was just twelve years old in 1953, but remembers his father 'was very concerned' about Tommy because 'he wasn't a well man. I think he was coming home to say goodbye to his brothers and sisters.' During the same visit Tommy presented President Seán T. O'Kelly with the code used in the message to Clan na Gael announcing the date of the Rising.[22] Eileen admitted that she has on occasion used the cypher to keep her nineteen grandchildren amused.

Tommy died soon after his visit home in 1953, and his was a notable absence beside his brother and the veterans of 'F' Company on 'the stand in O'Connell Street' in 1966. His brother John, however, shared their story in several interviews during the anniversary year. Proinsias MacAonghusa 'interviewed Daddy for RTÉ', Eileen said, and he gave another interview, with Frank Shouldice and Tom Sheerin, to John Caulhan from WNAC Radio Boston.[23] O'Connor told his American interviewers that he was a sergeant in Fionán Lynch's 'F' Company, 1st Battalion, Dublin Brigade. His daughter knows that he was 'absolutely disgusted' by MacNeill's countermand and was 'devastated' that the Rising was called off 'after all their work [and] all their preparations', but he 'was delighted then' when 'it all happened on the Monday'.

Fionán Lynch sent word to his 1st Lieutenant, Jack Shouldice, to mobilise the company. Their orders were 'to hold and fortify the crossing at North King Street and Church Street', Jack's son Chris Shouldice explained, and to occupy and fortify the adjoining houses and erect barricades. The plan was to defend the crossing from enemy attacks coming from British barracks on the Smithfield side, and from military posts such as the Broadstone Railway Station and the North Dublin Union on the north and east sides, to keep the crossing open for Volunteer forces from the Four Courts, and maintain a line of communication with the GPO garrison. Sergeant John O'Connor was dispatched to mobilise 'the lads' in Drumcondra:

It was a nice sunny day apparently [and] he had to cycle around telling the lads that it was on. A lot of them had gone off to Fairyhouse [races] and so he gathered as many as he could – I think he said he got ten of them – and brought them in.

O'Connor told John Caulhan that he and his section of twenty men paraded at Blackhall Street at noon on Easter Monday. Carrying their Lee Enfield rifles, Howth Mausers and revolvers, the company moved out to 'build barricades to act as outposts for the Four Courts position … I was posted [at a barricade] at a place in May Lane (a side street perpendicular to Church Street) just beside the famous Jameson's Distillery'.[24] Three further barricades were erected to cover a large open area created some years previously by the demolition of old tenements. The first, at the junction of Church Street, May Lane and Mary's Lane, was constructed using timber from the ruins of some old houses. The second, at the narrow point of Mary's Lane, was composed of 'a lot of stuff out of yards and old furniture', and the last was placed in Cuckoo Lane, off Beresford Street.[25]

Vice-Commandant Piaras Béaslaí later commented on the unique nature of their position: 'In other parts of the city, buildings only were held [but] our troops were actually out on the streets in an area where a large civilian population resided and our military problems were added to by the problems of civilian administration.'[26] John O'Connor recalled that in the early days of the Rising, the Volunteers 'were greatly troubled' by the demands of people who had been at the Fairyhouse races to get through the barricades, a few of whom, Jack Shouldice observed, 'were inclined to be obstreperous at being held up'.[27] They also dealt with attempts by opportunistic looters to breach the barricades with parcels under their arms, 'rolls of tweed, woollen gowns and things like that'. The Volunteers were 'rather upset' at the disturbance, O'Connor said, because they 'were obsessed by the idea of a cavalry charge'.

Jack Shouldice recalled the difficulties in the early days of the week in regulating the 'hundreds of people who came clamouring for bread to Monk's Bakery in North Brunswick Street', one of the few in Dublin that remained in operation. He also remembered the antagonism of the local residents, many of whom were forced to evacuate their homes. Nonetheless, morale on the barricades 'was very high'. The Volunteers had not been informed about

Casement's failure in Kerry, and John O'Connor expected that 'there would be a similar movement right throughout the country. We [knew] that in Cork and in Limerick there were two very efficient, well equipped [and] well trained brigades. We thought they would come into action and … draw the British forces from the Curragh.'[28]

O'Connor was quick to dispel the suggestion that the Volunteers' high spirits were related to the abundance of alcohol available in Jameson's Distillery, and credited their abstinence to youth as much as integrity: 'We didn't know how to drink whiskey then.' They were further discouraged by the example of two local men who had come to help the Volunteers with the barricades. Unable to resist temptation, they 'tapped a barrel of stuff in [Jameson's] yard and … we had to cart them up to Richmond Hospital'. A month later, while lodged in Stafford Prison, John O'Connor 'read in the *London Opinion*' Sir Andrew Jameson's acknowledgement that, even though the Volunteers had access to enough whiskey to 'set Dublin mad', they didn't touch it. Jameson also, apparently, complimented their taste in cigars. Mr Jameson's Havana cigars, O'Connor admitted, 'were the best I've ever had before or since'. They sent a box to every barricade and a bottle of whiskey to headquarters. Some time later, O'Connor received 'a request from one of the officers to send more "hand grenades". I knew what he meant, so we sent a few more of these little bottles of whiskey.'[29]

As O'Connor augmented his barricade on Monday afternoon, Jack Shouldice took twenty men to occupy and fortify Reilly's public house at the corner of Church Street, 'looking down North King Street towards Bolton Street'. He told his son that 'they were covered in flour because … they had knocked out the windows and put up all these bags of flour' acquired from Blanchardstown Mills on the opposite corner. In the meantime, Volunteers under Frank McCabe and Maurice Collins had occupied a house on the opposite corner, and Jack's brother Frank stood sentinel on the Jameson's Malthouse Tower on Beresford Street.

The fighting in the early part of the week consisted mostly of sniping. 'Bullets spattered round the chimneys of Reilly's Fort,' Jack Shouldice recalled. 'The roof tops soon got too hot for our men who were forced to come down.'[30] On Wednesday Denis O'Callaghan's 'A' Company set the Linenhall Barracks ablaze. While the fire burned 'as bright as day', Frank Shouldice and his men in the Malthouse Tower trained their binoculars on a machine gunner on the roof of Jervis Street Hospital, whose commanding view of the battle zone had resulted in numerous Volunteer casualties.[31] Frank took careful aim and fired. The Vickers gun fell silent.

John O'Connor told his son and daughter about his dawning realisation on Thursday night that the tide was turning against the rebel forces. From his position at the barricade on May Lane, he saw 'a bright glow' in the upper storeys of the Jameson's building. It was 'as if somebody had turned on a light in each window'.

Lieutenant Diarmuid O'Hegarty saw the same light and sent a message requesting that O'Connor and his men ascertain the source. They discovered 'the glow from the fires in O'Connell Street had illuminated the glass in the windows of Jameson's'.[32] Church Street was also alight, 'rendering the men at the barricades a target for snipers', and O'Connor's Volunteers worked to reinforce their barricade with 'bales of hay and sheets of closely packed brown paper', which proved surprisingly effective at intercepting bullets.

> [Then on Friday we heard] the sound of terrific fire and of course we knew that the main battle was taking place in North King Street. I think the most bitter fight in the whole of Easter week was the fight for Reilly's Fort. Members of 'F' Company were under incessant fire for, I think, about thirty-six hours.[33]

The 'fight for Reilly's Fort' began on Friday morning, when the 2/6th Battalion of the South Staffordshire Regiment, under Lieutenant Colonel Henry Taylor, moved across the Liffey at Butt Bridge to seal the British cordon around the Four Courts. Their orders were to move westwards along North King Street and to link up with the 2/5th Battalion of the South Staffordshire Regiment from the east.[34] The soldiers erected barricades on Bolton Street and established a command post in the technical college. Unaware of the strength of the Volunteer position, Taylor dispatched a section into North King Street. They were easy targets for the Volunteers in Lagan's public house and 'Reilly's Fort', and retreated under a hail of rifle fire to Beresford Street 'where they came under fire from Frank Shouldice's men in the Malthouse'. It was, in Jack

Frank Shouldice
(*courtesy of Frank Shouldice jnr*)

Shouldice's words, 'a veritable death trap'.[35] The 'South Staffs' fell back further and the Volunteers in the partly built cottages backing onto Beresford Street and Stirrup Lane practically wiped out the remainder of the platoon. For Shouldice's men in 'Reilly's Fort', the lull in fighting was an 'opportunity to get some badly needed rifles and ammunition'. However, 'most of the rifles were found to have been shattered by the Volunteers' fire and were consequently useless'.[36]

Chris Shouldice explained that his father and uncle were generally 'extremely reticent' about discussing Easter Week with their families: 'As it happened, the best place to get them to talk was after a match on a Sunday when they were in a fully relaxed mood.' Jack and Frank Shouldice, Maurice Collins, George Geraghty and other 1916 veterans often gathered in Meagher's pub on Richmond Road to celebrate, or commiserate, after an afternoon in Croke Park: 'We would bring out our drinks and sit on barrels in the garden at the back of the pub. Then the stories would come and the songs and ballads … My father used to sing the old version of "Galway Bay" and my Uncle Frank, who had a lovely baritone voice, would sing "The Pride of Petravore" – the songs that he had sung during the Rising.' The traditional melodies evoked memories of brotherhood and barricades, and 'the curtains opened a bit here and there and you could look through. It [was] fascinating.'

During these relaxed Sunday afternoons, Chris was privy to some 'disjointed' accounts of his father's position in 'Reilly's Fort'. 'It was hard to string things together', but when he later gained access to his father's submissions to the Bureau of Military History, he was able to 'flesh out' his recollections and make sense of things that 'he didn't quite put together before'. He learned, for exam-ple, that the British forces launched an aggressive counterattack in North King Street on the afternoon of Friday 28 April. Paul O'Brien evocatively captured the scene in Reilly's Fort, which came under concentrated machine-gun fire:

> Bullets stormed along the roof and inside the room splashing clouds of yellow chips from the planking and plaster … Jack Shouldice and his men returned a rapid fire from the barricaded windows. Empty shell casings flew through the guns' ejection ports and tumbled down littering the floors. The battles were furious and attack after attack was abandoned. Each time the British fell back, dragging their dead and wounded.[37]

A frustrated Taylor dispatched a convoy of makeshift armoured personnel carriers, which progressed as far as a Volunteer barricade at a midpoint on North King Street. The soldiers piled out and proceeded to fire into the houses on either side. They forced entry to gain a foothold in the street and vicious house-to-house fighting ensued, with what Chris described as 'Stalingrad-type intensity'.

Chris Shouldice recorded that, at one point, when there was a lull in the fighting, 'an impromptu concert broke out. Uncle Frank was to be heard singing "The Men of the West" and "The Pride of Petravore". Daddy recognised his voice up on the Jameson's Malthouse Tower … and, apparently, the men on the barricades and Daddy's own people in Reilly's Fort joined in'. The South Staffordshire infantry must have been 'absolutely shocked' and 'not a little irritated', Chris said. 'These are some of the tiny incidents that stuck in my mind as a kid.'

In the early hours of Saturday morning, Lieutenant Colonel Taylor ordered his soldiers to begin tunnelling through the interior walls of the houses in North King Street towards 'Reilly's Fort'. Progress was slow and, at dawn, an impatient Taylor told his men to charge the rebel stronghold with fixed bayo-nets. The platoon ran into a wall of bullets fired from several directions, inclu-ding the Malthouse Tower, and lost nine men with many more wounded. 'It was terrible slaughter,' Frank Shouldice said, 'and to this day I can't understand why they tried to rush things.'[38] In 1964 Captain Fionán Lynch told the BBC:

It was, of course, a tragic thing in many ways. One had to be sorry for them, they were only very young boys and in fact Lieutenant Shouldice told me that when he went to collect the rifles with others, he heard one lad saying 'Oh Mammy, Mammy', which was terrible.[39]

After two days of continuous fighting, Shouldice's garrison had been reduced by 'death, wounds and illness' to eight wearied, 'almost stupefied men' who were rapidly running out of ammunition.[40] At 9 a.m. on Saturday morning, left with little choice, they dashed across the 'fire-swept North King Street' to the barricade at Father Mathew Hall, where they received the unwelcome instruction to fall back to the Four Courts for the unconditional surrender. 'Nevertheless,' Jack said in 1948, 'there was a feeling of pride amongst us that we defied the might of England for a whole week.'[41]

As Shouldice and his men evacuated the besieged 'Reilly's Fort', John O'Connor's section abandoned their barricade in May Lane for the main barricade at the end of Church Street:

> We got it pretty hot there … A house [on the corner] had fallen down from the rifle fire … and we were lying on rubble [and] broken bricks and firing up the street firing on what [had been] our own chief stronghold, 'Reilly's Fort' … I [eventually received word] to bring all my men back into the Four Courts… It meant that we would have to go out into Smithfield and come under fire there and then come down Hammond Lane.[42]

O'Connor led his men down Hammond Lane 'which must be a hundred yards' with 'rifles banging behind' them. They reached a 'small barricade near the Four Courts' which 'everyone of [them] jumped, except one poor fella got a bullet in the leg. Two others went back for him.'[43] They were eventually able to gain access to the building through a hole in the internal wall of Coughlan's shoemakers. When O'Connor saw his commandant, he realised:

> Ned Daly's object in getting us into the Four Courts was that he didn't want to have us surrendering in isolated groups. He was afraid that we might get badly handled by the British [and] he wanted to do the thing in the proper formal manner.

Dressed in his full uniform, he paraded us in the Four Courts and then sent word to the British to come in. The soldiers filed in and surrounded us. It must have been about six or seven on Saturday evening.[44]

'Daddy had a great admiration for Ned Daly,' Eileen explained, '[and] absolutely would have laid down his life for [him]. He thought he was a fantastic man. … I think [Daly] had a chance to escape after the Rising and he wouldn't, he stayed with the men. He told the people that were not in uniform to try to get away as best they could … but he made sure he had full uniform and he was arrested.'

John O'Connor told Proinsias MacAonghusa about his journey from Richmond Barracks to the North Wall on the Sunday night after the surrender:

Dublin was in a shocking state; the whole place seemed to be on fire. There was none of the city left. As soon as we got down close to O'Connell Bridge, we saw the fires were still burning. It was the most horrific fire I have ever known, and we … were all fully convinced that we would never set foot in Ireland again.

He remembered the 'hostile crowds around Inchicore' and being glad of the 'continuous line of British soldiers who stood close together with bayonets fixed. … Those British soldiers,' he claimed, 'saved us from our own people … [and] getting on to the ole cattle boat was quite a relief.' When 'we got to the railway station at Stafford, there was a crowd of women and they were yelling out to the soldiers to bayonet us. It was the most hostile reception, it was even worse than the women in Dublin.'[45]

John and Tommy O'Connor were reunited in Frongoch, the internment camp in Wales about which Eileen and John 'heard many tales'. Their father and uncle served mass in the camp 'because they used to be altar boys in Gardiner Street [but] … there were a lot of other things went on in Frongoch besides serving mass. There was football and discussions and learning of Irish', but there was also 'planning'. They weren't going 'to lie down and let the whole thing die. Tommy, I think, was sent on to Knutsford' and John was sent home in August 'with a shilling and a [train] ticket'.

John resumed his law studies, 'but he couldn't afford to be a [full-time] student', so he took employment with a coal merchant named MacNeice. In 1925 he married Patricia Willis, 'known as Pattie', from Avondale Road in Glasnevin, and in the following year he 'finally qualified as a solicitor'. According to her daughter, Patricia 'didn't play an active part' in Easter Week and 'wasn't a member of Cumann na mBan', but later 'she did hide guns and bring guns from one place to another under her skirt and little things like that'.

For Eileen and Johnny, stories of the 1916 Rising were part of the fabric of childhood. Johnny recalled that 'all the people on the barricades off North King Street remained great pals afterwards'. Eileen added that her father was 'always very close' to the Shouldice brothers, who 'were frequent visitors' to their childhood home in Howth Road, and Piaras Béaslaí 'was another one that came up to the house for the sandwiches and the whiskey'.

While the 1916 Rising was a 'frequent topic of conversation' in the O'Connor household, John never spoke much about the War of Independence and uttered 'not a word' about the Civil War. 'As far as we know he was active in the War of Independence', because he had 'a medal with a bar on it' and 'I can't imagine him not taking part [in the Civil War], but they just didn't want to talk about it, you know, certainly [not] to us'. Eileen 'naturally regrets' not asking questions, but is convinced that, even had she done so, her father, who died in 1967, would have avoided answering them.

Her brother agreed that 'there were certain things you didn't ask my father … I remember playing an LP by Eddie Calvert [featuring 'Lad of 18 Summers', a song about Kevin Barry]. I thought my father would be delighted with it but he just walked out of the room and my mother turned to me and said, "Turn that off".' When John asked why, she told him that in the 1920s 'every drunk coming out of every pub in Dublin was singing it'. On another occasion, John O'Connor's young son was bold enough to ask how many people his father had shot: 'I didn't get an answer anyway.'

John worked as election agent for both Éamon de Valera and Seán T. O'Kelly in the 1930s and 'was very close to Dev and his family. He admired him tremendously,' Eileen said, 'and [thought] anything that Dev did was right.' As a staunch Fianna Fáil supporter, John O'Connor 'absolutely hated' the Blueshirts. 'That was something we grew up with … He didn't [have] a personal animosity [for] any of the Fine Gael people, but there was a distance definitely because they took one side and he took the other.' Eileen's maternal aunt married 'a man called Murphy and ... it was only in later years that I realised that the little bit of stand-offishness was because he was a Blueshirt'.

John O'Connor's daughter described him as 'a very kindly man, very intelligent [and] a real family man'. He also had a very successful career as a solicitor, and Eileen worked in his office at 4 Upper Ormond Quay near the Four Courts in the years before she married: 'You felt you were part of history, working in there.' He was also 'president of the Incorporated Law Society' and solicitor to the attorney-general in the late 1930s and 1940s. As a Fianna Fáil TD for Dublin North Central during the 'Emergency', O'Connor 'supported the policy of neutrality' because, as his daughter explained, 'he didn't want to give back what we had already fought for and he didn't want to take part in the world war. We were a very young nation at that stage.'

WILLIAM ARCHER

When William (Liam) Aloysius Archer joined the Irish Volunteers in August 1914, he embarked on a lifelong military career. As a member of 'F' Company 1st Battalion, he stood at the barricades with John O'Connor until he was wounded on the morning of Thursday 26 April. He evaded arrest, and, after the Rising, was appointed O/C of the 5th (Engineers) Battalion, Dublin Brigade, and later deputy director of GHQ Engineering Department. In 1918 he organised an intelligence section in the GPO and continued to work in close association with Michael Collins until the Treaty. In March 1922 he joined the National Army and served as O/C Army Signal Corps during the Civil War. Archer retired from the Defence Forces on 31 January 1952 at the rank of lieutenant general, having served as chief of staff from January 1949.[46]

His son, also named Liam Archer, has little source material for his father's revolutionary past. Archer submitted an unembellished testimony to the Bureau of Military History, characterised by the prosaic formality of a military mind, but he did not speak 'at any stage' to his children about 1916. Liam suggested that his father's involvement in the intelligence section of GHQ in 1920 'would have kept him from letting too much out'.

Born in 1892, William Archer was the third son of Edward Archer. He grew up with his older brothers and three younger sisters, Claire, Eileen and

William Archer in the 1920s
(*courtesy of Liam Archer*)

Mary, in Aughrim Street, near the Cattle markets in Smithfield, Dublin.[47] The family had a 'tradition of working in the post office'. His brothers Robert and Edward were telegraph messengers and his father was a telegraph inspector, so, at fifteen years old, 'after he finished national school in Phibsboro', he started work as a sorter in the sorting office. 'Then he [moved] to the telegraph office and then worked in the [General] Post Office in 1916.'

Liam recalled that his father identified some of his fellow employees in the telegraph office as 'Cawstle Cawtholics'. 'Basically, these were Catholics that were strongly pro-government and, apart from those people, there was no chance of a Catholic reaching a position of authority in the Post Office.' His brother was a 'head postman' and his father an inspector, but 'that was the limit of the type of position that they could attain'.

Archer was conscious of his limited prospects, but also of the atmosphere of suspicion and tension in the years before the Rising. 'The supervision in the post office was so strict,' Liam said '[and] they had to be very careful [not to step] on anybody's toes.' At the outbreak of the First World War in 1914, a strict system of censorship was introduced on post coming from America and Europe, an armed guard was provided for the telegraph system, and the secretary of the Irish General Post Office, Arthur Hamilton Norway, regularly reviewed police and intelligence reports concerning Post Office officials. Archer was one of a 'small group who were strongly nationalist in sympathy', and they passed out as many copies of John Devoy's *Gaelic American* as they could before they 'were removed from the sorting staff as suspect'.[48]

According to his son, William Archer's immediate family would not have been 'specifically nationalist', rather they were 'anti-the-ascendancy'. His uncle Robert, or Bob as he was known, 'had more of an influence on him in terms of his nationalism', and 'guided him in these ideas'. After Archer joined 'F' Company, 1st Battalion of the Irish Volunteers in early 1915, his uncle 'helped him to buy his first rifle and even bought leather straps to hold the ammunition pouches ... He wasn't supported by his parents', but they didn't object either. 'I suppose if you start working at fifteen, they presume that by the time you're twenty you have enough common sense.'

In 1915 membership of the Irish Volunteers was deemed incompatible with civil service loyalty, and a standard letter was issued to Post Office employees. It informed them that 'such an attitude in the time of war on the part of persons entrusted with business of the state is fraught with risk to the country' and warned that, if they did not sever their connection to nationalist organisations, they would face instant dismissal.[49] The warning, together with the increased police surveillance placed on Volunteers' manoeuvres, prompted concern among the civil servants in 'F' Company about parading 'openly with the normal company'. Instead, they organised into a special section under William Archer as section commander and paraded on Sunday mornings at 25 Parnell Square: 'They had to be very careful,' his son said, 'both in and out of that sorting office.'

Archer was inducted into the IRB shortly before Easter Week and he prepared for action with the acquisition of a 'Lee Enfield cavalry carbine, ... a .25 Harrington and Richardson auto, and a large hunting knife'. He also personalised his Volunteer uniform with 'leather buttons, and a soft hat instead of a peaked cap'.[50] 'The photographs show them with different uniforms but once they were out and had their gun they were part of the team.'

Like his fellow members of 'F' Company, Archer was assigned to armed guard duty for the protection of some of the members of the Volunteer Executive in Holy Week. On the night before Easter Sunday, he was on duty at the Keating Branch of the Gaelic League at 18 North Frederick Street, where he learned of the cancellation of manoeuvres for the following day. He spent a restless Sunday night playing cards in 'the small guard room' with Piaras Béaslaí, Fionán Lynch, Diarmuid O'Hegarty, Floss O'Doherty, Con

O'Donovan and Paddy McNestry. The game of 'Nap' had been 'going for some time' when they were interrupted by the dramatic entrance of a 'rough young Corkman', introduced to Archer as Michael Collins:

> His entrance was characteristic of him, as I later knew him. He forced his way to a seat at the table, produced two revolvers and announced he would ensure there would be nothing crooked about this game. Not to be outdone, we all produced our weapons.[51]

On Easter Monday morning Lieutenant Diarmuid O'Hegarty instructed Archer to mobilise his section at Columcille Hall, Blackhall Place at 10 a.m. He 'took his brother's motorcycle' as far as Clonliffe Road, at which point 'the machine broke down' and he was forced to abandon his task and walk to Blackhall Place. Deputising for Lieutenant Jack Shouldice, who had not yet arrived from Clontarf, William Archer led his men into Church Street. His son's understanding is that he was in charge of erecting barricades in the area: 'There were a lot of hostile people there at that time; a buxom lady came out when he was escorting Piaras Béaslaí [down Mary's Lane] and proved most hostile.' Archer recalled:

> V.C. Beaslaoi [Béaslaí] ordered me to fix my bayonet. This I did and immediately a very fat dame in spotless white apron and voluminous shawl leapt in front of us and beating her ample bosom with clenched fists called on me to 'put it through me now for me son who's out in France'. We steered past her.[52]

He and Diarmuid O'Hegarty also met with hostility from two Franciscan friars, who were 'very perturbed' at the prospect of the Volunteers using seats from the church to block a passage that led through the church grounds from Bow Lane to Church Street, but their 'Superior drew them away, saying it was better they should be ignorant of what we did'.[53] They need not have worried, however, for the idea was abandoned, and instead Archer was instructed to help with the erection of a barricade at the junction of Church Street, May Lane and Mary's Lane using timber from the ruins of some old houses.

Archer remembered the 'holidaymakers' and 'looters' who demanded passage through the barricades on Easter Monday: 'The former we passed through in convoyed groups; the latter we stripped of all their loot and tried to frighten with dire threats.'[54] As the week went on the Volunteers also had to contend with increasingly limited rations. In his son's words: 'There was basically very little food around. They had made a local bakery operate so the local people could be fed', but other than intermittent deliveries of bread to the barricades, 'some mugs of strong tea', and the opportune discovery of a bowl of stewed figs in the offices of Jameson's Distillery, William Archer had no other food for the week.[55] They were also deprived of sleep 'because they had to be prepared for everything', and the combination of hunger and exhaustion made him more careless than he might otherwise have been with his gun:

> He was talking to his friends and he put this gun [a Lee Enfield cavalry carbine, minus the orthodox safety catch] on to his foot with the muzzle up. After a while, he realised that if the gun went off [his] hands would be blown off so he turned it over and put it on his toe. He must have done something [because], while still talking to his friends, the gun went off and blew one of his toes away.

Members of Cumann na mBan, whom Archer described as 'outstanding in their courage and devotion', transferred the more seriously injured Volunteers on stretchers to Richmond Hospital, and Archer was taken into the care of the staff at about midday on Thursday.[56] He 'was well looked-after' there, but the combination of pain, stress and medication made for a restless convalescence. According to the family history, he was 'hysterical' while he was in hospital: 'I suppose after the injections [of] morphine and things like that, but apparently he was crying out trying to convince Commandant Daly not to set fire to the Jameson's Distillery.'[57] Fr Albert Bibby, of the Church Street Capuchins, tried to calm him down and told him that Commandant Daly knew what he was doing: 'It didn't happen anyway, but he was upset at the idea of the damage that would be done.'

Once he recovered enough to understand the failing fortunes of the Volunteers, Archer began to consider a means of escape. His son was privy only to the highlights of what happened next, but it is Liam's understanding that when one of the DMP came around to look for well-known people, a sympathetic surgeon, Sir Thomas Myles, instructed the wounded Volunteer to feign sleep and told the officer that he wasn't there. 'My father realised the danger of his situation but the difficulty was to try to get out because the nurses took his uniform and boots away. But his sister came in [wearing his] trousers underneath her skirt and so he was able to get out, and that's how he survived.'

After narrowly escaping arrest, Archer was faced with having to explain both his absence and his leg wound to his superiors in the Post Office. 'They were very strict about who was out,' his son said, and he had to convince an investigation team – a number of senior gentlemen from England – that he wasn't involved in the Rising. He 'bluffed his way' through and 'convinced them that he had been out roaming and got caught up in the crossfire'. After a brief suspension, he was permitted to return in August to his work as a Post Office telegraphist. The GPO lay in ruins and a temporary sorting office was established in the Rotunda buildings in Parnell Street. The telegraph staff were relocated to the top floor of the Parcel Offices in Amiens Street.

In mid-summer 1916 Archer helped in the reorganisation of 'F' Company. Contact was established with Volunteers who had escaped the general round-up; the company was augmented 'with the trickle coming from internment', and 'paraded 70-strong for Fionán Lynch's inspection on his release from Lewes Gaol in 1917'.[58] Liam felt that the swelling of the Volunteer ranks after the Rising was because of the 'big change' in opinion after the executions, and there were 'more people interested in it and probably joined up'. In October his father was assigned the role of brigade signal officer under Diarmuid O'Hegarty and 'was an instructor in arms and things'.

On the threat of conscription in 1918, Archer was transferred to Rory O'Connor's staff. The director of engineering organised a company of engineers under the direct control of the GHQ. Known as the 5th (Engineer) Battalion, the four platoons were trained in the use of explosives, 'with the special mission of carrying out extensive sabotage of communications' should conscription be imposed.[59] In 1919 the 'specialist unit' was also involved in a raid on the *Irish Independent* on 21 December, the attempted rescue of Seán MacEoin from Mountjoy in 1920 and the destruction of Maynooth Town Hall. They also cut off communications to the Custom House before it was set alight by the IRA on 25 May 1921.

Archer was able to maintain his position in the Post Office during this period and was responsible for the transfer of cyphered messages from 'different sections of the police'. His son described the incident that first brought him to the attention of the GHQ director of intelligence. On 21 August 1918 Archer intercepted a message from the inspector general of the RIC to the chief of police in Glasgow about the arrest in that city of 'two sisters and a brother', Brigid, Anne and Charles Kelly, for attempting to smuggle arms into Ireland. The newspapers eventually reported the discovery of 'a portmanteau full of guns and ammunition' but 'my father received the message first' and took it to Michael Collins at the Keating Branch; Collins realised his usefulness and thus began his service:

> My father tried to organise within the telegraph section [of the Post Office] a num-
> ber of people to help him out but they had to be very careful, as supervision of the
> staff was very close.[60] There was a large number of telegraphists and they sat with
> one another [so he] couldn't take copies of the cypher messages. [Eventually] he
> was able to arrange that handwritten copies [were] taken out in [their] socks. So it
> was a hard time. He had to try to be a normal civil servant and be out 'on the run'
> in terms of not sleeping at home from October 1920 until the Truce.

Archer was lucky when, in 1918, a raid on his home failed to uncover a revolver and 'a lot of very incriminating papers'. He was lucky again in early November 1920, when the raiders missed a large cache of papers left there by 'my aunt [who] would have been assisting Diarmuid O'Hegarty'.

November 1920 was, according to Archer's witness statement, his 'most profitable period'. A night-time military curfew was in place and 'each morning for three weeks' he smuggled out in his socks copies 'of every police cipher message that had passed through the office the previous day'.[61] Once the cyphered messages had been smuggled from the post office, the codes (key) provided by Ned Broy were used to decipher them.[62] Members of Cumann na mBan then took the deciphered messages to GHQ. 'As time went on,' his son explained, 'the RIC changed their code system and sent it in [a] more complicated manner but they were able to crack them relatively easily. The insiders … copied the codes and passed them on to Collins, who sent them on to Dad. He would then return the deciphered messages to Collins and his intelligence group … Some people might think they were fantastic,' Liam laughed, 'but it was just the life that they lived.'

In his witness statement, Archer reported that, on 28 November 1920, he took a call 'from an Auxie' at Beggar's Bush Barracks who told him 'we are all in a bad way' before giving him the story of the ambush at Kilmichael.[63] Archer 'duly sympathised' and 'took a spare copy for [himself] of each of several cipher messages he sent'.[64] 'There was another message,' his son recalled, '[which] revealed that [Timothy] Quinlisk was a double agent.' Quinlisk had been a member of Sir Roger Casement's Irish Brigade in Germany, so after 1916 he was readily accepted into Sinn Féin circles and appointed as an IRA training officer. In November 1919, motivated by the prospect of a reward, Quinlisk offered his services as a spy for the Castle, and Ned Broy promptly supplied Collins with a copy of his statement. Quinlisk had attempted to pre-empt suspicion by telling Collins he had gone to the DMP to acquire a passport, and when the 'G' men put pressure on him to inform, he pretended to comply. Collins, however, was unconvinced and supplied Quinlisk with false information about a trip to Cork, including the name of the hotel at which he intended to stay. His suspicions were confirmed when, in February 1920, William Archer intercepted a telegram from the inspector general of the RIC to the county inspector in Cork: 'Tonight at midnight surround Wren's Hotel, Winthrop St, Cork. Collins and others will be there. Expect shooting as he is a dangerous man and heavily armed.'[65] On 18 February 1920 a member of Cork No. 1 Brigade lured Quinlisk to the outskirts of the city where he executed him. 'And that,' said Liam, 'was the end of our friend Quinlisk.'

Liam Archer found it significant that his father's witness statement finished 'abruptly' just before Bloody Sunday. 'I won't say [he was] involved – but he was maybe a bit upset about it occurring … Some consider the "elimination" of the British Intelligence people a callous shooting, but others might consider [it] a war situation.'

After his father died in July 1969, Liam discovered among his papers a personal memoir about his 'services and experiences in the Dublin General Post Office'. The pages reveal a pride in his intelligence work that Archer never articulated to his family. He made particular reference to his discovery that, during the War of Independence, 'a small red card was affixed above every telephone in [Dublin] Castle. It read: "Your conversation can be overheard by the rebels on any line that goes outside this building. Private lines are not immune". This,' Archer wrote, 'is what Collins's Intelligence service produced and I am not, I think, claiming too much if I say that the group that worked with me contributed something to this state of mind.'[66]

In March 1922 William Archer left the Post Office to join the National Army: 'He would have had a reduction in salary but being of a nationalistic view, I suppose he thought [the Army] would be the best thing for him.' In the same year he proposed to Mary Carr from Maynooth. The couple met for the first time in 1916 when Mary nursed the wounded Volunteer in Richmond Hospital, but she was subsequently 'posted to Egypt with the British Army' so they didn't see each other again until 1922, when Archer was visiting hospitals in an official capacity. They married early in the following year and moved into the house in Portobello Barracks vacated by the secretary to the Provisional Government, Diarmuid O'Hegarty, who incidentally had just 'married my father's sister', Claire Archer.

Liam was born in 1931 and spent much of his childhood in Portobello Barracks. While he finds it difficult to 'visualise' his mother, who died when he was just six years old, Liam described his father as 'a quiet man' who was 'very handy with his hands'. He shared a particularly fond childhood memory of his father 'working on a pair of shoe trees', shaping the wood into toe and heel and telling his 'inquisitive' young son: 'I'm making a wee wing to hang up the sun.'

'In about 1938 my father became director of military intelligence,' Liam explained, 'and he was in charge of G2 at the outbreak of the Second World War.' He revealed little to his family about this period except 'for the odd time' when he spoke about 'some German spies who were captured in a house in Terenure Road'. In January 1949 Archer replaced Lieutenant General Daniel McKenna as chief of staff (Irish Defence Forces) and retired three years later, after almost forty years of military service. Liam is proud of his father's distinguished career, but Archer was a man schooled in discretion who forged a career in the acquisition and maintenance of secrets. His son, like many of his generation, was privy only to the carefully censored version of his father's history.

CHARLES AND THOMAS BEVAN

A photograph of the Four Courts garrison marching in the 'big parade through Dublin' on the twentieth anniversary of the 1916 Rising features five members of the Bevan family. Joseph Bevan recognised his father, Charlie, and his uncles, Thomas and Séamus, immediately, but he was able to verify 'only late last year' that the two women marching in front of the banner were his aunts, Molly and Caitlín. Seán Prendergast, who knew the Bevan sisters as members of Cumann na mBan in 1916, described them in his witness statement as 'forceable [*sic*] and yet humorous' characters, and based on their nephew's interview, humour and determination seem to have been characteristic of the Bevan family.[67]

Joseph Bevan's understanding of his family's role in Easter Week is drawn from fragmented stories and his father's short personal memoir, written forty years after 'the rising had been crushed in blood and fire'.[68] The question of a memoir arose one day in 1956 during a conversation between father and son:

> I said, 'I wouldn't have the guts to do what you did and put a gun on my shoulder and walk out that Easter Monday not knowing if you were ever going to come back.' He answered me quite sharply: 'Nobody's asking you to … That was my job. Your job is to study, qualify and help to build up the economic life of this country and finish the job we started … Then I said, 'Well, okay Da. Write it all down', and he did … It's almost like a school-boy essay.

In December 1913 Charles Stewart Bevan, an apprentice compositor in Hely's Print Works, Dame Lane, in Dublin, joined his father, Joseph, and his brother Thomas in 'C' Company, 1st Battalion. Eager to emulate his older brothers, fourteen-year-old Séamus Bevan enrolled in Fianna Éireann in 1914, just in time for the Howth gun-running in July. 'It was beautifully timed,' Joseph explained. 'They marched past the west pier, along the front and turned left down the other pier just as the yacht was coming around the head … They passed out the rifles and got the hell out of there as fast as they could.' When the front guard was stopped, 'the rest of them disappeared [over] the garden walls'. Charlie ended up with a Mauser rifle, 'an ignorant looking thing', which he stored under the floorboards in his bedroom. He carefully cut out a section of the wooden floor, 'probably a foot square', underneath which he screwed a picture hook. 'Then he screwed a second hook into the butt of the rifle' rendering it 'quickly and easily' accessible.

'My grandfather, who I never met, and his three sons turned up for the get-together on Easter Sunday morning.' They were demobilised by Captain Frank Fahy and ordered to stand to. Early the next morning, Thomas left the family home at 9 Geraldine Street to visit a friend and returned to find his father and brothers engaged in the excited activity of preparing for manoeuvres.

Charles Stewart Bevan in Volunteer uniform (*courtesy of the Bevan family*)

They had divided Thomas' equipment between them and, deaf to his frustrated protests, left the house to mobilise with 'C' Company at Blackhall Street. 'They went off fully equipped,' Thomas told the Pensions Advisory Committee in 1936, '[and] I was left with none.'[69]

'They didn't know, of course, that the rebellion was about to start,' Joseph explained, 'they were only told that morning by their commanders.' In his memoirs, Bevan recalled that, when Edward Daly gave his Volunteers the option to withdraw, 'C' Company responded by cheering loudly.[70] 'There was nothing heroic about it,' Bevan wrote, 'for who but a veritable poltroon would turn tail in the face of danger?'[71] And so, charged with revolutionary zeal, Captain Frank Fahy led his men to Church Street and on to the Four Courts, which was empty because court sittings had been suspended for Easter. Lieutenant Thomas Allen, revolver in hand, 'relieved a solitary policeman of his keys to the building',[72] and, according to Joseph, 'my father was the first man into the Four Courts'. He added, 'He was about 5ft 3in [and] I've always reckoned that they sort of pushed him over the railings' at Chancery Place.

Section Commander Charlie Bevan, whose picture now hangs in the Law Library, told his son that, once inside, they moved immediately to 'fortify the whole place as much as they could'. They cut the telephone lines, secured the gates and barricaded the windows with tables and chairs. 'They ripped all the law books off the shelves [in the chancellor's office] and made barricades with them, and Dad found a brass coal scuttle and he used that too.' Beds from the nearby Four Courts Hotel were commandeered and carried to the chancellor's office, where the Volunteers established a makeshift first-aid post, while the snipers took up their positions on the roof:

> I know nothing about military tactics, but [their position] was very cleverly worked out. They could see Reilly's Fort from their vantage point in the Four Courts, and further up the road to Constitution Hill they could see the King's Inns …. He said that a lot of the time they were doing nothing, other than trying to get enough to eat [and] trying to keep in touch with their immediate commandant, Ned Daly.

Thomas Bevan finally reported to the Four Courts on Tuesday morning, armed with the prized Lee Enfield rifle he had won some weeks previously in a company draw. On Wednesday his captain instructed him to replace the wounded Paddy O'Daly as sergeant of the section guarding the prisoners. Among his charges was noted playwright and officer in the Inniskilling Fusiliers, Lord Dunsany, whom Thomas and Peadar Clancy had 'taken from his motor car at the Arran Quay church' on Tuesday.[73] Another officer later testified that Daly's men treated their prisoners with courtesy and, while food was in short supply, the cellars were well stocked so they 'subsisted for several days on sherry, champagne, port and claret'.[74] While his older brothers were taking their positions in the Four Courts, Séamus Bevan ran messages between there and the GPO. On Wednesday, for example, he returned to the 'boys', bringing 'big news' of the 'new flag' flying from the Henry Street corner of the GPO.[75]

In the early days of the week, the Four Courts garrison came under sniper fire from 'the British forces in the [cupola of] the Blue Coat School' [Blackhall Place] and a ceaseless bombardment of rifle fire from the Lancers who had taken refuge in the Medical Mission on Charles Street on Monday. The situation worsened on Wednesday, when a section of the Royal Dublin Fusiliers occupied buildings on the opposite side of the Liffey and opened fire on the west wing of the Four Courts. Commandant Daly fell back to the Four Courts on Friday and that evening the British forces began artillery shelling from the direction of Exchange Street. 'At one point the room under Dad was blown out,' Joseph said, but 'I think they held out for at least a day longer than Pearse did … They didn't want to surrender, I know that, [but] the aftermath is the part that my father would never forget.'

The Bevan brothers spent an uncomfortable night outside the Rotunda before being escorted to Richmond Barracks. Charlie Bevan's memoirs include a description of their arrival, when 'the officers were separated from the rank and file – the important from the less important prisoners. For some unaccountable reason,' he wrote, 'I was considered important.'[76] On their first night at Richmond Barracks, the 'important' prisoners were 'given a meal of tea, bully beef and hard tack, with the admonition to "make the best of it, it's the last meal you'll ever eat"'.[77] Charlie was court-martialled on Thursday 4 May and transferred to Kilmainham Gaol to await the verdict of the court. His son maintained that the trials were 'the biggest joke the world [had] ever seen [because] the verdicts were decided long before anybody ever got into a court martial'.

Like many of the second generation, Joseph tried to imagine how his father must have felt as he awaited his sentence: 'I think they prayed a lot. Don't forget you were in the middle of Holy Catholic Ireland then.' He must have been frightened, but 'he concealed it well [from] me. I don't think I would have had his courage.' He continued:

I think he must have been there for some days. He told me that it would get barely light in the morning and you would hear tramp, tramp of feet, rattling of keys, cell door opening and then afterwards keys, tramp, tramp and five minutes later you would hear a volley of shots. I think he was in Kilmainham on the morning that Seán Heuston (whom the Bevan brothers had known since childhood) was executed.

[The pattern continued] until one morning [when it was] just barely getting light – the rattle of keys, soldiers marching, your door opens and in comes the same officer but instead of being lugged out, he then tells you that your sentence has been commuted [to three years of penal servitude] and [to] count yourself bloody lucky.

He never forgave them for that; they left him there for days thinking he was going to be executed … I suspect that his sentence was commuted on the day he was convicted and they knew all about that.

Charlie and Thomas were 'shifted' to Mountjoy where they spent a week before boarding the boat to Portland Prison, aboard which, according to Robert Brennan, they infuriated a British NCO with a rousing version of 'The West's Awake'.[78] Portland was the first of a series of English prisons to host the 'brothers Bevan' between the spring of 1916 and June 1917, and where, in Charlie's words: 'I lost my identity and became just a number – q143.'[79] In common with many of the veterans of Easter Week, Charlie only ever told his son about 'the little tricks they used to get up to', and his impression is that 'generally they were treated fairly well. My father had a great deal of respect for the British Tommy, who [was] simply doing a difficult job.'

Joseph's understanding is that after Charlie and Thomas were released and 'once they got sober, they mobilised nearly straight away and got on with it'. Charlie actually took some months to recover 'from diminished health as a result of a long period of imprisonment', before resuming his apprenticeship in Hely's and rejoining 'C' Company in February 1918.[80] Thomas made contact with his company in the summer of 1917, but embarked almost immediately on a tour of the country with Gerald Crofts, Séamus Hughes and the other members of his singing group, the Lewes Concert Party.[81]

Both Bevan brothers were noted for their vocal talent. Charlie was an eleven-year-old soprano when he joined Edward Martyn's famous Palestrina Choir. While awaiting sentencing in his cell in Kilmainham in 1916, he distracted himself with memories of 'the consecration of St Patrick's Cathedral, Armagh, the wedding of the Marquis of Bute at Castlebellingham, County Louth [and] the consecration of the Bishop of Galway, at all of which the choir had been privileged to assist. In my 23 years,' he wrote, 'I had seen and done things not given to every lad.'[82]

Tommy was the bass to his brother's baritone and during the War of Independence 'their singing group raised money for the movement'. On 8 September 1917, for example, the Bevan brothers featured on the programme of performers at an *aeridheacht* in support of the Irish National Aid and Volunteers'

Dependants' Fund in the Round Room of the Mansion House.[83] They sang 'all around the country'. Tommy left active service soon after taking part in the guard of honour at Thomas Ashe's funeral on 30 September 1917, and told the Pensions Advisory Committee, 'I had no more service after that. I joined the O'Meara Opera Company and was away with them until April 1923.'[84]

While his brother saw limited service in the post-1916 period, Charlie returned to duty with 'C' Company under Captain Seán Flood and 1st Lieutenant Seán Prendergast.[85] They 'operated in the north inner city, starting at Capel Street and upwards to the Phoenix Park,' Joseph explained, '[and] as far as I can see they did a lot of patrols and observation duty during the War of Independence.' His father 'was certainly involved in one rescue of a fella called Matt Brady' from Richmond Hospital in October 1920.[86] In the same month he was ordered to 'stand to' in North Frederick Street in preparation for the attempt to rescue Kevin Barry from Mountjoy. He waited, 'armed with a Webley revolver until [his unit] was dispersed when the plans miscarried'.[87] 'Maybe somebody had squealed,' Joseph suggested, 'but something went wrong with the plot [and] they stood down.'

Bevan himself claimed that, while he served in the War of Independence, he 'never really got into the centre of activities', and his son was able to recall only 'one lovely story' about the Black and Tan period:

> Himself and his squad were out on patrol with their rifles somewhere around the Capel Street, Queen's [sic] Street, Four Courts area maybe about 10 o'clock at night … and the scouts came back and said: 'We're in trouble lads; the Tans have the whole area surrounded.'
>
> There were eight [or] ten of them [and] they broke into an undertakers called Bourke's in Queen's Street, stole a coffin [into which] they put the rifles … and marched down the centre of Queen's Street carrying this coffin. The Tan patrol stood back … and as this coffin was coming past them they doffed their caps. Dad used to tell that one with great glee but not very often. It sounded like boasting.

Another anecdote that Joseph could 'certainly remember' for its disturbing detail involves 'C' Company's activities from a position 'on the roof of Searson's [wine merchants] of Portobello Bridge':

> It was totally out of his area but the Tan lorries would come down from Portobello Barracks and the favourite pastime was lobbing grenades from Searson's roof into the trucks as they went past. Eventually the Tans got wise to this [and] they [covered the lorries with] chicken wire, so the lads would put hooks into the bombs … and they would catch on it. It only got to that stage when the Tans arrived … Even the British Army apparently, the Regulars, hated the Tans, who were thugs.

It was also during this period that Charlie married Rosie Costello, 'quietly, a very strong lady', and a member of Cumann na mBan under May Gibney. 'She used to go out with Tommy first,' Joseph smiled. While the wedding was a happy occasion for the family, they were simultaneously mourning the loss of Joseph's grandfather and namesake, who died in 1919. The newlyweds also had to contend with frequent raids on their home in 9 Geraldine Street, which 'was well known' to the military authorities, Joseph explained. From April 1920 it was used as company headquarters for 'B' Company, 2nd Battalion. They held lectures there and it was used on several occasions as a first-aid station.[88] From January 1921 until the Truce in July, it also served as an arms dump for 'C' Company. 'It actually still exists,' Joseph smiled, 'and I could tell you exactly where his rifle was hidden.'

Charlie's tenure with the IRA came to an end during the Truce in the summer of 1921. According to his pension application, he resigned from the company after Captain Seán Prendergast asked him about his 'attitude in the event of hostilities'.[89] 'Dad could see the Civil War coming … he was unable and unwilling to take arms against his former comrades.' He was 'horrified' by the conflict and 'thought it was the biggest tragedy that had ever hit this country … It became nasty [and] it divided families.' He also said 'that there were some personal scores settled during that Civil War. They glossed over that quite a bit.'

Joseph was born in 1932, while his parents lived in 4 Upper Mount Pleasant Avenue in Rathmines. The family moved to Beechwood Park in 1938, 'which is where I grew up really'. In the 1940s and 1950s young Joseph Bevan was introduced to some of the veterans of the independence movement: 'The eldest son of an ex-Volunteer was always known as "the lad"… so I was never known by my name'. However, Charlie Bevan hosted few visitors from his revolutionary past at his family home:

> Dad committed the unforgivable sin of moving from the north side to the south side of Dublin city, [but] I suppose if the truth be known, part of the reason that we didn't [have] too many of his comrades over to our house when we were growing up was that maybe they felt that he had let them down. He would definitely have been on the republican side [even though] he was not active in the Civil War.

Joseph does recall the occasional visit by Fionán Lynch, who was 'in the same battalion in 1916 but took the Free State side in the Civil War'.[90] There was 'a certain amount of circling around one another until they both became old pals' in the late 1940s.

Charlie Bevan was a monotype operator all his life 'and very proud of it'. He worked in the Hely, Juverna and Fodhla printing companies, and joined the case room staff of *The Irish Press* on its foundation in 1931. 'My father was the proud landlord of the monotype machine', and in 1937, when *Bunreacht na hÉireann* replaced the 1922 Constitution of the Free State, 'he set the new Constitution in Irish type. He was one of the few guys in *The Irish Press* who could speak Irish so he did all the Irish typesetting … loving every second of it.' Except

Fionán Lynch, captain of 'F' Company, 1st Battalion, in 1916 *(courtesy of the Lynch family)*

for a brief sojourn at the *Irish Independent* in the 1940s, he continued to work on typesetting and translating in *The Irish Press* until he got too old to operate the machine. Then he served as a proof-reader until he retired in August 1967, after thirty-eight years of service.[91]

In the year before his retirement, Bevan attended the fiftieth anniversary celebrations of the 1916 Rising. 'There were only thirteen survivors of the

Rising that had been printers,' his son explained, and they all received a replica statuette of the Cúchulainn memorial in the GPO from the Irish Graphical Society.[92]

> I took a week off work, had a medium-sized national flag attached to the wing of my car and made myself available to drive my father around – to be important. On Easter Monday I drove him, proudly wearing his medals, into O'Connell Street, being allowed to drive through the closed off streets to the GPO because of the flag on my car. He was so proud when an Army officer saluted smartly, opened the car door and escorted him to the viewing stand.
>
> That afternoon, after the parade, I took him up to Kilmainham Gaol ... Again he was greeted by an Army officer and escorted straight past the waiting crowds into the jail. It was the first time he had been inside the jail since the day he was marched out of it down to Mountjoy ... but he walked straight to what I now know is the East Wing and then straight to the iron steps in the middle of that slightly forbidding room. He turned his back to the stairs and pointed to the fourth door on the left on the first floor and said: 'Joe, that was my cell when I was sure I faced execution.'

Charlie Bevan died suddenly in December 1969, but his son was consoled by the fact that he had lived to see the fiftieth anniversary of the Rising. 'It was all he wanted to do [and] we treated him royally.'

PADDY O'DALY[93]

Séamus and Paddy O'Daly, the sons of a retired DMP officer, met their future wives at a Gaelic League dance in McDunphy's pub in Bolton Street in Dublin in 1906. Sisters Daisy and Nora Gillies, daughters of the general manager of *The Freeman's Journal*, married the O'Daly brothers in a double wedding on 16 May 1910. Paddy and Daisy had four children: Patrick, Máire, Bríd and Colbert. Their half-sister, Sr Philomena O'Daly, is Paddy O'Daly's daughter from his third marriage to Norah Gillies (his first wife's niece).

Philomena took her vows with the Little Sisters of the Assumption soon after her father's death in 1957. According to the rules of the congregation, she relinquished all her material possessions and lost contact with everybody except her immediate family. The loss of her father when she was just twenty-one, combined with the solitude of religious orders, meant that Philomena did not know the full extent of her father's involvement in national affairs until the late 1990s, when she began to investigate his story. A Christian Brother put her in contact with Commandant Peter Young, director of the Military Archives, who explained that Paddy O'Daly had served in the Four Courts in 1916; he was leader of Michael Collins' counter intelligence unit, or Squad, during the War of Independence, and commander of the Free State forces in Kerry during the Civil War:

> I remember my Dad as a very caring man, but a very sad man and it was only after-wards when I discovered his history that I realised how sad. I knew it affected me … and I had to go for counselling in my forties because that sadness was beginning to seep into my life.

Paddy O'Daly joined the IRB in 1907, and by late 1914 he was an organising officer with Fianna Éireann and a member of 'B' Company 2nd Battalion under Thomas MacDonagh. Two years later, at noon on Easter Monday, twenty-seven-year-old Paddy O'Daly led thirty men, drawn from the ranks of the Volunteers, Fianna Éireann and the Irish Citizen Army, towards the Phoenix Park to orchestrate an explosion in the Magazine Fort (the site of the British Army's principal armoury in Dublin) to signal the beginning of the Rising.

During his brief employment as a carpenter with Thompsons' Building Contractors, O'Daly had carried out repairs on the complex, and on Seán MacDermott's orders, 'had been able to ascertain a lot of information about the Fort, such as the strength of the garrison, the layout and where the keys were kept … and what the various stores contained'.[94] He gained additional intelligence from an officer who proved 'very friendly' when presented with 'the odd half pint of whiskey'. On Palm Sunday 1916 MacDermott asked O'Daly to attend a meeting of the Military Council in the Town Hall at Clontarf, where the Volunteer presented his information 'and proposed a plan' for gaining access, commandeering the arms and ammunition, and setting explosives in the main explosives store.

Thomas MacDonagh favoured seizure of the Magazine Fort and its armaments, but MacDermott and Clarke argued successfully for detonation.[95] Once the objective was agreed, MacDonagh gave O'Daly sole command of the operation, which involved approaching the complex disguised as a group of football players and their supporters. Tom Clarke asked O'Daly to select his 'football team' and on Connolly's objection that O'Daly's group comprised only Fianna officers, O'Daly was assigned 'a few hefty [ICA] men to add weight to the team'.[96] O'Daly's grand-nephew, Tony Roche, added:

> Paddy's first wife, Daisy Gillies, and her sister, my grandmother, Nora Gillies (a founding member of the Fairview Branch of Cumann na mBan) and the woman who would become Paddy's second wife, Bridget (Bríd) Murtagh, went to the Magazine Fort [on Easter Sunday] and basically chatted up the British soldiers on sentry duty. They had these buttons from British Army uniforms from the First World War and they asked the [guards about them]. Of course they were happy to tell them [about] the great deeds of the British Empire on foreign ground ... [The women were able] to find out the sentry roster and to suss out the number of guards that would be on the gate at any given time.

Daisy Gillies and Paddy O'Daly (*courtesy of Tony Roche*)

On the morning of 24 April, wearing civilian clothes and armed with revolvers, Paddy O'Daly and Gary Holohan stopped at Whelan's shop on Ormond Quay to buy a football. This important prop completed the illusion that they were a football team and allowed them to make a casual approach towards the heavily fortified complex on Thomas's Hill.[9] O'Daly distracted the sentry by enquiring about the whereabouts of a football pitch and Paddy Boland seized his rifle. The Volunteers surprised and disarmed the ten soldiers in the guardroom and the sentry on the parapet, but discovered that the officer in possession of the key to the high explosives store had gone to the Fairyhouse races. With no time to dwell on the frustration of their carefully laid plans, O'Daly and his men gathered any small ordnance they could find and placed five bags of gelignite against the wall of the main magazine. Having set the fuses, the Volunteers hastily departed, loaded the captured arms into a stolen horse-drawn hansom cab and dispersed to their designated battalion areas.

'That was their first mission,' O'Daly's grand-nephew Tony explained, and 'unfortunately or fortunately, depending on your way of looking at it, it didn't succeed.' They had 'failed to ignite the main explosives store signalling the beginning of the Rising' and the improvised explosion was muted. Afterwards, Paddy O'Daly, Barney Mellows and Jack Murphy made their way to the Four Courts, where they distributed the twelve captured rifles, and the majority of the others reported to North Brunswick Street. Captain Frank Fahy directed O'Daly to the east wing, where he remained on duty with Joseph Leonard until he was wounded on Wednesday 26 April.

That morning the officers in the Four Courts had decided to launch an attack on the Medical Mission opposite the east wing in an attempt to drive out the Lancers and to capture their ammunition. O'Daly smashed a window in the Mission and was just about to lob an incendiary through when he was shot in the arm. He slumped to the ground and, under heavy sniper fire, managed to pull himself to the Chancery Place gate, from where he was hauled back into the Four Courts. Like William Archer, he was taken to Richmond Hospital on Thursday and moved a few weeks later to the Castle hospital, where he remained until his discharge on 4 June. He was rearrested at his home a few days later and shipped from the North Wall to Frongoch in Wales.

After his return on Christmas Eve 1916, O'Daly was active in the reorganisation of the Volunteers; he served as a member of the executive of Fianna Éireann between 1918 and 1919 and as a company commanding officer and battalion vice-commandant with 'B' Company, 2nd Battalion, Dublin Brigade. On 1 August 1917 he suffered the first of many personal tragedies when his eldest daughter, four-year-old Máire, died of tubercular meningitis. 'There wasn't a coffin to be had in the city,' Tony said, and Paddy, who was a carpenter, had to make one: 'Imagine having to make a coffin for your child – horrendous!'

A second heartbreak followed in 1919, when Daisy O'Daly contracted tuberculosis. Her husband did not witness her deterioration, having been arrested for illegal drilling with Joseph Leonard and eleven other members of 'B' Company in Clonliffe Hall in February and sentenced to twelve months' hard labour in Mountjoy. While there, O'Daly was actively involved in orchestrating the 'famous' jailbreak of 26 March 1919. The original plan involved his making an application for parole, which O'Daly knew would be accepted because his 'wife was a patient in the Hospice for the Dying [in Harold's Cross] at the time'.[98] Once released, he made contact with Dick Mulcahy and Peadar Clancy to discuss plans for the escape of Piaras Béaslaí, Padraic Fleming and J. J. Walsh from Mountjoy.[99]

They met at O'Daly's brother-in-law's house in Rathmines, Tony said, and Mulcahy and Seán MacEoin decided that Peadar Clancy was to be in charge of the outside party. They also agreed that a Saturday evening would be the best time to make an escape attempt because there were fewer guards on duty. At the appointed hour, O'Daly would signal to Clancy by waving a handkerchief from an upstairs window in Mountjoy, and Clancy would throw 'a rope ladder with a stone on the end of it over the wall'. O'Daly told them that he would assist in the escape of the other prisoners but would not partake himself as he 'wanted to be able to visit the Hospice if given parole'.[100]

There were three 'friendly' warders on duty in the prison yard on Saturday 29 March and, in order that they would not be accused of collusion, three prisoners, including Paddy O'Daly and Joe Leonard, remained behind to 'restrain' them. They marshalled the guards with spoons rolled in handkerchiefs to resemble revolvers and Leonard pulled a button from a prison guard's coat to suggest a struggle.[101] Another warder, named Jones, 'was doing his best to get a punch on the jaw'.[102] Piaras Béaslaí's relative, John Beasley, picks up the narrative:

> Béaslaí went up first. He was a slight man and a rope ladder is quite hard to climb, so he got to the top and he couldn't get his hand around the wall. The next guy up was Walsh and he just dove over Piaras' head and landed on the other side in a blanket. [The three men ran along the canal bank to the Innisfallen Parade, where Seán Nunan and others were waiting with bicycles.] The planning was very clever. They had a small [bicycle] for Béaslaí and a large one for Walsh, but Béaslaí jumped on the large one and he couldn't reach the pedals and Walsh jumped on the small one [and] hit his knees off the handlebars and the two of them crashed bikes.

The dangling rope ladder proved too much of a temptation for the remaining prisoners. 'The fellas [were] looking at it and they said, "Sure why not?" No less than twenty prisoners got out and got away safely on bicycles and trams.'

Daisy O'Daly died two days later. 'The authorities clamped down after the escape,' Tony explained, 'and [Paddy] didn't get to see her before she died … The family had to contact the archbishop of Dublin at the time, a great man called William Walsh, and he had to intercede with the authorities to allow Paddy out for three hours to attend his wife's funeral.' Then he returned to serve the remainder of his sentence.

'The family was very split up' after Daisy died, Sr Philomena explained, 'Paddy, the eldest child, was seven and he stayed with his father. Bríd went to my father's two sisters, Molly and Susan, and Colbert went to the Holland family who were close friends of my father's.' In later years the O'Daly children 'built up a friendship but there wasn't the closeness of family because they had all grown up separately … It affected Paddy, Bríd and Colbert throughout their lives', and even though their mother had died of TB, 'they seem to have almost blamed the Troubles' for their disrupted childhoods.

While her father never spoke to Philomena about the War of Independence, she was able to glean a certain amount from her eldest brother, Paddy, who died in 2008 aged ninety-six. He remembered, for example, that 'if there was a raid on the house they would have to hide in the attic', which is where Joe Leonard taught him how to play chess when he was seven. It was a difficult time and 'to the day he died he could cry about his childhood' and how 'the Troubles affected his family circumstances'.

On 19 September 1919, a month after O'Daly's release from Mountjoy, he and Joe Leonard reported to 46 Parnell Square, where Michael Collins, Dick Mulcahy and Dick McKee invited them to join an IRA GHQ 'special unit' or 'Squad' to 'deal with spies and informers'. They took orders directly from Collins, who told O'Daly, Leonard, Seán Doyle and Ben Barrett to leave their employment and gave them 'a list of enemy agents who were to be eliminated'. McKee warned the recruits that 'their work would not be suitable for anyone with scruples about taking life'.[103] Two months later, on 19 December, the Squad was involved in a failed attempt to assassinate the lord lieutenant (Lord French), and on 21 January 1920, after the ranks had swelled to include Tom Keogh, Jim Slattery, Mick O'Reilly and Vincent Byrne, Paddy O'Daly shot and killed the newly appointed assistant commissioner of the DMP, William Redmond. They continued to target members of the plainclothes 'G' Division of the DMP, and on 2 March 1920 assassinated the British double agent John Charles Byrnes. On Saturday 20 November 1920, 'Bloody Sunday', O'Daly, his Squad and other IRA men shot fourteen British intelligence officers at various locations in Dublin, instigating brutal reprisals.

Joseph Bevan's abiding memory of being introduced to two of the 'Twelve Apostles' when he was seven years old is that 'those gentlemen had cold, sad eyes'. The adult Joseph considers that the 'burden they were carrying' was immense. According to Tony Roche, however, 'these were people who were … willing to sacrifice everything for their country as they saw it … I think that it is good for people to know that it wasn't thuggery'.

When he thinks of his childhood, Tony is reminded of a line from the chorus of Ronnie Drew's ballad, 'When Margaret was Eleven': 'They served us war for breakfast and soldiers' songs for tea'. He explained:

> We were raised on stories of Uncle Paddy and Joe Leonard … My mother had a fascination for her father [Séamus] and Uncle Paddy – I was indoctrinated as a child. Paddy and my grandfather went on to serve in the National Army [and] I was given my grandfather's army issue leather holster … We didn't play cowboys and Indians; we played IRA and Black and Tans.

After the burning of the Custom House, when the Dublin Brigade active service unit endured heavy losses, the remaining IRA men amalgamated with the Squad to form the Dublin Guard under O'Daly as O/C. Most of them took the pro-Treaty side and joined the newly formed Irish National Army in 1922. According to Joseph Leonard's son, Jimmy, 'most of the leaders of Michael Collins' Squad would have been appointed leaders because there was nobody to run the army'. On 31 January 1922 his father and Paddy O'Daly were among the officers who entered Beggar's Bush Barracks, the erstwhile Auxiliary headquarters and 'the first British barracks to be handed over to the Free State by the British … It was very historic.'

Paddy O'Daly 'was definitely a Michael Collins man,' his daughter said. 'I remember that there were two huge photographs in an alcove at home. One was Michael Collins and the other was Arthur Griffith. I grew up with [the understanding that] Michael Collins was our hero [and] … that de Valera wouldn't be someone who would be welcome in our house.' Tony agreed and added that his grand-uncle's 'absolute allegiance to Collins was unshakeable … he was their idol.'

Paddy O'Daly in Free State uniform
(*courtesy of Tony Roche*)

When the Civil War broke out in June 1922, O'Daly commanded the Free State troops that secured Dublin, but Sr Philomena was clearly uncomfortable when asked about her father's association with the atrocities in Kerry in the latter stages of the conflict. Tony, a generation apart, seemed more able to address the topic, and explained that after the Four Courts surrender, Liam Lynch, commander-in-chief of the republican forces, planned to seal off the greater part of Munster: 'The roads and the railway lines were disrupted to the south and Collins realised that the only way to get a group into Kerry was by sea.' On 2 August 1922 the men of the Dublin Guard, under Brigadier Paddy O'Daly, landed in Fenit. The 450 men took Ballymullen Barracks, driving the No. 1 Kerry Brigade IRA out of Tralee, and enforced martial law. The Dublin Guard earned a fearsome reputation for brutality in Kerry. They were implicated in a number of atrocities perpetrated against republican prisoners, including a series of killings with landmines in March 1923 that left behind a deep anger and bitterness, remarkable even in the context of civil war. O'Daly later commented, 'nobody asked me to take kid-gloves to Kerry, so I didn't'.[104]

This period of cruel violence began on 6 March, when a republican trap mine killed five Free State troops, including three officers, at Knocknagoshel near Castleisland in north-east Kerry. O'Daly issued a memorandum to GHQ stating: 'As a result of mine tragedy at Castleisland this morning, the GOC Kerry command has issued an order that in future all mines will be lifted and all dumps cleared by Irregular prisoners.' To the officers of the Kerry command he wrote: 'The taking out of prisoners is not to be regarded as a reprisal policy but as the only alternative left to us to prevent the wholesale slaughter of our men.'[105]

On 7 March nine IRA prisoners were taken from Ballymullen Barracks in Tralee and driven about three miles out on the Killarney road to clear a mine obstruction at Ballyseedy Cross. Republican accounts indicate that when they reached their destination the prisoners were tied together around a pile of stones and Free State soldiers detonated the mine that had been placed inside. Eight men were killed but the ninth, Stephen Fuller, was blown clear and survived to tell IRA officer John Joe Sheehy that the prisoners had been shown nine coffins in the barracks before their departure and that the intentions of their escort were clear.[106] Sheehy publicly contradicted the Free State claims that the killings had been the result of an accident. Public outrage ensued and the bereaved families smashed the military coffins to pieces.[107] Later that day, four republican prisoners were killed at Countess Bridge, near Killarney, and on 12 March, at Caherciveen, five more republicans were killed using the same brutal method.

Paddy O'Daly was appointed to preside over a military court of inquiry convened on 7 April 1923. The Free State commanders denied that the incidents had been reprisals for Knocknagoshel and rejected the allegations of brutality and mistreatment of prisoners. In the words of O'Daly's grand-nephew:

> It is often forgotten that Paddy didn't have the luxury of presiding over a well-disciplined army … At the Court of Inquiry, [he] acknowledged what was done was wrong, but he pleaded with Mulcahy for leniency for the men based on their national service … it is difficult to understand from today's perspective but if you go back to their time, he regarded these men as having done wonderful stuff for the War of Independence.

Dick Mulcahy, chief of staff of the Free State army, replied to attacks in the Dáil by defending O'Daly and his army in Kerry, and said that he accepted the findings of the military court, which exonerated the troops.[108]

Many years later, in his posthumously published *Kerry Landing, August 1922: An episode of the Civil War*, Captain Niall C. Harrington of the Dublin Brigade confirmed that Ballyseedy had been a reprisal, and that the 'mines used in the slaughter of prisoners were constructed in Tralee under the supervision of two senior Dublin Guards Officers'.[109] Tony Roche, who is strongly of the opinion that 'all history is written out of perspective and, indeed, prejudice', is disinclined to accept Harrington's assertion at face value and insisted on his grand-uncle's innocence of any knowledge of the plans: 'You see, they had been ambushed two nights previously, a horrific ambush' and for a couple of weeks before that they had received messages 'almost nightly' at Ballymullen Barracks 'about activity or trap mines'. They had 'lost a horrendous amount of people', but there 'was no order given to land-mine Ballyseedy. It was a wildcat action … [and] Paddy seems to [have been] oblivious'.[110] The only accountability he acknowledged for his grand-uncle was inattentiveness:

> Pádraig O'Connor's wife came to him and said, 'They are bringing down buckets of ash.' That was a euphemism for explosives. Paddy, I suppose a bit carelessly, said, 'Find out what's happening and come back to me', and she never did. Maybe he should have investigated himself.

The events of the Civil War 'are extraordinarily painful,' Tony added, 'and Paddy has never been able to defend himself, [but] I believe from what I have heard and researched that [he] was an extraordinarily upright man.'

In late 1997 Sr Philomena O'Daly and her brother Paddy, then in his eighties, were alerted to the scheduled broadcast of a 'programme on television' about what became known as 'the Ballyseedy Massacre'.[111] Director Frank Hand embedded into his documentary emotionally charged dramatised segments which proved distressing for O'Daly's family. Paddy was unable to watch it and Philomena turned off the television set. 'It's a black spot,' she said, 'and I didn't want to look at it.'

Soon after the documentary aired on RTÉ, O'Daly's daughter was again faced with the evidence of the persistent bitterness surrounding the events in Kerry. She was attending a counselling training course, and during a mock therapy session, one of the group divulged that his father had been killed in Kerry during the Civil War. 'We had to work through it then,' Philomena remembered, 'because he was saying that it was my father that had killed his father.' Her voice shook as she relived the emotional strain: 'It was a terrible thing to come up against.'

The Civil War also precipitated a split in the O'Daly family. Séamus and Paddy joined the Free State army, but their brother Frank was staunchly anti-Treaty:

> When his nephew died, Paddy went to his brother Frank's house to sympathise before the funeral. He met his sister-in-law, May – who was a bit of a firebrand. He held out his hand to her – that was the kind of man he was – and she said: 'I won't shake hands with you until you go down on your knees in front of me and apologise for killing Irishmen.' Paddy said, 'Let bygones be bygones,' but she wouldn't. It was a difficult time.

Major General Paddy O'Daly resigned from the army in March 1924 and attempted to settle into civilian life with his second wife, Bríd Murtagh, whom he had married three years before. In July 1928 he accepted the job of overseer at the governor-general's residence [Áras an Úachtaráin] and the couple moved into a house in the Phoenix Park. For O'Daly, it seems, sorrows came not as single spies, but in battalions, because Bríd died two years later and soon afterwards O'Daly lost his job with the Office of Public Works. De Valera 'sacked him', his daughter said. 'I think he was accused of stealing a fireplace but, you see, my father and Dev were enemies from the Civil War. There was always sadness about that.'

Having lost both his job and his home, O'Daly went to live in Naas Road in Inchicore. On 27 September 1934 he married Norah Gillies, and their daughter Philomena was born in August of the following year. Tragedy stalked O'Daly's life once more when his third wife died just ten months after the birth of her daughter. 'My grandmother wanted to take me to look after me,' she said, 'but he had been parted from his other children because of the Troubles so he wouldn't part with me … He was both mother and father to me.' Even though he didn't share the details of his military service or articulate his feelings about his many losses, O'Daly's daughter detected his sadness in everything he did: 'I used to see my dad with tears in his eyes [but] I didn't ask questions.'

Prominent personalities in Sr Philomena's childhood included Dick Mulcahy and Joe Leonard. The latter in particular was a 'frequent visitor'. He and Paddy 'were like two peas in a pod … and Dan Holland's family provided a second home after my father returned to the army during the "Emergency". He was missing from Monday to Friday, so Catherine Holland was instrumental in my upbringing.' It was actually 'like history repeating itself' because after Paddy's first wife, Daisy, died in 1919, the Holland family took one-year-old Colbert O'Daly into their care.

Sadness invaded Phil's home again in the late 1950s, when Paddy O'Daly was diagnosed with bone cancer. The doctors discovered that it originated at the point where he had been shot in the arm in 1916, 'so it eventually killed him on 16 January 1957'. Philomena, who nursed him in his last months, said that he was a religious man and 'was prepared for death'.

BLOODLINES

❧ DEATH IN BATTLE ❦

The story of the Easter Rising, with its powerful resonances of birth and redemption, exerted a tenacious grip on the nationalist imagination in the post-Rising decades. The names of its leaders, 'sacrificed to the cause of Irish freedom', were indelibly inscribed in the annals of republican martyrology. But beneath the veil of romantic reinterpretation lay the brutal reality of Easter Week during which 485 people died.

Captain Seán Connolly of the ICA was shot dead in the opening act of the bloody drama of insurrection, and Michael J. O'Rahilly fell in Moore Street during its closing scene. Their deaths in the heat of battle were somehow less sanctified than 'martyrdom' by an executioner's gun, and their children were bequeathed a more visceral inherited memory of rebellion. Niamh O'Sullivan and Proinsias Ó Rathaille are another generation removed from the violent reality of the Rising, and they retell their grandfathers' stories with all of the contradictory emotion inherent in W. B. Yeats' refrain: 'A terrible beauty is born.'[1]

The parents of the Volunteers who fell with The O'Rahilly in Moore Street were not afforded the dubious consolation of a son's immortalisation in verse. They mourned in private. For the families of Henry Coyle, Patrick Shortis, Michael Mulvihill and Patrick O'Connor, the legacy of 1916 was defined more by fear and penury than by pride.

Séamus Brennan has deeply conflicting feelings about the death of his grand-uncle, Private Francis Brennan of the 10th Battalion, Royal Dublin Fusiliers, just yards from his mother's house in Usher's Quay on Easter Monday 1916. His story represents the complexity of the opening decades of the twentieth century, and the reality for thousands of Irish families whose sons and brothers were faced with multiple loyalties but forced to choose one side.

SEÁN CONNOLLY

Margaret (Madge) Connolly, who was born on Valentine's Day 1916, never knew her father, Captain Seán Connolly of the ICA, 'the first rebel shot in Easter Week'. In fact, 'Seán Connolly had three children at that stage,' his granddaughter, Niamh O'Sullivan, explained. 'Aiden was six, Kevin was two and my mother, Margaret.' While Madge knew little about the events of Easter Week, Seán Connolly's widow, Christina (Cissie), was 'very forthcoming' in response to questions from her curious granddaughter. She told her, for example, about the 'consternation' on the morning her husband left for Liberty Hall:

> My grandfather, dressed in a uniform, was leaving the house [in Fairview]. My grandmother, her two little boys holding on to her skirt, called [after] him: 'What are we going to do, Seán?' There would be no help if he didn't come back. If you didn't have relatives or friends, you would be on the breadline … So he turned at the garden gate, he looked back at her and he said, 'I'm sorry Cissie, my country needs me', and he walked away.

Christina said that she had a 'feeling' that this would be the last time she would see her husband. 'But you couldn't dissuade him,' Niamh said sadly. 'In the early days, he had told her, "Accept me as I am … and if a call comes I will go, irrespective." So she had accepted the fact that if it did come to the crunch he would definitely go and do his bit.'

The couple had met six years earlier at 'a Gaelic League gathering in Parnell Square' and they were married, after a brief courtship, on 19 October 1910. Three years later, Christina's thirty-year-old husband joined the ICA, because, according to his granddaughter, he had a deep admiration for James Connolly, who was 'a union man' and 'believed in the people'. Seán Connolly was a dedicated member of the ICA but he was also a celebrated singer and performer, and in the years before the Rising, he shared the Abbey stage with fellow 1916 combatants Helena Molony, Máire Nic Shiubhlaigh, Arthur Shields and Peadar Kearney. According to Niamh O'Sullivan:

> He would have been a firm favourite of Lady Gregory's and he played in Manchester, Liverpool and Birmingham, and he even got an offer to go to Broadway … I

215

remember asking people who had seen him on stage what kind of an actor was he and they said, 'When he got on stage, you forgot that it was Seán Connolly.' He had the ability to encourage and enhance the plot itself and to entice an audience into it, which is a tremendous talent.

In April 1966 ICA member Emily Norgrove recalled Seán Connolly's last performance in Liberty Hall fifty years before:

> About 4 p.m. [on Easter Sunday] we were ordered out on a route march. Everyone was tensed up and prepared for action, but nothing happened. On our arrival back in the [Liberty] Hall … we had tea followed by an impromptu concert. Michael Mallin played tunes on the flute. Seán Connolly, who could hold an audience in rapt attention with his recitations, made his last appearance on [the] platform that night. In a few short hours, the voice we loved to hear would be stilled in death.[2]

The next morning, Norgrove and her fellow members of the ICA paraded in Beresford Place, where James Connolly issued final orders to his officers and shook hands with Seán Connolly for the last time. The newly promoted captain led thirty ICA men and ten members of its Women's Section, including his sister Kathleen (Katie) Connolly, away from Liberty Hall towards Dublin Castle. The column breached the outer gates 'but they were beaten back', Niamh explained. 'They retreated to City Hall', where fifteen-year-old Matthew Connolly took up a position on the roof with the older brother he 'idolised'.

The ICA came under heavy fire during the afternoon and, ignoring his own warnings about keeping low, Connolly 'fell mortally wounded by a sniper's bullet from the Castle'.[3] In Niamh O'Sullivan's received version of her grandfather's last moments, the truth is painted liberally with the shades of satisfying symbolism:

> Seán Connolly was raising the Republican flag on the roof of the City Hall and he was shot by the sniper … The play he was in [in 1916] was called *Wrap the Green Flag Around Me*, so it's very ironic that it should be the very flag he was raising when he was shot … He fell on the glass roof of the main central building [under which] … there is a marble statue of [Michael] Davitt [who was] one of my

216

grandfather's heroes. It was ironic that his blood should have dripped down onto the shoulder of the statue.[4]

In the closing days of Easter Week 1916, Christina Connolly waited anxiously for news of her husband. When Niamh asked 'how she coped with the uncertainty' she replied, 'You have no idea! The worst part was not knowing if he was dead or injured somewhere.' Niamh continued:

Christina Connolly and her sons, Aiden and Kevin (*courtesy of Niamh O'Sullivan*)

> She could actually hear the gunfire. It revolved around the city [and] you could see the smoke and the flames [at] night-time. [By the end of the week], he still hadn't returned and news was very sketchy. There [were] no telephones and nobody could run anywhere, [because] there were a lot of barricades [and] gunfire and snipers in the city itself. Eventually, [after six long days] news did get back to her that he had been shot, but they couldn't confirm whether he was dead or alive. Finally, news came through to my grandmother that a body had been recovered.

Connolly's remains had been hastily buried in the yard of City Hall, and after the exhumation Christina faced the grim task of going to the city morgue to identify a body 'in very bad condition'. The 'bodies were stacked high and the gentleman in charge of the mortuary said that if she had sixpence she could have any one of them. So my grandmother paid the money and collected the body and that is why my grandfather is buried in Glasnevin in his own private grave.'

Without any means of providing for her family, Christina was forced to abandon her 'lovely' home 'out towards Inchicore' and take her three young children to live with her in-laws in Gloucester Street. It was a difficult compromise, not least because the Connolly home 'was known as a republican hotspot'. They 'kept people and they held guns,' Niamh explained, '[and] it was raided many times by the Tans' during the War of Independence. And so Seán Connolly's widow sent her children out of the city to Spiddal in Connemara. 'She wanted them to learn Irish and to keep them safe', but she didn't realise that 'Spiddal was also a hotspot for the rebels'. The children were 'farmed out [to] different houses. My mother went to Finnertys and my uncles, Kevin and Aiden, went to Thorntons', an elderly couple who lived in a 'big stone farm house' on a hill above the village:

> Kevin, who would have been seven years of age, was a bad asthmatic. One day (14 May 1921) when he wasn't feeling very well, he was upstairs in bed. The Thorntons' son, Martín, who was on the run, had come back in to get food. He would have been back over the fields but somebody tipped off the Tans that he was inside in the house. When they arrived … he jumped out the back window [and] down through the fields to a dyke and pulled the rushes over him.
>
> The Tans gave chase but when they couldn't find him they got irate and came back down to the house. They got the two old people and locked them into the barn outside and then went upstairs and tied my uncle to the bed. They set a bomb under [it and another] at the end of the stairs, pulled the pin and drove off in the truck.
>
> Providentially, the bomb under the bed didn't go off, but the one at the bottom of the stairs … blew the bed straight [into the air] and my uncle knocked his head off the ceiling. It knocked him out cold. The bombs set fire to the stairwell [and] because the house was high up the people in the village could see [it] and they came rushing up … They released the Thorntons [and] got into the house through the back window. That's how they eventually got the young child out. So they weren't safe going to Spiddal, they should have remained in Dublin.[5]

The children spent two years in Galway and returned to Dublin when Margaret was five years old. In the meantime, Christina had secured a job as an official of the School Attendance Department of the Corporation. 'That's how she managed to keep the children with her,' her granddaughter explained. There were also 'certain people in the city [who were] financially well off, and gave assistance to anyone who 'had gone out for the Movement'. It was through these connections that Christina met a wealthy fruit merchant and ex-alderman, Walter Leonard Cole. The Connolly house in Gloucester Street was 'full of people', so Walter Cole offered Christina the upstairs floor of his home at No. 3 Mountjoy Square: 'My mother and her two brothers grew up in that beautiful old Georgian house.'

After the Dáil was declared an illegal assembly and forced underground in September 1919, its members convened several times in Cole's large dining room on the first floor. 'Anyone who was anyone at that stage came through his door … [He was] one of the biggest supporters of the Movement and my mother would tell you, if she was still alive, that Arthur Griffith used to come every morning for coffee.' Cole's grandson, Simon Walker, told broadcaster Joe Duffy that 'when Griffith and Dev [stayed] here, Griffith would polish his own boots but Dev would leave them outside the door'.[6] Apparently, Christina's three children 'did not take kindly to de Valera' and 'found him an austere man', but Margaret told her daughter that 'Michael Collins was full of fun' and 'she would sit on his knee as he read the comic strips from the newspaper'.

Walter Cole's home was also 'a safe house' and arms store during the War of Independence, Niamh adds, and its location in 'a very wealthy area of Dublin' city made it an ideal setting for clandestine meetings: 'You couldn't prove that there was anything under the counter being done in there.' Its residents were 'very discreet people' who received sundry visitors 'for tea or to play cards or maybe a dance'. Even if the house was being watched, they could never be '100 per cent sure about who was there or what their business was … The two female servants were loyal and trustworthy and the children would have been strictly warned' about the importance of discretion. 'They stuck together and … wouldn't discuss anything with any stranger.'

Nevertheless, 'the house was raided constantly'. There is a story in the Cole family about how the front door had 'to be repainted seven times within the space of the year [as a result of] the military attacking it with hatchets and rifle butts'.[7] Christina's brother, Patrick Swanzy, and Walter Cole were arrested in one such raid in September 1920. *The Freeman's Journal* reported:

In the course of the raid, Mrs Connolly's young son, Kevin, who is ill, was lifted out of his bed, which was thoroughly searched. Photographs of Mrs Connolly's late husband, the late Lord Mayor [Tomás] MacCurtain and Mr James Connolly were removed from frames and smashed.[8]

During the same period, Christina used her 'very fine singing voice' to raise money 'for the cause. She sang in the Theatre Royal in Tralee and performed in Manchester and Birmingham and [at] quite a few events in Dublin.' The song 'The Tricoloured Ribbon' 'was written for my grandmother' by Seán Connolly's friend, fellow Abbey actor and ICA member Peadar Kearney, and 'she used to sing [it] because the words were so real [to her] and emphasised her situation':

> For all around my hat I wear a tri-colour ribbon,
> Oh, all around my hat until death comes to me,
> And if anybody's asking me why do I wear it,
> It's all for my own true love I never more will see.
>
> In praying and watching the dark hours passed over
> The roar of guns brought no message to me
> I prayed for Old Ireland, I prayed for my lover,
> That he might be safe and Old Ireland be free …

No. 3 Mountjoy Square was host to the Treaty delegation on the night before they left Dublin in October 1921:

> They all met in [the house] and they said to the children, 'You know we are go-ing to London, what do you want?' And so the boys asked for soldiers and one of them asked for a truck and my mother said she wanted the Dáil. Remember, she was only about six but a small child listens and picks up things very easily… They thought she meant 'a doll' but she didn't, she meant the *Dáil* …
>
> But they went off and they signed [the Treaty] and I asked my grandmother why. And she said, 'If you had taken six years of hell on earth, you'd have signed any-thing for peace.' The city was still volatile and they were tired. So from that point of view, [it was] better to make the best deal you could rather than keep fighting.

Niamh once asked her grandmother why de Valera refused to accompany the delegation to London, to which she replied: 'A fit of pique!' and suggested a certain jealousy felt by the 'tall, austere man' clad in black who 'rarely smiled' towards the charismatic, 'broad-shouldered, slim-hipped' young Collins, who 'walked with a swagger' and 'had that natural leadership'. Like her little daughter, Christina was disappointed at the failure of the delegation to return with 'the Dáil', but Niamh feels that she would have 'mostly supported Collins' in his endorsement of the Treaty.

In the years that followed, Christina always took her children to the 1916 commemoration ceremonies and was 'quietly' proud of Seán Connolly's role. They were present, for example, at Glasnevin Cemetery in November 1937, when Dr Kathleen Lynn unveiled a limestone memorial stone to Captain Seán Connolly, and 'they received a great boost' in the following year when W. B. Yeats published 'a wonderful poem about my grandfather'. The poet mourned the unrealised potential of 'the player Connolly' in 'Song Three' of *Three Songs to the One Burden*.

MICHAEL J. O'RAHILLY

In December 1983 Séamus Scully imaginatively reconstructed for the Old Dublin Society the frenetic scene in the GPO on Friday 28 April 1916:

> It was almost six o'clock. Clarke, MacDermott, Plunkett and The O'Rahilly had gathered around the bed of the wounded James Connolly to prepare a plan of evacuation from the burning building ... The wild suggestion of escape through the filthy, choked sewers was impossible. Headquarters had lost contact with the main outlying posts. The enemy now had a clear field for military attack. They were trapped. It was agreed that their only chance of escape was through the Moore Street area, in the vague hope of taking up quarters at Williams and Woods' factory in Parnell St and perhaps eventual escape. Apparently, they were unaware that Parnell St was already under enemy control since Thursday.[9]

Forty-one-year-old Michael Joseph O'Rahilly (The O'Rahilly) from Ballylongford, County Kerry, was chosen to lead the front guard.[10] Despite his initial opposition to what he considered an inexpedient uprising, his leadership and integrity during Easter Week in the GPO elevated him 'to an almost heroic status'.[11] The O'Rahilly chose twenty-five Volunteers to form the vanguard of the retreat from the GPO and, according to his grandson, Proinsias Ó Rathaille, he turned to his friend Desmond FitzGerald and 'more or less said it's better than dying of cold on top of the Howth tram'.

At 7:30 p.m. The O'Rahilly and his men emerged from the side entrance of the shell-damaged GPO into Henry Place. Their desperate mission, conceived in chaos, was to mount a frontal attack on the British barricade at the intersection of Moore Street and Parnell Street, in an attempt to distract the British military long enough for the rest of the garrison to escape the blazing GPO. They rushed for the corner of Henry Street, turned right onto Moore Street and into the sights of the machine guns of the 6th Sherwood Foresters at the barricade at the end of the street. The first volley cut through their ranks.[12] They scattered, frantically seeking shelter in the narrow doorways on both sides of the street. The O'Rahilly made it to within thirty yards of the barricade and swerved into a doorway at the corner of Sampson's Lane. Volunteer Thomas Devine's party took cover in an alleyway a short distance behind, but the remaining Volunteers were stranded halfway down Moore Street. When the shooting subsided, The O'Rahilly blew twice on his whistle, signalling to his men to advance, and with a Mauser pistol in one hand and a sword in the other, he dashed out into the middle of Moore Street. According to Devine:

Michael J. O'Rahilly
(*courtesy of Mercier Archive*)

> He had covered only a few yards when he was hit from the barricade and fell face forward, his sword clattering in front of him. He lay motionless for a few seconds and we thought him dead. Then with great effort he raised himself a little on his left arm and with his right made the sign of the Cross. Again he lay down and such was the greyness of his face, we thought him dead; then minutes, seconds – I cannot tell

– later he stirred and, by supreme efforts, slowly and painfully dragged himself inch by inch into Sackville Lane a few yards away where he lay down for the last time.[13]

Aware of his inevitable fate, The O'Rahilly reached into his pocket to retrieve the note that had been sent to the GPO on Wednesday by his eleven-year-old son Aodogán. It read: 'Dear Dada … I heard from Nell and Anna that the Volunteers are winning. I don't suppose they will ever get the GPO for as long as you are in command.'[14] On the reverse of the crumpled page, Michael J. O'Rahilly penned his last words to his family:

> Written after I was shot. Darling Nancy I was shot leading a rush up Moore Street and took refuge in a doorway. While I was there I heard the men pointing out where I was and made a bolt for the laneway I am in now. I got more [than] one bullet I think. Tons and tons of love dearie to you and the boys and to Nell and Anna. It was a good fight anyhow. Please deliver this to Nannie O'Rahilly, 40 Herbert Park, Dublin. Goodbye Darling.

Proinsias Ó Rathaille finds it difficult to discuss the suffering and indignity of his grandfather's prolonged death, but has always been moved by the pathos of his final act:

> There were two holes in the note from the Maxim machine gun on Parnell Square … and the blood was flowing down his hand when he was writing it. As far as I remember, he just folded the note and managed [to] put it back in his pocket and [then] … he wrote on the wall with his finger covered in blood: 'The O'Rahilly died here' … He was a brave man.

Proinsias knows that his grandmother, Nancy (Nannie) O'Rahilly 'was totally devastated when the note finally came out to her'. It had been discovered on the body and 'ended up in this general's office in Dublin Castle I think'. There are 'a lot of stories' about how the note finally made its way to Nancy, but Proinsias is inclined to believe that 'this girl was in the [office] tidying up or whatever and she saw the note. She just took a chance and took it and just delivered it out to Nancy.'

Private William Richards told the *Evening Herald* on 15 May 1916 that he 'spoke words of comfort to them during the bombardment'.[23] In the context of his grandfather's 'careful and decent' treatment of his prisoners, Proinsias found it even more 'hurtful' that 'the British wouldn't let anyone near his body as he lay fatally wounded'. He also despaired at the ignominious theft of The O'Rahilly's rings and watch while he lay dying in the doorway.

For Desmond FitzGerald, The O'Rahilly was 'the most tragic figure in that tragic gathering of men' because 'he was devoted to his wife and family with a rare devotion, but he had decided to leave them to serve Ireland when the call to service came'.[24] It was small consolation for his wife, who was six months pregnant with their fifth child. Her distress was compounded by rumours that her 'house was going to be attacked by the separation allowance women' – the wives of soldiers in the British Army.[25] Her sisters-in-law, Áine O'Rahilly and Nell Humphreys (*née* Rahilly), rescued Nancy and the children, and on Thursday Nell took responsibility for the grim task of identifying her brother's body. Proinsias knows that his grandmother, who he remembers as 'quiet and very elegant', was heartbroken at the news and, as with Catherine Colbert, her grief was manifest in the fact that her piano 'stayed silent ever after'.

The children were 'devastated that they had lost their father so young,' Proinsias said, '[but] my father always [considered it] the ultimate gesture'. His uncle, Aodogán O'Rahilly, echoed this sentiment in 1991 when he told *The Irish Times*:

> One of my brothers used to say that it was irresponsible for a man to go out and leave his wife and four young children and go into a fight in which he was going to get killed. I never felt that. I felt that he did what had to be done ... [He was] a heroic figure [and] my brothers and sister and I were brought up as dyed-in-the-wool republicans.[26]

Aodogán was active on the anti-Treaty side in the Civil War and Niall O'Rahilly, whom his son describes as 'a deep thinker', also remained staunchly republican into adulthood. In July 1940 Niall married fellow activist Brigid (Bridie) Clyne from Dormond, County Leitrim, and they lived for a short period with Maud Gonne 'in a mews out in the garden in [Roebuck House], Clonskeagh'. Neither

Bridie nor Niall O'Rahilly ever discussed their politics with their children, but Niall 'would be always scribbling his thoughts on pieces of paper' which, in later years, he elaborated into poetry. The lines of ragged verse revealed, in his son's opinion, his disappointment with what he considered de Valera's 'hypocrisy' in the 1930s.

The couple eventually made their home in the majestic eighteenth-century Ballinascorney House in the foothills of the Dublin mountains. 'I believe that old Joe [McGrath] gave it to my mother as a wedding present,' Proinsias said, 'because she was involved with him in Cumann na mBan and the [Belfast] Boycott.[27] I must say it was some wedding present.'[28] The house is steeped in history and has strong associations with Robert Emmet, who took refuge there after his abortive rebellion in 1803. Some people refused to stay there because it was said that you could hear the 'sounds of [ghostly] footsteps upstairs'. Proinsias, however, describes his childhood spent roaming the seventy-three acres of forestry and fishing in the lakes, as 'Nirvana':

Proinsias Ó Rathaille and his mother Bridie O'Rahilly (*courtesy of Proinsias Ó Rathaille*)

> I had no realisation of how famous [my family] were. It [eventually] dawned on me because of the people who used to come and go. It was a who's who of republicans … after that I just learned through the family, bit by bit, what had happened. Then I got very interested in the history of it.

HENRY AND THOMAS COYLE

ICA member Thomas Coyle was wounded on the roof of City Hall on Monday 24 April 1916, and four days later his brother, twenty-eight-year-old Henry Coyle of 'F' Company, 2nd Battalion, fell mortally wounded behind The

Henry Coyle
(*courtesy of Harry Coyle*)

O'Rahilly in Moore Street. Henry's grandson, Harry Coyle, feels that it must have been 'horrific' for their parents:

There were only two sons and one was cripplingly injured and in jail in Frongoch and the other [was] dead outside the GPO …[29] You can imagine all the horror when you think of just your own family. My own son, Henry, is twenty-eight years old and I can't imagine him picking up a rifle and going into the GPO and barricading [himself] in. They were different people; they were old before their years. Whether it was right or wrong, I think they were very heroic and it was just something that needed to be done at the time.

The whole family was 'very republican-minded', Harry explained, and 'my grandfather, a true teetotaller, was a prominent member of the Davis hurling team from 1903'. The brothers' immersion in the philosophy of cultural nationalism led to their membership of the Irish Volunteers, but in 1915 nineteen-year-old Thomas, a slater from the north inner city, was drawn to the socialist ideals expressed in the constitution of the ICA. On Easter Monday 1916 both men prepared for action. Thomas left his home in Rutland Street and Henry said goodbye to his wife, Alice Coffey, who was six months pregnant with their first child:

My grandmother lived until I was in my late twenties and I spoke to her several times about it. She told me… that he had been absent quite a bit leading up to the Rising and … [on] the morning of the Rising he told her that he was going off [and] wasn't sure when he would be back but if anything happened, she was to go to his sister [who] would take care of her and the baby. She got alarmed but he assured her that there was nothing to worry about. That was the last time she saw him.

Henry joined Frank Henderson in Fairview on Easter Monday. The next day he followed his captain to the GPO, unaware that his brother had received a crippling head wound on the roof of City Hall that morning and had been brought under armed guard to the field hospital in Dublin Castle. Henry stood with his company in the GPO until Friday, when he answered The O'Rahilly's call for Volunteers. Alice told her grandson that 'after the Rising she knew that something had happened':

> He had been missing for a week and she visited two hospitals without success. Eventually, she found the body in the City Morgue [in Store Street]. There were several covers pulled back and one of them was her husband. [She said] that she would never forget that moment. She recognised him … He had been killed by gunfire [and] either two or three bullets had penetrated his body. She heard anecdotally from people who had been in the vicinity that he had died in close proximity to The O'Rahilly and, in fact, had tried to assist The O'Rahilly with a third man but was caught with gunfire himself.

Oblivious to his brother's fate, Thomas lay immobilised in Dublin Castle. He is actually featured in the 'famous' postcard, circulated after the Rising, of 'the wounded Volunteers in [the] Infirmary'. Thomas Coyle sits upright in his truckle bed, flanked on one side by a priest and on the other by a British soldier, but smiling in defiance of his physical confinement. The photograph 'appeared on the front of the *Daily Mirror* of the day' and was subsequently reproduced as a picture postcard – part of the flood of rebel Sinn Féin sponsored memorabilia in the wake of the Rising, which contributed significantly to the wellspring of sympathy and support for the rebels following the executions.[30]

Henry Coyle's image also appeared in print after 1916. His was one of a series of obituaries published by the *Catholic Bulletin* between 1916 and 1919 in which the fallen rebels were celebrated as paragons of faith and sacrifice. The laudatory articles, accompanied by photographs or drawings and modelled on the familiar hagiographical saints' lives, emphasised the Volunteers' manliness, courage, faith and purity, and appealed to earnest Catholic Ireland. The message was clear: the rebels died not for a workers' republic or an independent Gaelic Ireland but for a Catholic nation. For Harry Coyle, however, the significance of his copy of the *Catholic Bulletin* is that it contains one of the few images he has seen of his grandfather.

In the immediate aftermath of the Rising, Alice Coyle's preoccupations were with her husband's burial and the imminent arrival of their child. Her grandson explained:

> They were allowed to bury them [because] at that stage there had probably been a bit of a realisation by Britain that they had made an error in [the] summary execution of the leaders. [The] National Graves Association paid for graves for people that were killed. In later years, when things had quietened down, [and] the men were given the proper recognition for what had happened, [my grandmother] was asked if she would like him to be reinterred in the Republican Plot but she said that it would be a very traumatic exhumation and she didn't do it.

Alice's son was born on 4 July 1916. 'That child was my father. His full name was Henry O'Rahilly Coyle because of the connection with the death of The O'Rahilly', and Henry is a Coyle family name. 'My great-grandfather's name was also Henry Coyle, I'm Henry, my son is Henry and his first-born is Henry, so it gets confusing … but we've always respected the name and the sacrifice of not alone my grandfather, but all the men that went out.'

Harry was forcibly reminded of his grandmother's 'sacrifice' when he happened upon a photograph in 'a rather interesting book'. He turned the page to find a studio photograph of Alice Coyle, clad in widow's black, balancing her infant son on her knee. The poignant vignette, enclosed in a decorative border, was one of a collection of souvenir photographs published in early 1917 in aid of the Easter Week 1916 Widows and Orphans' Fund and 'it was sold for 3 pence to raise money to provide a seaside holiday for the children of the men who died for Ireland in 1916'.[31]

Alice told her grandson that, shortly after the birth of her child, 'there was a knock on the door' and outside stood a lady 'who was obviously a well-off person':

Alice and Henry O'Rahilly Coyle
(*courtesy of Harry Coyle*)

She turned out to be the widow of The O'Rahilly and she said to my grandmother that she had heard that [Henry] had been killed while trying to assist her husband. She was aware that the baby had been born and asked if [my grandmother would] permit him to be christened in the O'Rahilly christening robe … So my grandmother said she would be privileged.

In September 1920 Alice married for a second time. Her choice of suitor led to a fracture in the family because the Coyles refused to accept Joseph Coughlan, who 'had been in the British Army during the 1916 Rising'. 'But,' Harry said, 'you can't really point a finger at anyone [because] John Redmond was exhorting Irishmen to join the British Army and there were tens of thousands of young Irishmen fighting in the British Army at the time.' The couple had two children, Maureen and Joshua, between 1921 and 1923.

In 1922 Coughlan was a sergeant in the National Army stationed in the Curragh, and Alice sent her seven-year-old son to live with 'an elderly aunt' who was 'a very charitable woman'. Even though Henry O'Rahilly Coyle grew up without his father and separated from his mother, his son insisted that 'he had no animosity or bitterness towards anybody'. There are two things, however, that Harry does regret on his father's behalf. First, he never got to know his uncle Thomas; and second, other than his father's medal, Henry had few physical reference points for his father's memory. He was proud of the medal, which always had 'a prominent place in our home', but 'everything else stayed with his mother. [That was] wrong because he was Henry Coyle, and they were now a new family.' Harry recalled a visit to his grandmother's house in 1956, when she showed him 'the O'Rahilly family's christening robe. Alice had wrapped it carefully in tissue paper and stored it in a large brown cardboard box on top of an old wardrobe'. The significance of the object 'didn't register' with fourteen-year-old Harry, and many years later a casual conversation with his cousin, Stephen Coughlan, led to the revelation that Alice's daughter, Maureen, had donated the precious family artefact to 'the Museum'. Unfortunately, Stephen was 'not sure which museum' and 'that was the last that anybody heard of it'.

The christening robe represented an important symbolic link with his father's past, but the human link was similarly broken for Henry O'Rahilly Coyle. His uncle, Thomas Coyle, remained in Dublin Castle for three weeks after the Rising and was then lodged in Kilmainham Gaol to await deportation to England. After his release from Frongoch in December 1916, Thomas rejoined 'B' Company, 2nd Battalion, Dublin Brigade and, according to his pension application, he 'taught [the] company how to make bombs'.[32] He enlisted in the National Army in October 1922 and was discharged as medically unfit in March 1924. He had to leave, he said, 'owing to my wounds coming against me'.[33] Thomas died nine years later on 19 October 1933 'as a result of the wounds he received in 1916'.[34] 'I didn't know about him,' Harry said sadly, '[until] a short few years ago [when] a lady contacted me and [said] she was his great-granddaughter.' For Harry Coyle, the 'real tragedy' is that 'my father would have been interested in his Uncle Thomas' and he did not realise that Thomas' widow 'lived until the mid-seventies in a house in Donnybrook', just two miles from where Henry lived:

> He would have passed her door three or four times a day and didn't realise she was his father's sister-in-law. He would have loved to have spoken to her [about Thomas and Henry] but it was only in recent years that her descendants contacted me [and] … we put the family together again.

Harry was recently struck by another unusual coincidence:

> One of my sons was in St Michael's College and they were given a choice of subjects [on which] to do a historical essay. Naturally, knowing my interest in the 1916–21 period, [he] elected to do an essay on that … When he handed it in, the teacher asked: 'Where did you get all your background knowledge?' He said: 'My father is very interested in it because my great-grandfather was killed in 1916.' So the teacher said, 'What was his name and where was he killed?' and he told him that his name was Harry Coyle and he was killed during the evacuation of the GPO with a man called The O'Rahilly. The teacher said, 'My grandfather [Francis Macken] was killed beside him.'

MICHAEL MULVIHILL, PATRICK SHORTIS AND PATRICK O'CONNOR

Three young Kerrymen answered The O'Rahilly's call for volunteers on Friday 28 April 1916, and less than an hour later they fell under a hail of machine-gun fire on Moore Street. The nieces and nephews of Patrick O'Connor from Rathmore, Michael Mulvihill from Ballyduff and Paddy Shortis from Ballybunion described the bittersweet legacy of 1916.

Margaret Mulvihill attended a ceremony in the Golden Jubilee year, during which a plaque to her brother was unveiled at their old homestead in Ardoughter.[35] The tribute to the fallen rebel was little comfort to his sister, who was profoundly bitter about what she perceived as a lack of respect shown by the government to the families of the men who gave their lives 'gloriously' in 1916.[36] Her grand-nephew, Liam Hutchinson, who spent his childhood summers with the 'remnants of the Mulvihill family' in Kerry, is more conscious of their material sacrifices than he is of his uncle's 'patriotic sacrifice'. Likewise, Patrick O'Connor's niece, Kitty Murphy, is aware that her family's suffering was not confined to personal grief. The O'Connor farm was a target for raids and reprisals during the War of Independence, and the family 'were marked people all their lives'.

Paddy Shortis from Ballybunion in North Kerry was the eldest in a family of seven children. His siblings mourned his death and acknowledged his bravery, but were reluctant to 'go around beating a drum about it'. His niece and nephew, Mary and Richard Johnson, are pragmatic about their connection to the 1916 rebel, and similarly disinclined to invest in the romantic eulogy. Richard observed: 'As you know, dead men tell no tales, and the vast majority of the mythology of 1916 was produced by live men and women telling tales.'

The three Kerrymen all left their native county in the early 1900s to find work in London. 'They had to go,' Mary explained. 'You must remember, people would have starved if it hadn't been for England, there was no work here.' Shortis, in fact, had intended to embark on a path towards the priesthood. In the early 1900s he won 'a first class scholarship in his entrance exam to St Brendan's seminary in Killarney', where he received both ecclesiastical instruction and 'an education in nationalism'. His vocational path led him to All Hallows College in Dublin, but after two years, and having gained a BA from the National University, he acknowledged that he found more inspiration in Marconi's experiments in wireless telegraphy than in theological debate. The young Kerryman returned to his native county to train as a wireless operator in the Atlantic Wireless College in Caherciveen and left for London soon afterwards to sit his examinations for certification.

Paddy's prolonged absence from home meant that Ann Shortis, born in 1904, had very few memories of her eldest brother. 'She was very young when he left,' her daughter Mary said. 'She remembered saying goodbye to him [but] that was it'. Ann's young life had already been scarred by loss. Both her parents, William and Annie Shortis, died before she was seven years old and she and her siblings were placed in the care of 'two maternal aunts'.[37] Norah and Mary Browne cared for the children and employed managers 'to look after their father's successful public house on the main street in Ballybunion', but Ann's eldest brother left almost immediately and she did not see him again.

Paddy Shortis passed his examinations in London but was denied his certificate 'owing to his views on Irish affairs'.[38] Those views drew him into the orbit of the Irish nationalist movement in the city, and very possibly into the same Gaelic League halls frequented by Michael Mulvihill from Ardoughter, a townland less than eight miles south of Ballybunion. Mulvihill, described by his nephew as 'an athletic man … with a scholarly face and penetrating eyes', had left home in 1897 in search of employment.[39] He secured a job as a 'sorter in the Post Office' at £295 per annum, £2 of which he sent home to Ardoughter every week.[40] The money was essential to his parents and eight siblings, who subsisted on John Mulvihill's meagre pension.

In 1903 Michael's father had retired 'prematurely' from his job as the principal of Ballincrossig National School after a series of disputes with the school clerical manager about the appropriateness of 'Fenianism' in the classroom. This 'left the family in very poor and straitened circumstances,' Liam Hutchinson explained, and Michael's 'dedication to his family's survival' was, in his opinion, just as noble as his dedication to his country. During his time in London, Mulvihill, 'a renowned hurler' and 'fluent Irish speaker', was an active member of the

Michael Mulvihill
(*courtesy of the Mulvihill family*)

GAA and the Gaelic League. He was also a member of the London Volunteers and was sworn into the IRB soon after he arrived in the city. 'My grandfather [John Mulvihill] spent a lot of time travelling over and back to America, [so] there is every reason to believe that he was an IRB man as well. But he was a man of mystery like an awful lot of the men at that time were.'

Eighteen-year-old Patrick O'Connor from Rathmore was similarly involved in nationalist circles in London after his arrival in the city in 1900.

Patrick O'Connor
(*courtesy of Kitty Murphy*)

Like Michael Mulvihill and Patrick Shortis, O'Connor had received an early 'education in nationalism' in County Kerry, where the powerful combination of a Fenian heritage and a resilient social memory of land agitation and the Famine fuelled his early radicalism. O'Connor grew up with six siblings on what his niece, Kitty, called a 'reasonably good farm'.[41] 'They had about ten or twelve cows but were more interested in education than they were in the farm. They were all bad farmers.' Kitty's father, Daniel O'Connor, was disinclined to speak about his brother, but her mother, Annie O'Leary, told her 'occasional things that a man wouldn't'. She learned, for example, that even though things were 'quite lively' in Rathmore when Patrick was a young man, he 'was not a person for socialising':

Maybe my father wouldn't talk about how distant he found him or how unfriendly, because they were all one family. But my mother said he might come visiting and if you talked about political things he was geared up but [otherwise he] didn't talk.

He was a very distant, silent person [and] he rarely laughed. He never had a girl, he never went dancing; all he wanted was history and to be involved in something. His brother Denis ('Dinny'), on the other hand, was totally different and had girls all over the place. He was an accordion player and he played for every house dance that was around the place.

Patrick O'Connor's mother, Mary O'Donoghue from Glenflesk, had a significant radicalising influence on her 'serious' son. She had lived through the Great Famine in the 1840s and 'remembered the people cutting the nettles and taking them home to … keep them from the hunger'. She often told Patrick about what she considered 'the cruelty of the English that time'. He was also inspired by Irish-Ireland propaganda and the gospel of self-reliance preached in the pages of Griffith's *United Irishman*. He refused to buy anything other than Irish-manufactured goods and 'one time he walked ten kilometres to Barraduff to buy a box of Irish matches. There was determination there.' He was also 'an intellectual. He came first in Ireland, England and Scotland in his Civil Service exam' and at eighteen years of age he took a position in the Post Office in London. 'It so happened that the people he was working with were very involved in Gaelic things and he didn't have any other interest in life. Then he got transferred to the GPO in Dublin in 1915 and, of course, he got very much involved there again.' O'Connor joined 'F' Company, 1st Battalion, in Dublin, and in April 1916 he returned to Kerry for the last time:

> His father and his brother died within seven days of each other and he came down from Dublin for the funerals. His father was more or less an alcoholic and he got pneumonia. His brother, Denis [who had also been in the Civil Service in London], was only about thirty-six I'd say. He was an athlete and he ran in a race over in London. The heavens opened and he got all wet and he left on the wet clothes [when] he [went out] to celebrate that night. He developed TB and he died of it. He was buried on the Good Friday and his father was buried on the Tuesday or Wednesday before that.
>
> At about two or three o'clock on Good Friday, Patrick got a telegram to tell him come back, they were very near the Rising … He [came to Rathmore] to say goodbye to my father, who told him: 'If you're in it, be in it to the end.' He had the same mentality … He said that he didn't think he'd see him any more. His country was what he lived for. So he went to Dublin and 'tis history.

Both Michael Mulvihill and Paddy Shortis returned to Dublin after conscription was introduced in England in January 1916. Shortis left London immediately and joined Henry Coyle and Frank Henderson in 'F' Company, 2nd Battalion, Irish Volunteers. Mulvihill waited until early April, when he was called up for military service. According to his brother-in-law and fellow member of the London Volunteers, Austin Kennan:

> He discussed with me the strong rumours of an early insurrection and we decided to go to Dublin. We did this on Good Friday, accompanied by Seán McGrath,

who carried a gun in a travelling rug. The three of us stayed at the Kincora Hotel in Parnell Square [and] Mick signed his name as 'O'Connor' [his mother's maiden name] for the benefit of any DMP men who might inspect the register. We knew that certain members of that force were making a speciality of tracing Irishmen who left Britain rather than join the British Army.[42]

The London exiles arrived in Larkfield, Kimmage, on Saturday and were disappointed to find that George Plunkett had 'no definite news about a rising'. They returned to the city, and on Easter Monday were delighted to learn that the rebels had taken the GPO. Kennan and Mulvihill came within sight of the rebel headquarters just as the Kimmage garrison marched into O'Connell Street. Kennan recalled: 'Denis Daly from Kerry waved to us and said, "This is revolution!" We entered the Post Office and Mick and I were given shotguns and a quantity of bombs ... and the two of us took up position on the front of the roof near the centre.'[43] Patrick O'Connor and 'a number of his comrades' joined them in the GPO on Monday night and on Tuesday, Henry Coyle and Patrick Shortis arrived with 'F' Company from Fairview.[44]

Mulvihill and Kennan, together with members of the Kimmage garrison and Éamonn Bulfin's Rathfarnham Company, exchanged fire with the troops in Trinity College. They complained about Desmond FitzGerald's 'meagre rations', and when it rained on Wednesday they used their overcoats to keep the incendiaries dry. Kennan recorded that they were visited on the roof by Patrick Pearse and Michael Collins, 'with whom [they] had been closely associated in London' and by 'a priest who gave [them] general absolution'.[45] In the meantime, Patrick O'Connor assisted in the futile attempts to put out the raging fires in Clery's stables and adjoining buildings.[46] On Thursday, after the shelling intensified, Mulvihill and Kennan were ordered to the ground floor and posted to new positions at the windows to prepare for the expected frontal assault. Paddy Shortis was also posted at the barricaded windows, where Aoife Burke found him on Friday:

Between 3 and 4 p.m. I got the smell of burning and knew the GPO had taken fire. About this time the shelling was terrific; sometimes the whole place shook ... I remember a Volunteer asking me would I say the Rosary with him at his post of duty. I did so and got some other girls to join … and every minute I thought a bomb or a bullet would put an end to the lot of us …

Some months later, I think, I recognised the Volunteer of the Rosary … from a photo in the *Catholic Bulletin*; and there, I'm sorry to say, I learned he was shot in the rush out from Headquarters; his name was given … as Shortis: poor fellow, the Rosary he asked me to say with him was probably his last and fervently he said it.[47]

Austin Kennan searched unsuccessfully for his brother-in-law amid the chaos of the evacuation, and only afterwards learned that he had volunteered with Shortis and O'Connor to join The O'Rahilly's vanguard. They dashed into Moore Street with Henry Coyle, Éamonn Dore, Francis Macken and Denis Daly from Caherciveen, who had gestured so encouragingly to Mulvihill and Kennan on Easter Monday. Patrick Shortis was fatally wounded in the first furious volley of machine-gun fire from the British barricade, and Thomas Devine dragged him to the relative safety of an alleyway on the left side of the street.[48] Éamonn Dore watched as The O'Rahilly fell wounded and 'my nearest comrade, Pat O'Connor, was killed just in front

Patrick Shortis in Volunteer uniform
(courtesy of the Johnson family)

of me and falling on me pinned me under him.'[49] In 1947 Margaret Mulvihill stitched together in a letter the various threads of truth and conjecture about her brother's death and concluded that 'his body, until buried by the military authorities, laid [*sic*] stretched, dead face downwards in Moore Lane at the junction of Henry Place'.[50]

Patrick O'Connor's niece regrets that the family missed an opportunity to speak to people who might 'have given them the story from the start'. Her father and his brothers, being 'men of their day', refused to board a train for Dublin because 'that wasn't done by farmers at that time'. So they only had 'second-hand information'. Notwithstanding Dore's testimony, Kitty feels that the most 'authentic' version of events is that 'he was shot in Moore Street' but 'apparently he was not dead at the time they removed his body and he died later in the hospital'. They were able to identify him because he 'had got a poisoned finger [which] had to be amputated and one nurse said that she attended to a dying man who had only three-quarters of his index finger'.

Paddy Shortis' nephew, Richard Johnson, is also deeply frustrated by the dearth of information about his uncle's last days:

> There is nothing much to research. I mean his name is in the Roll of Honour in the National Museum in Kildare Street. I've been in there and seen that, but that's as far as any of us can go really. My mother talked to me but she didn't have much to say because none of the family knew where he was or what he was involved in. In fact, he had been dead for some considerable time before they heard about it; they never knew it.

According to family history, Paddy's brother, Archie Shortis, who was a student of chemistry in Dublin in 1916, developed TB 'as a result of being out at night looking for Uncle Paddy's body'. In a tale of grim coincidence, Richard said that it was actually his father, also called Richard Johnson, who was the first person to find Paddy's body in the city morgue:

> My father was a student in Limerick in 1916 … but when he heard about the Rising he came up to Dublin to see what was happening … He saw the women in the street outside Jacob's factory cursing the Volunteers coming out. This, of course, was down near the Liberties in the city of Dublin where almost every single house would have had a member of the British armed forces among them. [He was not a member of the Volunteers but] had attended The O'Rahilly's Irish classes and knew the family, and Madam O'Rahilly asked Richard to look for her husband. He didn't find him, but in the morgue he came across a tall blond guy called Shortis. He came

across [him] completely by accident, and then nearly twelve years later, he married my mother, the sister of the man he had seen lying out on the slab in the morgue.[51]

News finally reached Ballybunion that Paddy Shortis' body had been found, and in Rathmore, Patrick O'Connor's mother, Mary, mourned the loss of a second son. Kitty, who was born in 1922, 'was only six or seven' when her grandmother died, but can still visualise the diminutive, 'lady-like' woman who had a living memory of the Famine and was so generous to her grandchildren:

> She was a dotey woman [with] rather a quick temper but she had a hard life … She lost three of her family in one week from Monday to Friday … She wasn't bitter [but] she refused to take the pension. She would take nothing. As a matter of fact, she asked them not to put the Tricolour on her coffin. She was 105 per cent with [Patrick] but she didn't want any honour for it.

Michael Mulvihill's death 'devastated' his family in Ardoughter, and his grand-nephew was not 'surprised' to hear that the 'independently minded' John Mulvihill refused assistance from the White Cross, despite the fact that the family had been so dependent on his son's financial assistance. Apparently 'old John Mulvihill' said: 'We never took money for killing people and we are certainly not taking money for being killed.' He died in June 1923 and a month later his widow, Mary Mulvihill, made an application for Dependants' Allowance under the Army Pensions Act 1923.[52] By May 1924 she was becoming increasingly anxious about 'the undue delay in dealing with [her] claim' because, at seventy-one, she was supporting her 'invalid' son Thomas and daughter Margaret, who was in 'ill health, suffering from the effects of acute pleurisy contracted some years before'. Why, she asked, was she being 'allowed to starve by the government of the country for which [her] son fought and died'?[53]

Mary Mulvihill died in 1944 and the payment of the vital allowance of £1 per week was terminated. In 1947 her daughter, Margaret, 'destitute and extremely worried', was moved to invoke her brother's memory in a letter to P. J. Lyons on behalf of her brother Thomas who, at forty-seven, was passed over for civil service employment in the Department of Industry and Commerce in favour of 'ex-army men'. She wrote with bitter sarcasm: 'All I can say is that we got great thanks from the Government for Michael's patriotism.'[54] Two years later, when the family received 'an ejectment order' for non-payment of council rates, Margaret made an emotional appeal to local Labour Party TD Dan Spring to lobby on her behalf for the allowance to be reinstated in her name.[55] Unsuccessful in 1949, Margaret wrote again in August 1953, claiming to be 'in dire circumstances'. Based on the provisions of that year's amendment to the Military Service Pensions Act, she asked for a 'special allowance in respect of the death and services of my brother Michael Mulvihill … who was gloriously killed in action in the GPO on Easter Saturday [sic] 1916'.[56] She was finally successful, but her long struggle with penury bred a deep resentment towards the institutions of the state for which she considered her brother had 'sacrificed his life'.

Margaret Mulvihill's residual bitterness was patently obvious in the Golden Jubilee year. In February 1966 she responded to an appeal in the national press for the relatives of men killed during Easter Week who lived outside Dublin to make contact with the government so that they could be brought 'free of charge' to Dublin for the 'ceremonies'. She wrote to inform the secretary to the Department of Defence that she was 'the only one now living in Kerry. Patrick O'Connor's brothers, I heard, are long since dead, also his sisters. The Shortis family are gone from Ballybunion and O'Rahilly lived in Dublin years before his death.'[57] However, she declined Seán Lemass' subsequent invitation to attend the ceremony in Arbour Hill in April, when a commemorative plaque featuring her brother's name was due to be unveiled. In a letter sent to Tom McEllistrim TD in March 1966, she explained:

> I think now all this is for leaders' relatives or the Queen Bees of the Rising … Miss Pearse etc., are the only ones to be treated by any Government we have had. Yet, in a quiet way, Michael brought in more arms each year than any of these … He got the death he wished and we could not stop him but I think now, like [Daniel] O'Connell, that any country is not worth a drop of human blood.[58]

Lemass' letter of invitation arrived in the same month as a letter refusing Margaret's application for an increase in the £190 per annum Dependants'

Allowance she received under the Army Pensions Act. Her frustration is unmistakable in the last line of her letter to McEllistrim: 'I am sorry about cancelling the visit to Dublin, of course my health is poor, besides I will not be of bother to any one if I possibly can help it. I may go there some other time when I can afford to do so.'[59]

The Kerry Volunteers bequeathed a legacy of loss and a material burden on their families, but their names also carried a political weight that propelled their brothers and sisters into the midst of conflict during the War of Independence and the Civil War. Archie and Arnold Shortis both emigrated to America in the 1920s, ostensibly for 'health reasons' and 'to find work', respectively, but Richard feels there may have been more to the story of his uncles' emigration: 'They were both on the run [during] the War of Independence.' The Black and Tans 'raided the house in Ballybunion a number of times and they were looking for them'. The brothers, like so many others, 'disappeared' in America.

'Uncle Bill', another of the Shortis brothers, 'didn't get involved in the War of Independence but got involved in the Civil War on the Irregular side.' He told his nephew that 'he was studying medicine in Galway University at the time', and he and his flying column 'occupied two very nice houses, Carton being one and the other being Lyons. He moved in very high quality circles,' Richard laughed. He was interned in the Curragh in 1922, 'but he never wanted to talk about it, too many unhappy memories and too many bitter memories.'[60]

Even though 'nobody was turned away from the Mulvihill home in Ardoughter', the family was not actively engaged in the War of Independence. Michael's brother, Tom, felt that 'the substantial contribution of his family was completed in 1916'. Despite his abstention, Tom Mulvihill was 'badly beaten by the [Black and] Tans' who, according to his grand-nephew, 'had a habit of going back to families that had participated [in the rebellion] and giving them some special treatment'. He received 'very bad chest injuries and always had breathing difficulties [and] was never really fit for full-time work after that'. Liam regrets that during his youth he didn't ask his grand-uncle 'more pertinent questions', but feels that even if he had, he would have found that Thomas Mulvihill was from a generation 'that was quite reticent' about talking of what happened: 'I suppose they saw some terrible things and maybe they just wanted to leave it behind.'

Patrick O'Connor's brothers similarly avoided active involvement in the struggle for independence. 'They all had children that time,' Kitty Murphy explained, 'and I suppose for their mother's sake they didn't do any more.' Nonetheless, Daniel told his daughter that the family would 'gather round at night … afraid that they could be raided or shot at night on account of [Patrick] taking such an important part. They were living in fear.' The Black and Tans 'targeted' the O'Connor farm and 'raided our house, I suppose, three times every week to see were we keeping people'. The raids were not entirely arbitrary, as the O'Connors provided a safe house for the local flying columns. 'People used to stay in our house and sleep under the beds and things', but there was 'a great woman down in the Bridge Bar' who would alert the family if she heard about a potential raid, and 'tell my father and mother don't keep anybody tonight'.

Kitty recounted an incident during one of the raids: 'My grandmother had a beautiful tick of feathers on her lovely bed and they took it out in the yard and with a bayonet they slit it [and] threw paraffin oil on it and they burned it on account of her son being involved.' But having lost two sons, 'I suppose she could bear anything after that'. Despite the harassment and the family's support for the local Volunteers, Kitty's father 'never took up a gun':

> He wore an Easter lily all the time and he was president of the local Fianna Fáil Cumann. He canvassed at every election and represented the party in the polling booth … He didn't think much of Collins [and] even though I would have loved to visit Béal na mBláth, I didn't dare mention it because my father would kill me. De Valera was the person in his eyes, very much so. I was never in my life asked for a vote by Fine Gael canvassers … that's how we were recognised.

Thomas Mulvihill, who 'wasn't a narrow nationalist by any stretch of the imagination', agreed with Michael Collins' assessment of the Treaty as a 'stepping stone', but refused 'to recognise Fine Gael'. He welcomed debate, and his grand-nephew, Liam Hutchinson, can clearly recall the political 'to-ing and fro-ing' during his childhood. The Mulvihills had 'tremendous respect for anyone who had a strong opinion and would stand up for themselves [and] if you had an opinion and it was diametrically opposed to my Uncle Tom, he would argue to the ends of the earth but he'd never disrespect you for it'.

Ann Shortis' children were served 'the Civil War for breakfast every day'. Her son, Richard, smiled at his parents 'illogical' union, because 'they were totally antipathetic from the point of view of politics'. Their father, Richard Johnson, was a staunch Fine Gael supporter and Ann was 'republican more than anything else'. The domestic conversation was 'volatile' but 'wonderful'. They had 'extremely heated arguments'. Ann's support for de Valera was short-lived and ceased when 'he went into the Dáil. That didn't suit her at all,' her son explained: 'They fought a Civil War about the oath and the six counties and suddenly [de Valera] discovers [the oath] is "an empty formula".' She felt that he 'betrayed them'.

Patrick O'Connor's niece Kitty was born on 6 September 1922 'at the very end' of the Civil War. 'Pity I wasn't older,' she smiled ruefully, because 'I know very little about it. You see, my father and mother had suffered so much that I think they would rather have forgotten it.' In 1957 Kitty knew enough about her family's politics to conceal the fact that her fiancé, John Murphy, was '110 per cent Fine Gael', and after they married he was 'wise enough' to avoid conversations about politics. Kitty laughed at the memory of polling day, when she and her husband 'went up to the school [and] he voted Fine Gael and I voted Fianna Fáil and we came out of the polling place and we talked about the weather'.

Michael Mulvihill, Patrick O'Connor and Paddy Shortis are buried together in the Republican Plot in St Paul's Cemetery in Glasnevin, Dublin. 'The grave was unmarked for a number of years,' Liam Hutchinson said, until 1929, when the National Graves Association cordoned off the area and put up a headstone. This was replaced in 1966 with a monument on which is inscribed: 'We know their dream … they dreamed and are dead.'[61]

FRANCIS BRENNAN

Just before noon on 24 April 1916, newly recruited Private Francis Brennan was engaged in drill practice with the 10th Battalion, Royal Dublin Fusiliers in the Royal (Collins) Barracks in Dublin. The battalion was due to depart for France in September, and on that spring morning the Royal Dubliners had assembled for training on the grassy slopes of the barracks facing the River Liffey. From his elevated vantage point, Brennan could almost make out his mother's house at 24 Usher's Island. At 12.10 p.m. Colonel Cowan at military headquarters at Parkgate Street received a call from Dublin Castle: 'the Sinn Féiners' were attacking the Castle. He quickly sent orders to Richmond, Portobello and the Royal Barracks to dispatch regiments to relieve the garrison in the Castle. At 12.15 p.m., in response to the sharp blast of a bugle, eighteen-year-old Francis Brennan shouldered his standard-issue service rifle and marched with the fifty men of 'B' Company behind Lieutenant Neilan out of the barracks and eastwards along Ellis Quay towards the city. In the words of his nephew, Eddie Brennan:

> They had only gone three or four hundred yards along the quays and hadn't even reached Queen Street Bridge when they were fired upon from the Mendicity Institute [*sic*] across the river, and that's when Francis was shot and mortally wounded, less than ten yards from his mother's front door.

Eighty-three-year-old Eddie Brennan knew that his father, Edward, served with the Irish Guards in France during the First World War, but until the late 1990s, he was oblivious to the full details of his family's military history. A chance exchange with 'a Royal Dublin Fusiliers man' led to the 'surprising' revelation about his Uncle Francis, and, during the same conversation, he learned that another of his father's brothers, Eugene Brennan, was one of more than 35,000 Irishmen who fought and died with the British Army during the First World War. His feelings about the Rising, he said, are now 'confused, to say the least':

> As a young man I was a rabid republican, [largely due to the influence of] my teacher, Mr O'Connor, who was an ex-IRA man. I revelled in the stories about all the 1916 heroes [and the efforts] to bring about Irish freedom and independence. I knew that my father was in France with the British Army in 1916 and had nothing to do with the Rising [but] you can imagine the surprise I got when I discovered that one of my uncles was actually killed in the Rising …
>
> I never felt any bitterness or anything about it … I know that both sides were doing what they had to do. I just got more keenly interested and started to delve and dig in and ask the questions and go into the records and go to the library.

He learned that in 1913 his grandparents, Eliza and Charles Brennan, lived with their six children at 24 Usher's Island. Charles was 'a sail-maker' and he 'looked after the tarpaulin covers of railway wagons … My father, Edward, began work with the railway as a labourer in Inchicore Works and he was later promoted to a footplate fireman, shovelling coal on the steam trains.' The outbreak of war in Europe in August 1914 caused great excitement. Thousands of Irish reservists were called up to join the 20,000 Irishmen already serving in the regular British Army, and British soldiers arrived in boatloads at the North Wall for the training camps in Ireland. 'War fever had gripped Ireland', newspapers served up graphic descriptions of German 'atrocities' in Europe, and recruitment propaganda was ubiquitous in the streets.[62] The majority of the Irish population, from all social and cultural backgrounds, supported the Allied cause and, like 80,000 other Irishmen in the first twelve months of the war, Eugene and Edward Brennan were seduced by Kitchener's imperative to 'Join an Irish Regiment Today'. Eddie cannot say for certain what motivated their enlistment, but in 1914 Irish recruitment to the British Army was driven by a series of varied and often complementary factors. Some joined up for the 'king's shilling', while others, like the Irish Volunteer and poet Francis Ledwidge, enlisted because the British Army 'stood between Ireland and an enemy common to our civilisation'.[63] Thousands of Irish nationalists felt a sense of duty or a moral obligation to 'do their bit' in a conflict that was sold as 'an Irish War' in which Irish interests were at stake. IPP leader John Redmond delivered the message forcibly at a public meeting in Woodenbridge, County Wicklow, on Sunday 20 September 1914:

> The interests of Ireland – the whole of Ireland – are at stake in this war … [It] is undertaken in the defence of the highest principles of religion and morality and right and it would be a disgrace forever to our country and a reproach to her manhood and a denial of the lessons of her history, if young Ireland confined her efforts to remaining at home to defend the shores of Ireland from an unlikely invasion, and to shrink from the duty of providing on the field of battle that gallantry and courage which has distinguished our race all through its history.[64]

Other recruits, such as Tom Barry, were 'not influenced by the lurid appeal to save Belgium or small nations' or to secure Home Rule for Ireland. Rather, they went to war 'to get a gun, to see new countries and to feel a grown man'.[65] Whatever the reason, or combination of reasons, for their enlistment, the Brennan brothers did not have long to wait before they were called into action. In September 1914 Eugene was mobilised with the 1st Battalion, Royal Irish Rifles and dispatched to the Western Front, and Eddie's research revealed that, in December, his uncle 'was part of the famous Christmas truce' – a series of unofficial ceasefires along the Western Front:

> His commanding officer [Lieutenant Colonel George Brenton-Laurie] recorded in his diary that his men were directly opposite the German lines. The Germans shouted across first: 'English, we won't fire if you don't fire. We would like to keep Christmas Day totally free of fire.' He said that when the Germans began to sing, he could not stop the Irish from singing in reply.

In early 1915 Francis Brennan's future seemed bright. He had just left school, and at seventeen 'he won a scholarship ... to go into the Civil Service and he was posted to the offices of the Land Commission' in Mornington House in Upper Merrion Street, Dublin. His happiness was short-lived, however, because in March 1915 the Brennan family received the devastating news that Eugene Brennan was one of 450 Irishmen who had fallen at the Battle of Neuve Chapelle in northern France. Less than a year later, in February 1916, Francis joined the newly formed 10th Battalion, Royal Dublin Fusiliers.

On Easter Monday morning, as Seán Connolly's ICA column marched towards the gates of Dublin Castle, twenty-five-year-old Seán Heuston led 'D' Company, 1st Battalion, to the two-storey Mendicity Institution on Usher's Island. Their task was to hold the complex for at least two hours to 'prevent all troops from passing into the City from the Royal Barracks'.[66] Captain of 'D' Company Richard Balfe was 'putting out a Tri-colour flag' when 400 Royal Dubliners, headed by an officer with a drawn sword, erupted onto the quays. From his position at a window on the second floor, Volunteer Patrick Stephenson watched as they 'continued to pour out in khaki like a sausage coming from a machine', marching in fours along the northern quays:

The brass band alone was missing as the column came still nearer to us, and to add to the air of festivity a tram came running along the tracks from the Park. The Tommies had reached half way between Ellis Street and Blackhall Place, when possibly the strain becoming too much, someone fired. At that, the reaction of the rest was instantaneous and we all let go.[67]

'Heuston had told [the Volunteers] that nobody was to fire until he blew his whistle,' Eddie explained, 'but they got so excited when they saw the Tommies that somebody started off and then everybody joined in.' The driver of the tram 'realised that they were in the firing line. All the passengers ducked out and fled up the side streets.'

The Volunteers poured several volleys into the soldiers' ranks: 'It was a case of fire and one could not miss,' Balfe recorded. He watched as Lieutenant Gerald Aloysius Neilan 'dropped' – a bullet in the head had killed him instantly.[68] Stephenson remembered 'the thundering reverberations that beat about our ears as the echo of the rifle explosions came back across the river from the houses opposite'.[69] The crown forces were 'driven back in disorder' and crouched in doorways, while others jumped for the cover of the tram.[70] Private Andrew Barry of the Royal Dubliners, who had helped to unload the *Asgard* at Howth two years earlier, recorded: 'Some of the lads dived for the quay wall. Myself and a few others scrambled on to the pavement. Bullets were smashing into the shops. A door opened, and an old woman dragged us inside.'[71] From his position at the window, Stephenson 'fired with the rest at nothing in particular':

> Through the gap that lay between the rounded roof of the tram and the side could be seen the movement of the Tommy as he crawled along towards the front of the tram. It was just a matter of waiting until he was at full stretch and let one go. The crawling stopped simultaneous with the sound of the shot …
>
> For a long time this kind of grim triangular target practice went on without a single shot being fired back from the tram as it stood there, mute and immobile. Then the sound of a whistle came across the river and the sandy coloured figures withdrew into the side streets, and silence beat down on your head and drummed in your ears. In those first sharp minutes we had been made into soldiers.[72]

'It was during that episode that Francis was shot.' His nephew, who found Stephenson's account 'very graphic', still considers it 'unbelievable' that he was shot 'almost across the road' from his home. Eddie also suspects that his grandmother may have witnessed the shooting:

> [She would have] heard the commotion … and she certainly would have seen the soldiers marching past the house on the opposite side of the quays … The family knew that Francis was stationed in the barracks so they might have known that he was among them. If they continued watching they would have seen the battalion scatter a couple of hundred yards further up when they were fired upon … Francis didn't die on the spot; he died later in the Adelaide hospital [and] the family lore is that Eliza spent a number of evenings trying to find what hospital he was in.

Soon after the first engagement, the British forces attacked the Mendicity Institution from a concealed machine-gun post on the top floor of a building in Queen Street. Curious about the site of his uncle's last moments, Eddie recently visited the area around Queen Street and identified what he presumes must have been the location of the British machine-gun post: 'I think the building was a pub in 1916, but it is now occupied by Bargaintown [a furniture shop].' With the manager's permission, he climbed to the second floor, 'had a good look' and found 'that there is an open field of fire from that angle'. Stephenson noted:

> It seemed as if some giant steel whip was lashing the stone work [of the Mendicity Institution] with a tremendous vindictiveness. Heuston shouted at us to hold our fire, but in truth all we could do was lie [there], watching the back walls of the room being riddled with bullet holes and the plaster float around the room in a fine grey mist.[73]

Inexplicably, the British forces did not take advantage of the machine-gun fire as cover for an attack on Heuston's position, and the rebels remained until the final assault came on Wednesday. Volunteer James Brennan testified: 'The British opened an attack from all sides … machine-gun fire and rifle fire kept up a constant battering on our position.' Outnumbered and trapped, Heuston 'knew the position was hopeless' and he was left with no option other than surrender.[74]

Eddie Brennan finds it 'hard to fathom' that it has been a century since those 'two people who were related to me were alive,' and that they were 'so easily written out of history'. Other than his recent discovery of Francis Brennan's name inscribed on a memorial plaque 'to all the government employees who gave their lives in the Great War' in the foyer of the Merrion Hotel, his exhaustive search of 'all the records and all the archives' for references to his uncle has proved disappointing:[75]

> I did find a photograph of a group of six soldiers taken in the Royal Barracks. Three are sitting and three are standing and there is a caption on a board beside them which states: 'Everybody's doing it'. It was a recruiting poster, but Francis could have been one of them. I like to think so anyway … In fact, if I remember correctly, some of his battalion was sent to Gallipoli, where they were wiped out, so he probably wouldn't have survived the year anyway.

Edward Brennan 'ended the war as a stretcher-bearer' and his son suspects that the relatively benign posting might have had something to do with the fact that his 'two brothers had been killed in action'. Eddie's uncertainty is based on his father's refusal to discuss his experiences during the war, and he regrets that 'there are still an awful lot of holes that need to be filled and gaps in the story. I don't know if I'm ever going to be able to fill them.' Despite his unwillingness to discuss his past, Eddie knows that his father was deeply affected by his experiences during the war:

> I was never sure whether he was actually shell shocked or not. I do know that he never got any pension from the British Army. I never spoke to him about it, but he told my brother Joe, who lives in Manchester, that he wouldn't take it. It was blood money. I can only guess that [he meant] that in order to achieve [a pension] you had to survive the war and that meant killing other people.

His father's unspoken resentment might also have been born out of his experiences in Ireland after his repatriation in 1919 when, like many ex-servicemen, he was subject to suspicion and discrimination. Edward Brennan had left Ireland in 1914 to the sound of cheering crowds, imbued with a spirit of adventure and convinced that he was fighting for Ireland's future, but having survived the trenches, he returned to find an Ireland that was, in the words of W. B. Yeats, 'changed utterly'.[76] The early enthusiasm for the Allied cause had been blunted in his absence by the enormous human and material cost of war. By 1916, when Brennan was 'on the train that brought the first tanks from the channel ports up to the Front', his countrymen were pioneering a different vision of fighting for Ireland. After the Rising, the mainstream of Irish nationalism was radicalised by the heavy-handed response on the part of the British military authorities, and by 1918 Home Rule was no longer enough to satisfy Irish ambition. The militant nationalism expressed by Sinn Féin was in the ascendancy, and its popular anti-conscription campaign and republican manifesto paid dividends at the polls in December.

At the outbreak of the War of Independence, some ex-servicemen, such as Emmet Dalton and Tom Barry, provided military training to the IRA, but most, including Edward Brennan, struggled to return to their pre-war lives in a largely unsympathetic country. The ten years between his father's return to Ireland and his marriage to Mary Marshall in 1929 are 'very much a mystery' to Eddie, but he presumes that he returned to his job on the railway. All Eddie knows for certain is that by the time he was born, in 1931, the family of six was living in one room in a house in Chapelizod.

As an adult, Eddie learned that his father experienced at first-hand the republican hostility towards ex-servicemen in Dublin:

> The landlord was an ex-IRA man, or probably still IRA, and there was a woman also lodging in the house in Chapelizod, and she was ex-Cumann na mBan. In early 1938 they were informed that my father [had] managed to get [a newly built Corporation] house in Drimnagh. They tackled him. They wanted to know why did a British Army man get a house from the Corporation before IRA and Cumann na mBan and they attacked him physically.

Eddie could not remember 'seeing any evidence' of the altercation, which happened when he was only seven, but smiled at the memory of moving to 'this wonderful new house', which 'at the time was brilliant'. It was from Drimnagh that Edward Brennan travelled to the Phoenix Park to attend the annual Armistice Day services:

> On 11 November every year they would bring out the famous Ginchy Cross and it was temporarily erected in front of the Wellington Monument [to act as an Irish Cenotaph].[77] I can honestly say that the only time I ever saw my father inebriated was on one of those occasions when he obviously [had] had a few drinks with his friends.

Their medals are the only physical remnants of the Brennan brothers' military service. Eddie's brother Joe is the custodian of their father's military service medal, and his cousins in Dunboyne have inherited 'Eugene and Francis' dead pennies'.[78] They are 'two bronze disks, about five inches in diameter and they have a figure of Britannia and the lion. Set into the bronze is a little oblong on which is inscribed the name of the recipient, the deceased soldier.' The medals are a provocative reminder of the complexity of the 1916 legacy for so many Irish families. Francis Brennan grew up in the same city, with the same formative influences and experiences as the men who occupied the Mendicity Institution on Easter Monday morning, but, in his nephew's opinion, he was simply 'in the wrong uniform at the wrong time'. His brother Eugene represents one of thousands of Irish war dead 'erased [for years] from official history [and] denied recognition because they did not fit into the nationalist myth and its "canonical" lines of memory'.[79]

'Keepers of the Flame'

Writing in *The Irish Times* on 27 December 2014, Roy Foster warned that 'the commemoration of the extraordinary events of a century ago … must not be excessively triumphalist or self congratulatory'. Rather, we should try to remember what kind of people these 'makers of the Irish revolution' were, and 'the sort of country they wanted'.[1] The inevitable comparisons between the actual Republic and the ideals expressed in the Proclamation of the Irish Republic may serve as an uncomfortable reminder of unrealised potential and compromised priorities, but there are inherent dangers of misinterpretation in making direct comparisons between the revolutionary generation and our own.

The signatories of the Proclamation of the Irish Republic grew up in a romantic, noble, chivalrous and militant world, and they were convinced of the moral imperative of fighting for Ireland's freedom from Britain. As a child of the 1950s, Nuala O'Faolain suggested: 'having been born free it's literally impossible to imagine what it was like to need freedom'.[2] Nonetheless, the descendants of the 'makers of revolution' have often attempted to imagine what motivated their ancestors to strike against British rule.

ICA leader Michael Mallin's son, Fr Joseph Mallin, suggests that the desire for 'justice and freedom' inspired his father's generation: 'Some [were] well off and higher-class people, others came from poverty [and] … they were willing to give up all in order to make it possible to live their lives not in poverty and oppression under the wealthy and powerful.' A grandson of Terence MacSwiney and Cathal Brugha, Professor Cathal Brugha, finds the genesis of revolutionary ideation in the realms of cultural nationalism:

> Most of them came together because of their interest in the Irish language. Their motivation was something deeply human … A lot of them had huge difficulties

with the whole idea of holding a gun. That's not where they started. Their starting point was almost with the mystical.

Michael O'Hanrahan's grand-niece, Áine Caffrey, is inclined to agree, and she gives added precedence to the devout Catholicism that underpinned the revolutionary ideal:

> These men weren't men of violence; they were men of great vision … So many of them were poets and writers and also men of very deep faith, which probably isn't understood very much now … They were people, I think, to be admired, and if we could get back to following many of their great ideals I think that Ireland would be a better country.

James Connolly's great-grandson, James Connolly Heron, also feels that 'it would be no harm to dust off the books and go back and read what those people had to say about society, because a lot of it is very relevant to where we are today, nearly a century later, and if James Connolly were alive today he would still be burning to change society'.

Thomas MacDonagh's granddaughter, Lucille Redmond, is distinctly aware that theirs was 'a different generation', but is inclined to find grounds for disappointment in the evolution of the Republic for which her grandfather gave his life:

> These people were idealists the same way that people all over Europe who wanted a new world and a new country [were]. The country that arrived with its Magdalene Laundries … and its persecutions of anyone who had taken the anti-Treaty side and its ultra-Catholicism and its utter unkindness was not at all the kind of world they had died for and they had worked for.

During the Decade of Centenaries 'the mirror of commemoration' should reflect our hopes and aspirations for the future, and Lucille is emphatic: 'I want our future to come out of the hope and idealism that brought Ireland into being.'[3]

ENDNOTES

INTRODUCTION: INDIVIDUAL TRUTHS

1   Keith Jeffrey, *The GPO and the Easter Rising* (Irish Academic Press, Sallins, 2006), p. 104.

2   *The 1916 Rising, Oral History Collection* (Irish Life and Lore, 2013).

3   Maurice O'Keeffe, interviewed by the author, 10 October 2014.

4   Initial Statement by the Advisory Group on the Decade of Centenary Commemorations Coordinated by the Department of Arts Heritage and the Gaeltacht. Available at: www.decadeofcentenaries.com/statement.

5   Richard White, *Remembering Ahanagran* (Hill and Wang, New York, 1998), pp. 4–5.

6   Maurice O'Keeffe, interviewed by the author, 10 October 2014.

7   Diarmaid Ferriter, 'In Such Deadly Earnest,' *The Dublin Review*, No. 12 (Autumn 2003), p. 40. Some of the testimony to the BMH was in the form of written statements or responses to a questionnaire.

8   *Ibid.*, p. 2.

9   Fearghal McGarry, '"Too Many Histories"? The Bureau of Military History and Easter 1916', *History Ireland*, Vol. 19, No. 6 (November/December 2011), p. 26.

10   Once the Irish Life and Lore interview is completed, the participants are asked to sign a consent form giving their permission for the interview to be released for commercial and educational purposes.

11   Fearghal McGarry, *Rebels: Voices from the Easter Rising* (Penguin, Dublin, 2011), p. xiv.

12   Tim Pat Coogan, *De Valera: Long Fellow, Long Shadow* (Arrow Books, London, 1995), p. 69. Questions about de Valera's military capability were first raised in Max Caulfield's *Easter Rebellion* (1964).

13   *Ibid.*

14   Three Irish ports, at Berehaven, Queenstown (Cobh) and Lough Swilly, retained by Britain under the terms of the Treaty (1921), were returned under the terms of the Anglo-Irish Trade Agreement (1938).

15   Michael Foy and Brian Barton, *The Easter Rising* (The History Press, Stroud, 2011), p. 275.

16   BMH WS 1043 (Joseph V. Lawless).

17   BMH WS 645 (Nora Ashe).

18   *The Kerryman*, 18 January 1985.

19   McGarry, *Rebels* (2011), p. xiv.

20   Dan Holland was a member of 'F' Company, 4th Battalion, Dublin Brigade and served in the South Dublin Union in 1916.

21   Sinéad McCoole, *No Ordinary Women: Irish Female Activists in the Revolutionary Years 1900–1912* (The O'Brien Press, Dublin, 2008), p. 13.

22 *Ibid.*, p. 15.

23 William Butler Yeats, 'Sailing to Byzantium', *The Tower*, (MacMillan & Co., London, 1928).

24 Michael Hopkinson (ed.), *Frank Henderson's Easter Rising: Recollections of a Dublin Volunteer* (Cork University Press, 1998), p. 10.

25 McCoole, *No Ordinary Women* (2008), p. 13.

26 Joseph Leonard of 'B' Company, 2nd Battalion, Dublin Brigade, was in the Four Courts in 1916, was a member of Michael Collins' counter intelligence unit, the Squad, and served with the National Army in Kerry during the Civil War.

27 Nuala O'Faolain, 'An Era beyond Imaginative Reach', *The Irish Times*, 29 April 1991, p. 12.

28 *The Irish Times*, 4 April 1991, p. 9.

29 John Waters, '1916 Rising Honoured in Nature', *The Irish Times*, 18 April 2005, p. 14.

MEMORIES IN CONTEXT: IRELAND 1890–1923

1 Roy Foster, *Vivid Faces: The Revolutionary Generation in Ireland, 1890–1923* (Penguin, London, 2014), p. 11.

2 Parnell was the leader of the Irish Parliamentary Party in Westminster. He pursued nationalist and agrarian policies aggressively, which resulted in a series of Land Acts between 1870 and 1903 and two Home Rule Bills defeated in the House of Lords. Thomas Clarke was imprisoned for fifteen years for Fenian activities, and was part of the drive to revitalise the Irish Republican Brotherhood in the early 1900s. He advocated the achievement of an Irish Republic by an armed insurrection.

3 BMH WS 249 (Frank Henderson).

4 Kevin Whelan, '1916 in Context', Papers from a conference entitled 'The 1916 Rising: Then and Now' held at Trinity College Dublin (TCD) on 21 April 2006. Available at: http://www.theirelandinstitute.com/institute/ (accessed 3 October 2014).

5 Michael Hopkinson (ed.), *Frank Henderson's Easter Rising: Recollections of a Dublin Volunteer* (Cork University Press, 1998), pp. 16–18.

6 BMH WS 249 (Frank Henderson).

7 Hopkinson, *Frank Henderson's Easter Rising* (1998), p. 22.

8 The UIL also played a significant role in the reunification in 1900 of the Irish Parliamentary Party, which had split after the Parnell divorce scandal in 1890.

9 BMH WS 249 (Frank Henderson).

10 *Ibid.*

11 Fearghal McGarry, *The Rising, Ireland: Easter 1916* (Oxford University Press, 2011), p. 18.

12 Hopkinson (ed.), *Frank Henderson's Easter Rising*, p. 19.

13 In 1896 Connolly founded the Irish Socialist Republican Party and by late 1913 James Larkin's Irish Transport and General Workers' Union (ITGWU) had 30,000 affiliated members.

14 Between 1880 and 1890 the Irish Parliamentary Party under Parnell introduced a significant measure of social-reform legislation and brought two Home Rule Bills for Ireland to the Parliament floor.

15 The IRB was organised in 'circles' of men of a limited number headed by a 'centre'. None of the men in the circle other than the centre would have known the identity of other members of the IRB. This was done to maintain the secrecy of the organisation and prevent general infiltration by British agents.

16 If Ireland were to be granted Home Rule it would remain part of the United Kingdom but have a separate parliament in Dublin with jurisdiction over the thirty-two counties.

17 In 1905 Griffith founded the Sinn Féin ('We Ourselves') party, which politicised the cultural nationalist agenda and advocated a policy of protectionism. The party performed disappointingly at the polls and went into decline after 1909.

18 The House of Lords' power of veto was replaced in 1911 by a two-year delaying mechanism on legislation.

19 Robert Kee, *The Green Flag: A History of Irish Nationalism* (Penguin, London, 2000), p. 456.

20 Asquith introduced the third Home Rule Bill into the House of Commons in April 1912.

21 *The Irish Times*, 18 April 1914.

22 Hopkinson, *Frank Henderson's Easter Rising* (1998), p. 26.

23 Gerry White, O'Shea, Brendan and Younghusband, Bill, *Irish Volunteer Soldier, 1913–1923* (Osprey Publishing, Oxford, 2013), p. 10.

24 In the summer of 1913 employers in Dublin attempted to impose on their workers a pledge not to join or belong to the ITGWU. This provoked strikes, which were countered by lockouts, until over 2,000 workers and 300 employers were involved. It was a long and bitter dispute, often erupting into violent clashes between the striking workers and the police.

25 Senia Pašeta, *Irish Nationalist Women, 1900–1918* (Cambridge University Press, 2013), pp. 162–3. Some historians have argued that the women who participated in ICA activities were never officially members, but most of the women who were afterwards interviewed or submitted testimony to the BMH identified themselves as such.

26 The *Chotah* landed with 600 rifles in Kilcoole, County Wicklow, a week later.

27 BMH WS 249 (Frank Henderson).

28 BMH WS 162 (John F. Shouldice).

29 Francis X. Martin, 'Writings of Eoin MacNeill', *Irish Historical Studies*, Vol. 6 (March 1948), pp. 227–8.

30 BMH WS 249 (Frank Henderson).

31 P. S. O'Hegarty, *The Victory of Sinn Féin* (Talbot Press, Dublin, 1924), p. 3.

32 Connolly was co-opted onto the Military Council in February 1916 because of concerns that the ICA would strike for a workers' republic unilaterally and prematurely.

33 Desmond Ryan (ed.), *The Collected Works of Padraic H. Pearse* (Phoenix Publishing Co., Dublin, 1924) p. 137.

34 BMH WS 400 (Richard Walsh).

35 *Ibid.*

36 BMH WS 249 (Frank Henderson).

37 *Ibid.*

38 Foy and Barton, *The Easter Rising* (2011), p. 47.

39 BMH WS 162 (John F. Shouldice).

40 On 21 April Bulmer Hobson had been lured to a spurious meeting of the Leinster Executive of the IRB at 76 Cabra Road, where he was detained at gunpoint until the Rising started.

41 BMH WS 007 (Liam Ó Bríain).

42 Tim Pat Coogan, *Ireland in the Twentieth Century* (Hutchinson, London, 2003), p. 52.

43 BMH WS 162 (John F. Shouldice).

44 BMH WS 249 (Frank Henderson).

45 *Ibid.*

46 Sources sometimes mistakenly call him Gerald, who was George's younger brother.

47 BMH WS 004 (Diarmuid Lynch).

48 BMH WS 357 (Kathleen Lynn).

49 Emily Norgrove Hanratty, 'Destination Dublin Castle', *The Irish Press*, 8 April 1966, p. 21.

50 Séamus Scully, 'Moore Street – 1916', *Dublin Historical Record*, Vol. 39, No. 2 (March 1986), pp. 58–9.

51 BMH WS 249 (Frank Henderson).

52 *Ibid.*

53 Stephen Ferguson, *The GPO: 200 Years of History* (Mercier Press, Cork, 2014), p. 143.

54 Brian Barton, *The Secret Court Martial Records of the 1916 Easter Rising* (The History Press, Stroud, 2010), p. 19.

55 BMH WS 249 (Frank Henderson).

56 BMH WS 162 (John F. Shouldice).

57 BMH WS 249 (Frank Henderson).

58 BMH WS 694 (Feargus (Frank) Burke).

59 BMH WS 249 (Frank Henderson).

60 Seán F. Lemass, 'I Remember 1916', *Studies: An Irish Quarterly Review*, Vol. 55, No. 217 (Spring 1966), p. 8.

61 Some accounts place the time of Pearse's surrender to General Lowe at 3.30 p.m. on Saturday 29 April 1916.

62 BMH WS 162 (John F. Shouldice).

63 BMH WS 249 (Frank Henderson).

64 Captain Percival Lea-Wilson, DMP, was killed on the orders of Michael Collins in Gorey, County Wexford, on 15 June 1920.

65 BMH WS 1494 (Mick McAllister).

66 BMH WS 162 (John F. Shouldice).

67 BMH WS 249 (Frank Henderson).

68 *Ibid.*

69 The number of dead in the Easter Rising is based on recent research carried out by the Glasnevin Trust, http://www.glasnevintrust.ie/; see also *The Irish Times*, 1 May 1916.

70 *Cork Constitution*, 1 May 1916.

71 Adrian Hardiman, 'Shot in Cold Blood: Military Law and Irish Perceptions in the Suppression of the 1916 Rebellion', in Gabriel Doherty and Dermot Keogh (eds), *1916: The Long Revolution* (Mercier Press, Cork, 2007), p. 226.

72 *The Irish Times*, 6 May 1916.

73 *Irish Independent*, 12 May 1916.

74 BMH WS 162 (John F. Shouldice).

75 *Ibid.*

76 Owen Dudley Edwards and Fergus Pyle (eds), *1916: Easter Rising* (MacGibbon & Kee, London, 1968) p. 77.

77 David Fitzpatrick, *Politics and Irish Life 1913–1921: Provincial Experiences of War and Revolution* (Cork University Press, 1998), p. 97.

78   Hardiman, 'Shot in Cold Blood' (2007), p. 226.

79   Whelan, '1916 in Context'. Available at: http://www.theirelandinstitute.com/institute/.

80   Hopkinson, *Frank Henderson's Easter Rising* (1998), p. 6.

81   Dick McKee was company captain, then commandant of the 2nd Battalion, and eventually brigadier of the IRA Dublin Brigade, a member of the GHQ Staff and, from July 1919, a member of Collins' Squad.

82   BMH WS 679 (John F. Shouldice).

83   *Ibid.*

84   Alvin Jackson, *Ireland 1978–1998* (Blackwell, Oxford, 1999), p. 248.

85   Because of the large number of arrests, the Squad and the Active Service Unit (ASU) of the Dublin Brigade were merged to form the Dublin Guard with Paddy O'Daly as O/C.

86   The delegation comprised Arthur Griffith (chairman), Michael Collins, Robert Barton, George Gavan Duffy and Éamonn Duggan. The delegates were styled 'Envoys Plenipotentiary' and given the power to negotiate and sign a treaty.

87   Francis Costello, *The Irish Revolution and Its Aftermath, 1916–1923: Years of Revolt* (Irish Academic Press, Sallins, 2003), p. 277.

88   *The Irish Times*, 8 April 1922, p. 5.

89   Hopkinson (1998), pp. 7–8.

90   *Ibid.*, p. 8.

91   The first editions of *An Phoblacht* were printed there, as was *Saoirse na hEireann*. The company was raided frequently by the Free State army.

92   Hopkinson, *Frank Henderson's Easter Rising* (1998), p. 9.

93   *Ibid*, p. 13.

94   *Ibid*, pp. 13–14.

LONG SHADOWS: EXECUTED LEADERS

1   W. H. Kautt, *The Anglo-Irish War, 1916–1921: A People's War* (Praeger, London, 1999), p. 50.

2   The Bishop of Ross, cited in Coogan, *Ireland in the Twentieth Century* (2003), p. 60, and John Dillon, for example, referred to the insurgents having fought 'a good clean fight, however misguided': John Dillon, in Kautt, *The Anglo-Irish War* (1999), p. 50.

3   Brian Hughes, *16 Lives: Michael Mallin* (The O'Brien Press, Dublin, 2013), p. 206.

4   Piaras F. MacLochlainn, *Last Words, Letters & Statements of the Leaders Executed after the Rising* (Kilmainham Jail Restoration Society, Dublin 1971), pp. 122–4.

5   Sinéad McCoole, 'Women were among the Chief Sufferers in the Ensuing Conflict', *The Irish Times*, 14 April 2006.

6   BMH WS 382 (Thomas Mallin).

7   Fr Joseph Mallin, SJ, on RTÉ's *Spirit Level*, first broadcast 2009.

8   *Ibid.*

9   Sinéad McCoole, 'The Heroic Wives who were Left Behind in 1916', *Sunday Independent*, 23 April 2000, p. 22.

10   *The Irish Times*, 7 April 1988, p. 8; Interview with Joseph Mallin on RTÉ, *Spirit Level*.

11 Fionnuala McHugh, 'My Life: Father Joseph Mallin', 13 September 2013. Available at: http://www.scmp.com/magazines/post-magazine/article/1308371/my-life-father-joseph-mallin (accessed 31 July 2015).

12 'Mallin's Vow', *The Irish Press*, 12 May 1980, p. 9.

13 *Ibid.*

14 BMH WS 733 (James O'Shea).

15 *Ibid.*

16 Foy and Barton, *The Easter Rising* (2011), p. 79.

17 BMH WS 733 (James O'Shea).

18 Foy and Barton, *The Easter Rising* (2011), p. 82.

19 Barton, *The Secret Court Martial Records* (2010), p. 275.

20 BMH WS 585 (Frank Robbins).

21 *Ibid.*

22 Foy and Barton, *The Easter Rising* (2011), p. 90.

23 BMH WS 733 (James O'Shea).

24 Alex Findlater, *Findlaters: The Story of a Dublin Merchant Family (1774–2001)* (A&A Farmar, Dublin, 2001), p. 282.

25 BMH WS 382 (Thomas Mallin).

26 Michael Mallin's trial proceedings, PRO WO71/353.

27 *The Irish Times*, 13 September 2013.

28 BMH WS 382 (Thomas Mallin).

29 Hughes, *Michael Mallin* (2013), p. 185.

30 MacLochlainn, *Last Words, Letters & Statements* (1971), pp. 122–4.

31 Rev P. J. Carroll, CSC, 'Touching Memories of Easter Week', *Limerick Leader*, 8 October 1932, p. 11.

32 *Ibid.*

33 BMH WS 382 (Thomas Mallin).

34 *Ibid.*

35 The White Cross was a non-political organisation set up during the War of Independence to assist the families of activists.

36 BMH MSP W1/D322 (Michael Mallin), Agnes Mallin to the Ministry of Pensions, 22 October 1928.

37 'A Daughter of the Easter Rising', *The Irish Times*, 23 April 2005

38 Easter 1916 Witness Statements. Available at: http://www.easter1916.ie/index.php/rising/witnesses/ (accessed 31 July 2015).

39 Hughes, *Michael Mallin* (2013), p. 220.

40 *The Irish Times*, 4 April 1991.

41 Seán Russell was a senior member of the IRA.

42 McHugh, 'My Life: Father Joseph Mallin'. Available at: http://www.scmp.com/magazines/post-magazine/article/1308371/my-life-father-joseph-mallin (accessed 31 July 2015).

43 Dan Mulcahy, 'Life and Death of Commandant Edward Daly', in Brian Ó Conchubhair (ed.), *Limerick's Fighting Story 1916–21, Told by the Men Who Made It* (Mercier Press, Cork, 2009), p. 60.

44   Annie Daly died in 1908 of typhus.

45   John Daly's release was precipitated by his hunger strike in protest about his harsh treatment and the vigorous campaign by the IRB for his release after 1889.

46   John O'Callaghan, *16 Lives: Con Colbert* (The O'Brien Press, Dublin, 2015), p. 115.

47   Helen Litton, *16 Lives: Edward Daly* (The O'Brien Press, Dublin, 2013), p. 42.

48   BMH WS 855 (Madge Daly).

49   Mulcahy, 'Edward Daly' (2009), pp. 57–8.

50   Interview: Proinsias MacAongusa with John S. O'Connor for 1966 RTÉ documentary series 'The Week of the Rising', donated by O'Connor's daughter, Eileen Butterly, from the family collection; Patrick Stephenson, cited in Litton, *Edward Daly* (2013), p. 53.

51   Litton, *Edward Daly* (2013) p. 131.

52   BMH WS 154 (Nora Dore (née Daly)).

53   BMH WS 153 (Éamonn T. Dore).

54   BMH WS 154 (Nora Dore (née Daly)).

55   *Ibid.*

56   Piaras Béaslaí, 'Edward Daly's Command, Dublin, 1916', in Ó Conchubhair (ed.) *Limerick's Fighting Story 1916–21* (2009), p. 69.

57   BMH WS 153 (Éamonn T. Dore).

58   MacLochlainn, *Last Words, Letters & Statements* (1971), p. 69.

59   *Ibid.*

60   Kathleen Clarke, cited in Tim Pat Coogan, *1916: The Easter Rising* (Phoenix, London, 2001), p. 160; MacLochlainn, *Last Words, Letters & Statements* (1971), p. 70.

61   Father Leonard, 'Memories of Easter Week', in Barton, *The Secret Court Martial Records* (2010), p. 169.

62   MacLochlainn, *Last Words, Letters & Statements* (1971), p. 71.

63   *Irish Independent*, 24 April 1937, p. 12.

64   'The Daly Family'. Available at: http://www.ul.ie/wic/content/daly-family#_ftn1 (accessed 5 December 2014).

65   Litton, *Edward Daly* (2013) p. 190.

66   BMH WS 855 (Madge Daly).

67   *Ibid.*

68   BMH WS 856 (Elizabeth Colbert).

69   *Ibid.*

70   Anne-Marie Ryan, *16 Dead Men: The Easter Rising Executions* (Mercier Press, Cork, 2014), p. 172.

71   BMH WS 856 (Elizabeth Colbert).

72   Madge Daly, 'Con Colbert of Athea, Hero and Martyr', in Ó Conchubhair (ed.), *Limerick's Fighting Story* (2009), p. 73.

73   Cited in Barton, *The Secret Court Martial Records* (2010), p. 266.

74   BMH WS 280 (Robert Holland).

75   BMH WS 856 (Elizabeth Colbert).

76   O'Callaghan, *Con Colbert* (2015), p. 166.

77 MacLochlainn, *Last Words, Letters & Statements* (1971), p. 151.

78 *Ibid.* p. 152.

79 *Irish Independent*, 1 June 1916.

80 BMH WS 856 (Elizabeth Colbert).

81 BMH WS 1272 (James Collins).

82 *Ibid.*

83 *The Irish Press*, 23 April 1937.

84 'Jim Colbert', Obituary, *The Irish Press*, 5 February 1970, p. 11.

85 'Remembering a Soldier of Freedom', *Limerick Leader*, 21 February 1970, p. 11.

86 Joseph Plunkett's siblings were Philomena (1886), Moya/Maria (1889), Geraldine (1891), George (1894), Fiona/Fina (1896) and John/Jack (1897).

87 Count George Oliver Plunkett was named after his ancestor, Oliver Plunkett, the Archbishop of Armagh who was martyred in 1681.

88 BMH WS 358 (Geraldine Dillon (née Plunkett)).

89 Honor Ó Brolcháin, *16 Lives: Joseph Plunkett* (The O'Brien Press, Dublin, 2012), pp. 354–5.

90 BMH WS 358 (Geraldine Dillon (née Plunkett)).

91 The first news of the rebellion was sent by Rosalie Rice in Kenmare post office to her cousins, the Ring brothers, at the Western Union cable station on Valentia Island, who forwarded the message to the United States on Easter Monday. The coded message read: 'Mother operated on successfully today.'

92 *The Irish Press*, 3 August 1972, p. 6.

93 *Ibid.*

94 Cited in *Southern Star*, 13 May 1916, p. 2.

95 BMH WS 257 (Grace Plunkett).

96 NLI MS 21594.

97 Florence O'Donoghue, 'Plans for the 1916 Rising', *University Review*, Vol. 3, No. 1 (Spring 1963), p. 10.

98 BMH WS 358 (Geraldine Dillon (née Plunkett)).

99 *Ibid.*

100 *Irish Independent*, 30 January 1953, p. 4.

101 Foy and Barton, *The Easter Rising* (2011), p. 188.

102 BMH WS 388 (Joseph Good).

103 *Ibid.*

104 BMH WS 156 (Seumas (Séamus) Robinson).

105 BMH WS 388 (Joseph Good).

106 BMH WS 244 (John McGallogly).

107 BMH WS 1744 (Seán Nunan).

108 BMH WS 358 (Geraldine Dillon (née Plunkett)).

109 *Ibid.*

110 *The Irish Press*, 3 August 1972, p. 6.

111 Waters, 'Children of the Rising', 4 April 1991, p. 9.

112 Ernie O'Malley, *The Singing Flame* (Anvil Books, Dublin, 1978), p. 119.

113 BMH WS 511 (Michael Lynch).

114 William Henry, *Éamonn Ceannt: Supreme Sacrifice* (Mercier Press, Cork, 2012), p. 134.

115 BMH WS 264 (Áine Ceannt).

116 *Ibid.*

117 *Ibid.*

118 Henry, *Éamonn Ceannt* (2012), p. 179.

119 Séamus G. O'Kelly, 'Éamonn Ceannt: Rebel Piper', *Connacht Tribune*, 20 August 1955, p. 18.

120 Henry, *Éamonn Ceannt* (2012), p. 167.

121 Dave Kenny, 'Time for Us to Draw on the Memory of the Heroes of 1916', *Irish Examiner*, 8 May 2013, p. 8. Máire nic Shiubhlaigh led Cumann na mBan at Jacob's during the Rising.

122 *Ibid.*

123 *The Irish Times*, 3 February 1954, p. 3.

124 NLI, Ceannt Papers, MS 13,069/1–9.

125 *The Irish Press*, 29 November, 1933, p. 8.

126 Sinéad McCoole, *Easter Widows* (Doubleday, London, 2014), p. 333.

127 Mary Gallagher, *16 Lives: Éamonn Ceannt* (The O'Brien Press, Dublin, 2014), p. 334.

128 *Ibid.*

129 McCoole, 'Women Were Among the Chief Sufferers', 14 April 2006.

130 *The Irish Press*, 29 November 1933, p. 8.

131 'Barbie MacDonagh Remembers', *The Irish Press*, 9 July 1969, p. 9.

132 *The Irish Press*, 6 December 1962, p. 12.

133 His vocational crisis was the subject of his first book of poetry, *Through the Ivory Gate* (Sealy, Bryers & Walker, Dublin, 1902).

134 *Sunday Independent*, 26 March 1978, p. 8.

135 Shane Kenna, *16 Lives: Thomas MacDonagh* (The O'Brien Press, Dublin, 2014), p. 50.

136 Michael Hayes, 'Thomas MacDonagh and the Rising', in Francis X. Martin (ed.) *The Easter Rising 1916 and University College Dublin* (Browne & Noland, Dublin, 1966), p. 39; Donagh MacDonagh, 'Thomas MacDonagh', *An Cosantoir*, Vol. V, No. 10 (October 1945), p. 528.

137 *Sunday Independent*, 26 March 1978, p. 8.

138 Clarke, cited in Peter Costello, *The Heart Grown Brutal: The Irish Revolution in Literature from Parnell to the Death of W. B. Yeats, 1891–1939* (Gill & Macmillan, Dublin, 1977), p. 84.

139 Frank Robbins corroborated MacDonagh's instruction in his witness statement: BMH WS 585.

140 'Events of Easter Week', *The Catholic Bulletin*, 1918.

141 BMH WS 445 (James J. Slattery).

142 BMH WS 335 (Joseph Furlong).

143 BMH WS 312 (Seosamh de Brun).

144 *Sunday Independent*, 26 March 1978, p. 8.

145 BMH WS 312 (Seosamh de Brun).

146 *Sunday Independent*, 23 April 2000, p. 22.

147 BMH WS 358 (Geraldine Dillon (née Plunkett)).

148 Kenna, *Thomas MacDonagh* (2014), p. 256.

149 *Ibid*, p. 272.

150 'Barbie MacDonagh Remembers', *The Irish Press*, 9 July 1969, p. 9.

151 Lucille Redmond, 'The Lady Vanishes', *Skerries News*, Vol. 19, No. 8 (October 2008), p. 15.

152 *Ibid*.

153 BMH WS 717 (Sr Francesca – Mary MacDonagh).

154 'Barbie MacDonagh Remembers', *The Irish Press*, 9 July 1969, p. 9.

155 McCoole, 'The Heroic Wives', 23 April 2000, p. 22.

156 BMH WS 717 (Sr Francesca – Mary MacDonagh).

157 MacLochlainn, *Last Words, Letters & Statements* (1971), p. 214.

158 *The Irish Times*, 2 January 1968, p. 7.

159 *Sunday Independent*, 26 March 1978, p. 8.

160 Louis N. Le Roux, *Life of Patrick H. Pearse*, translated by Desmond Ryan (Phoenix Publishing, Dublin, 1932).

161 David Thornley, 'Patrick Pearse', *Studies: An Irish Quarterly Review*, Vol. 55, No. 217 (Spring, 1966), p. 10.

162 Ruth Dudley Edwards, *Patrick Pearse: The Triumph of Failure* (Gollancz, London, 1977).

163 Roisín Higgins and Regina Uí Chollatáin (eds), *The Life and After-Life of P. H. Pearse* (Irish Academic Press, Sallins, 2009), p 11.

164 David Thornley 'Patrick Pearse and the Pearse Family', *Studies: An Irish Quarterly Review*, Vol. 60, No. 239/240 (Autumn/Winter 1971), pp. 332–46.

165 *Irish Independent*, 8 September 1900.

166 P. H. Pearse, 'Education in the West of Ireland,' in Ó Buachalla, Seamus (ed.), *A Significant Irish Educationalist: The Educational Writings of P. H. Pearse* (Mercier Press, Cork, 1980), p. 313.

167 United Irishman Robert Emmet led an abortive rebellion against British rule in 1803 and was executed for high treason. He is said to have courted his sweetheart, Sarah Curran, in the grounds of The Hermitage in Rathfarnham.

168 Max Caulfield, *The Easter Rebellion: Dublin 1916* (Roberts Rinehart, Colorado, 1995), p. 7.

169 Ruth Dudley Edwards, 'Willie Pearse – the loving shadow of his brother', *The Irish Press*, 10 November 1979, p. 14.

170 Sheila Walsh, 'Waiting for News at St Enda's', *The Irish Press*, 13 April 1966, p. 12.

171 MacLochlainn, *Last Words, Letters & Statements* (1971), p. 78.

172 Walsh, 'Waiting for News at St Enda's', 13 April 1966, p. 12.

173 MacLochlainn, *Last Words, Letters & Statements* (1971), pp. 79–80.

174 Dowling, in fact, ceremoniously placed the final slate on the roof of Kilmainham on 8 July 1964, four years after work had begun on its restoration.

175 Waters, 'Children of the Rising', 4 April 1991, p. 9.

176 *The Irish Times*, 30 December 2004, p. 4.

177 Carroll, 'Touching Memories of Easter Week', 8 October 1932, p. 11.

178 Mary Emily Pearse married Alfred McGloughlin on 5 July 1884.

179 Mary Brigid Pearse, *The Home Life of Patrick Pearse: As Told By Himself, His Family and Friends* (Browne & Nolan, Dublin, 1934), pp. 13–40.

180 Alfred McGloughlin emigrated to America where he subsequently married twice more before his death in 1945.

181 The document is filed in the National Library at NLI MS 15453.

182 David Fitzpatrick, 'James Connolly: A Full Life', *History Ireland*, Vol. 14, No. 2 (March/April 2006).

183 Barton, *The Secret Court Martial Records* (2010), p. 327.

184 McCoole, 'The Heroic Wives', 23 April 2000, p. 22.

185 BMH WS 919 (Ina Heron (née Connolly)).

186 *Ibid.*

187 McCoole, *No Ordinary Women* (2008), p. 26.

188 Countess Markievicz, 'James Connolly as I Knew Him', *The Nation*, 26 March 1927.

189 Helena Molony, *Women of the Rising*, RTÉ Radio 1 documentary presented by Donncha Ó Dulaing, first broadcast 16 April 1963.

190 McGarry, *The Rising* (2011) p. 135.

191 Foy and Barton, *The Easter Rising* (2011), p. 172.

192 *Ibid*, p. 199.

193 BMH WS 290 (Seán McLoughlin). Volunteer James Good (BMH WS 388) testified that, during the evacuation, there was 'no aggressive leadership' with the 'exception of perhaps one man', twenty-year-old Seán McLoughlin.

194 On Friday evening, MacDermott proposed that military command be given to McLoughlin. Connolly seconded the proposal – BMH WS 290. James Good later noticed that McLoughlin 'wore on his tunic shirt yellow stripes. I had the impression they were James Connolly's.' – BMH WS 388. After their arrest, the Dublin Metropolitan Police (DMP) considered McLoughlin an insignificant and junior figure because of his obvious youth and he escaped the fate 'of seven of the eight other commandants'. Charlie McGuire, 'Sean McLoughlin – the Boy Commandant of 1916', *History Ireland*, Vol. 14, No. 2 (March/April 2006).

195 BMH WS 290 (Seán McLoughlin).

196 BMH WS 388 (James Good).

197 Frank Byrne, 'Last Words Connolly Spoke to His Daughter', *Sunday Independent*, 16 April 1978, p. 13.

198 Lucinda McDermott to Ina Connolly, 8 February 1952, Connolly family private archive.

199 *Ulster Herald*, 17 April 1971, p. 11.

200 Nora Connolly and her husband, Séamus O'Brien, left the Labour Party when it dropped 'workers' republic' from its list of aims.

'No Hero Stories': The GPO Garrison

1 The full text was published by M. H. Gill in 1907. Patrick Callan, '*Rambles in Eirinn* by William Bulfin', *Studies: An Irish Quarterly Review*, Vol. 71, No. 284 (Winter 1982), p. 391.

2 BMH WS 1769 (Patrick J. Little).

3 Four issues of *An Macaomh*, St Enda's school magazine, were published between 1909 and 1913.

4 Patrick Pearse, 'The Murder Machine', written in 1912 and published as a pamphlet in January 1916.

5 *Ibid.*

6 Ryan, *The Collected Works of Padraic H. Pearse* (1924), p. 214.

7   BMH WS 497 (Éamonn Bulfin).

8   *Ibid.*

9   BMH WS 694 (Feargus (Frank) Burke); BMH WS 497 (Éamonn Bulfin).

10 BMH WS 694 (Feargus (Frank) Burke).

11 Walsh, 'Waiting for News at St Enda's', 13 April 1966, p. 12.

12 BMH WS 725 (Desmond Ryan).

13 BMH WS 694 (Feargus (Frank) Burke).

14 *Ibid.*

15 Ryan, *The Collected Works of Padraic H. Pearse* (1924), p. 98; BMH WS 694 (Feargus (Frank) Burke).

16 BMH WS 694 (Feargus (Frank) Burke).

17 BMH WS 497 (Éamonn Bulfin); BMH WS 370 (Fintan Murphy); another student, Frank Connolly, complied with MacNeill's request, a decision according to Margaret Pearse, 'he bitterly regretted afterwards'.

18 BMH WS 694 (Feargus (Frank) Burke).

19 BMH WS 359 (Aoife de Burca).

20 BMH WS 370 (Fintan Murphy).

21 In her witness statement, Aoife said that she was alerted by Cumann na mBan member Sorcha MacMahon that her help was required.

22 BMH WS 724 (Desmond Ryan).

23 *Ibid.*

24 Foy and Barton, *The Easter Rising* (2011), p. 175.

25 In his witness statement (497) Bulfin recorded: 'we had reached the entrance to Prince's Street when the Lancers came down O'Connell Street … We did not actually fire at the Lancers but, at that moment, firing took place from the Post Office and … the Imperial Hotel.'

26 BMH WS 370 (Fintan Murphy) and 'The GPO Flags in 1916', *The Irish Press,* 22 April 1966, p. 11.

27 BMH WS 359 (Aoife de Burca).

28 *Ibid.*

29 *Ibid.*

30 *Ibid.*

31 Desmond Ryan, 'The Week the Nation Was Reborn', *The Irish Press,* 11 April 1955.

32 BMH WS 724 (Desmond Ryan).

33 Foy and Barton, *The Easter Rising* (2011), p. 182.

34 BMH WS 359 (Aoife de Burca).

35 BMH WS 370 (Fintan Murphy).

36 BMH WS 694 (Feargus (Frank) Burke).

37 BMH WS 249 (Frank Henderson).

38 BMH WS 497 (Éamonn Bulfin).

39 *Ibid.*

40 *The Irish Press,* 22 September 1977, p. 10; BMH WS 359.

41 BMH WS 359 (Aoife de Burca).

42 BMH WS 370 (Fintan Murphy); BMH WS 497 (Éamonn Bulfin).

43 BMH WS 153 (Éamonn T. Dore).

44 BMH WS 370 (Fintan Murphy).

45 BMH WS 724 (Desmond Ryan).

46 BMH WS 497 (Éamonn Bulfin).

47 BMH WS 370 (Fintan Murphy).

48 BMH WS 004 (Diarmuid Lynch).

49 BMH WS 724 (Desmond Ryan).

50 *Ibid.*

51 BMH WS 497 (Éamonn Bulfin).

52 Walsh, 'Waiting for News at St Enda's', 13 April 1966, p. 12.

53 *The Irish Press,* 22 September 1977, p. 10.

54 *Irish Independent*, 14 December 1917, p. 4.

55 'Going to War in a Tram', *Sunday Independent,* 16 April 1967, p. 23.

56 Byrne, James, *et al.* (eds), *Ireland and the Americas: Culture, Politics and History*, Vol. II (ABC-CLIO, Santa Barbara, CA, USA, 2008), p. 134.

57 Frank Burke played for Dublin in three All-Ireland hurling finals between 1917 and 1919, and was a member of the Dublin football team that won three All-Ireland finals in a row between 1921 and 1923. He was also a member of the Dublin team that was playing against Tipperary at Croke Park on Bloody Sunday, 21 November 1920, when Michael Hogan, whom he was marking, was shot dead by the Black and Tans.

58 BMH MSP 34/1098, Bulfin to the Secretary to the Office of the Referee, Military Pensions Board, 10 February 1936.

59 'Going to War in a Tram', *Sunday Independent*, 16 April 1967, p. 23.

60 Caulfield, *The Easter Rebellion* (1995), p. 7.

61 Ernie O'Malley, *On Another Man's Wound* (Mercier Press, Cork, 2013), p. 43.

62 Scully, 'Moore Street 1916', *Dublin Historical Record* (1986), pp. 58–9.

63 *Ibid.*

64 BMH MSP 34/56 (Thomas Richard McEvoy), letter of reference from Hanna Sheehy-Skeffington, 28 February 1933.

65 Scully, 'Moore Street 1916', *Dublin Historical Record* (1986), p. 58.

66 *Ibid.* pp. 58–9.

67 *Ibid.*

68 BMH MSP 34/56 (Thomas Richard McEvoy).

69 *Ibid.*

70 BMH WS 821 (Frank Henderson).

71 Eileen McGough, *Diarmuid Lynch: A Forgotten Irish Patriot* (Mercier Press, 2013), p. 15.

72 Florence O'Donoghue (ed.), *Diarmuid Lynch, the IRB and the 1916 Insurrection* (Mercier Press, 1950), p. 12.

73 McGough, *Diarmuid Lynch* (2013), p. 32.

74 In the same year, John Devoy established the American Provisional Committee with the specific aim of raising money for the Volunteers.

75 O'Donoghue, 'Plans for the 1916 Rising', *University Review*, (Spring, 1963), pp. 3–21.

76 BMH MSP23/497 (Diarmuid Lynch).

77 Foy and Barton, *The Easter Rising* (2011), p. 33.

78 BMH MSP23/497 (Diarmuid Lynch).

79 McGough, *Diarmuid Lynch* (2013), p. 55.

80 BMH WS 004 (Diarmuid Lynch).

81 Diarmuid Lynch, *The IRB and the 1916 Insurrection* (Mercier Press, Cork, 1957), p. 175.

82 BMH WS 004 (Diarmuid Lynch).

83 *Irish Independent,* 9 March 1918, p. 2.

84 *Ibid.*

85 BMH WS 1770, part VI (Kevin O'Shiel).

86 BMH WS 510 (Frank Thornton).

87 BMH WS 939 (Ernest Blythe).

88 BMH WS 510 (Frank Thornton).

89 BMH WS 1068 (Michael Brennan).

90 BMH WS 939 (Ernest Blythe).

91 BMH WS 1068 (Michael Brennan); BMH WS 821 (Frank Henderson).

92 BMH WS 1068. The prisoners made a collection and Muriel MacSwiney arranged to buy a silver salver and to have the names of all those in the prison inscribed on it. This was presented subsequently to Diarmuid.

93 BMH WS 1068 (Michael Brennan).

94 BMH WS 510 (Frank Thornton).

95 BMH MSP23/497 (Diarmuid Lynch).

96 *Ibid.*

97 F. M. Carroll, 'De Valera and the Americans: The Early Years, 1916–1923', *The Canadian Journal of Irish Studies*, Vol. 8, No. 1 (June 1982), p. 41.

98 *The Freeman's Journal*, 2 August 1920, p. 4.

99 McGough, *Diarmuid Lynch* (2013), p. 85.

100 The Land Law Commission Act (1923) established the Irish Land Commission to facilitate the compulsory purchase of untenanted land, its division and distribution to local families.

101 McGough, *Diarmuid Lynch* (2013), p. 54. The replies are housed in the National Library in Dublin.

102 Clair Wills, *Dublin 1916: The Siege of the GPO* (Profile Books, London, 2010), p. 15.

103 *Ibid.*, p. 16.

WRITING THE RULE BOOK: THE FOUR COURTS GARRISON

1 Interview by John Caulhan, with Sherrin, O'Connor and Shouldice, WNAC Radio Boston, 1966.

2 The Defence of the Realm Act (DORA) was passed in the United Kingdom on 8 August 1914 and imposed strict press and postal censorship.

3   BMH MSP 34/16672/1 (Thomas O'Connor).

4   BMH WS 006 (Liam Ó Briain); Ó Briain knew Tommy O'Connor as 'bearer of messages to Devoy and I think of large sums in gold back to Tom Clarke' and Pat McCartan testified that 'O'Connor always delivered his dispatches and money safely from America'.

5   Piaras Béaslaí, 'The Fixing of the Date of the 1916 Rising', *Irish Independent*, 4 April 1952, pp. 6–8.

6   *Ibid.*

7   *Ibid.*

8   BMH WS 358 (Geraldine Dillon (née Plunkett)); BMH WS 741 (Michael J. Kehoe).

9   John Devoy, *Recollections of an Irish Rebel* (Chase D. Young, Co., New York, 1929), p. 462.

10 BMH MSP 34/16672/1 (Thomas O'Connor), Letter of reference from Kathleen Clarke, 5 September 1937.

11 BMH MSP 34/16672/1 (Thomas O'Connor).

12 BMH WS 192 (Fionán Lynch).

13 BMH MSP 34/16672/1 (Thomas O'Connor), Letter of reference from Kathleen Clarke, 5 September 1937. On the Saturday and Sunday of Easter Week Tommy provided an armed guard at the Clarkes' home.

14 Foy and Barton, The Easter Rising (2011), p. 150.

15 'F' Company occupied the area from North King Street along Church Street to May Lane.

16 BMH MSP 34/16672/1 (Thomas O'Connor). Letter of reference from Piaras Béaslaí, 30 August 1937.

17 BMH MSP 34/16672/1 (Thomas O'Connor).

18 BMH WS 597 (Edmond O'Brien).

19 BMH MSP 34/16672/1 (Thomas O'Connor).

20 *Ibid.*; official pardon from John Calvin Coolidge, 29 December 1927.

21 *An Tostal* was an Irish festival inaugurated in 1953 to celebrate Irish life. It took place annually during Easter until 1958. Its aim was to attract tourists and promote Irish culture.

22 BMH WS 836 (Tommy O'Connor).

23 Interview, Proinsias Mac Aonghusa with John S. O'Connor for 1966 RTÉ documentary series, *The Week of the Rising*. Donated by O'Connor's daughter, Eileen Butterly, from the family collection.

24 *Ibid.*

25 Interview by John Caulhan with Frank Shouldice.

26 Piaras Béaslaí, 'The North King Street Area', in Brian Ó Conchubhair (ed.), *Dublin's Fighting Story 1916–1921, Told by the Men Who Made It* (Mercier Press, Cork, 2009), p. 100.

27 BMH WS 162 (John F. Shouldice).

28 Interview by John Caulhan.

29 Interview by Proinsias Mac Aonghusa with John O'Connor, 1966.

30 BMH WS 162 (John F. Shouldice).

31 Paul O'Brien, *Crossfire: The Battle of the Four Courts, 1916* (New Island, Dublin, 2012), p. 46.

32 Interview by John Caulhan.

33 Interview by Proinsias Mac Aonghusa with John O'Connor, 1966.

34 O'Brien, *Crossfire* (2012), p. 55.

35 BMH WS 162 (John F. Shouldice).

36 *Ibid.*

37 O'Brien, *Crossfire* (2012), p. 58.

38 Caulfield, *The Easter Rebellion* (1995), p. 342.

39 Fionán Lynch's interview with the BBC, 1964, donated by Dr Gearóid Lynch from the family's personal collection.

40 BMH WS 162 (John F. Shouldice).

41 *Ibid.*

42 Interview by Proinsias Mac Aonghusa, 1966.

43 *Ibid.*

44 *Ibid.*

45 *Ibid.*

46 'Obituary, Liam Archer', *The Irish Press*, 23 July 1969, p. 14.

47 The 1911 census places Edward John Archer and his family at Cabra Road, Glasnevin.

48 Other members included Paddy Walsh, Seán Hayes, Paddy O'Connor and Brian Fagan.

49 Stephen Ferguson, *'Self Respect and a Little Extra Leave': G.P.O. Staff in 1916* (An Post, Dublin, 2006), pp. 12–13.

50 BMH WS 819 (Liam Archer).

51 *Ibid.*

52 *Ibid.*

53 *Ibid.*

54 *Ibid.*

55 *Ibid.*

56 BMH WS 568 (Eilis Bean Ui Chonaill (née Riain)).

57 Archer's distress may have been related to the fact that on Thursday he was given orders to take two tins of petrol and burn down the footbridge linking the administrative part of Jameson's Distillery to the Distillery proper, to deny British troops access to the Volunteer positions on Church Street from the Smithfield side. The incendiaries failed to ignite and the Volunteers retreated.

58 BMH WS 819 (Liam Archer).

59 *Ibid.*

60 These included, among others, Jack Brennan, Seán Ó Consul, Eugene Smith, Chris Butler, Bob Frewen, Paddy Hughes, Nellie and Mollie Heffernan, Kitty Conlon, May Clarke and Lena Wilson.

61 BMH WS 819 (Liam Archer).

62 Sergeant Éamonn 'Ned' Broy worked inside 'G' Division, the intelligence branch of the DMP. He acted as a double agent, copying sensitive files, which he passed to Collins.

63 On 28 November 1920 Tom Barry's IRA flying column ambushed and killed seventeen Auxiliaries at Kilmichael, Co. Cork.

64 BMH WS 819 (Liam Archer).

65 T. Ryle Dwyer, *The Squad and the Intelligence Operations of Michael Collins* (Mercier Press, Cork, 2005), p. 86.

66 William Archer, 'My Services and Experiences in the Dublin General Post Office', unpublished memoir, p. 8.

67 BMH WS 755 (Seán Prendergast).

68 Charles Stewart Bevan, 'Through the Valley' (1956), unpublished personal memoir from the Bevan family archives, p. 1. A copy was also donated to the Military Archives in 2005.

69 BMH MSP 34/1249 (Thomas Bevan), transcript of an interview with Pensions Advisory Committee, 4 December 1936.

70 Foy and Barton, *The Easter Rising* (2011), p. 150.

71 Bevan, 'Through the Valley', p. 2.

72 O'Brien, *Crossfire* (2012), p. 9.

73 BMH MSP 34/1249 (Thomas Bevan); Testimony of Frank Fahy, 2 November 1936.

74 Litton, *Edward Daly* (2013), p. 141.

75 BMH WS 1058 (Séamus Bevan).

76 Bevan, 'Through the Valley', p. 1.

77 *Ibid.*

78 Robert Brennan, *Allegiance* (Browne & Nolan, 1950), p. 136.

79 In December 1916 Charlie Bevan was moved to Lewes Prison in Sussex, and after the strike in May 1917 to Parkhurst Prison on the Isle of Wight.

80 BMH MSP 34/8865 (Charles Stewart Bevan).

81 BMH MSP 34/1249 (Thomas Bevan).

82 Bevan, 'Through the Valley', p. 2.

83 *The Freeman's Journal*, 3 September 1917, p. 5.

84 BMH MSP 34/1249 (Thomas Bevan).

85 BMH MSP 34/8865 (Charles Stewart Bevan).

86 *Ibid.* Testimony by Longford Volunteer Matt Brady and Charles Bevan, 17 June 1935.

87 BMH MSP 34/8865 (Charles Stewart Bevan).

88 *Ibid.* Testimony by Stephen Murphy, 19 November 1935.

89 *Ibid.*

90 Fionán Lynch was a captain of 'F' Company, 1st Battalion in 1916, a brigadier in the National Army and a minister in the Free State government.

91 *The Irish Press*, 25 December 1969, p. 4.

92 *Ibid.*, 1 September 1967, p. 4.

93 Paddy O'Daly is often also called Patrick Daly.

94 BMH WS 220 (Paddy O'Daly).

95 Foy and Barton, *The Easter Rising* (2011), p. 30.

96 BMH WS 220 (Paddy O'Daly).

97 BMH WS 328 (Garry Holohan).

98 BMH WS 387 (Paddy O'Daly).

99 *Ibid.*

100 *Ibid.*

101 Tim Pat Coogan, *Michael Collins: The Man Who Made Ireland* (Palgrave, New York, 2002), p. 99.

102 BMH WS 387 (Paddy O'Daly).

103 Coogan, *Michael Collins* (2002), p. 116.

104 Peter Cottrell, *The Irish Civil War, 1922–1923* (Osprey Publishing, Oxford, 2008), p. 24.

105 Michael Hopkinson, *Green Against Green: The Irish Civil War* (Gill & Macmillan, 2004), p. 241.

106 John Joe Sheehy was a senior IRA figure in Kerry in command of the republican garrison in Tralee before the arrival of the Free State troops. He retreated and led three flying columns in the Ballymacthomas area.

107 NLI MS 22956, Copy of enquiry into the Ballyseedy killings and General Price's report, 11 April 1923; Kerry Command report, 7 March 1923, MP p7/B/130

108 Maryann Gialanella Valiulis, *Portrait of a Revolutionary: General Richard Mulcahy and the Founding of the Irish Free State* (University Press of Kentucky, Lexington, 1992), p. 190.

109 Niall C. Harrington, *Kerry Landing, August 1922: An episode of the Civil War* (Anvil Books, Dublin, 1992), p. 149.

110 The bomb was constructed in Tralee under the supervision of Captains Eddie Flood and Jim Clarke. Commandant David Neligan selected the prisoners. Captain Ed Breslin was in charge of the Dublin Guard at Ballyseedy. 'An examination of the records for the period held at the Military Archives, strongly suggest that Paddy was not even in Kerry on the day prior to the Ballyseedy event. He had been called to a meeting with Mulcahy [at National Army Headquarters] in Parkgate Street [in Dublin]'; Tony Roche, correspondence with the author, 8 July 2015.

111 'Ballyseedy', RTÉ, Frank Hand, director, 12 November 1997.

BLOODLINES: DEATH IN BATTLE

1   W. B. Yeats, 'Easter 1916'.

2   Emily Norgrove Hanratty, 'Destination Dublin Castle', *The Irish Press*, 8 April 1966, p. 21.

3   BMH WS 357 (Kathleen Lynn).

4   Connolly actually starred in James Connolly's *Under Which Flag* a week before the Rising. Michael Davitt (1846–1906) was an Irish nationalist MP, agrarian agitator and labour leader.

5   *Connacht Tribune*, 2 July 1921. John Thornton claimed £2,000 for the burning by crown forces of his two-storey home in Spiddal on 14 May 1921.

6   RTÉ Radio 1, Documentary on One, *No. 3: Lessons in History*, presented by Joe Duffy, produced by Ronan Kelly (first broadcast 20 July 2013).

7   *Ibid.*

8   *The Freeman's Journal*, 10 September 1920, p. 2.

9   Scully, 'Moore Street – 1916', *Dublin Historical Record* (1986), p. 54.

10   The O'Rahilly was actually born Michael J. Rahilly, but adopted the moniker 'The O'Rahilly' himself in the early twentieth century.

11   Foy and Barton, *The Easter Rising* (2011), p. 196.

12   BMH WS 428 (Thomas Devine).

13   *Ibid.*

14   Ferguson, *The GPO* (2014), p. 144.

15   BMH WS 333 (Áine O'Rahilly).

16   Gallagher, *Éamonn Ceannt* (2014), p. 133.

17   The O'Rahilly's fourth son, Maolmuire, was born in 1911, and Ruairi in 1916.

18   The line that Aodogán O'Rahilly paraphrased as the title of his biography is drawn from the

third verse of W. B. Yeats' 1938 poem, 'Sing of The O'Rahilly': Then on Pearse and Connolly/ He fixed a bitter look:/'because I helped wind the clock/I come to hear it strike': William Butler Yeats, *Collected Poems* (Collier, New York, 1988), pp. 307–8.

19   Desmond FitzGerald, 'Inside the GPO', *The Irish Times*, 7 April 1966, p. 9.

20   John Brennan, 'The O'Rahilly, The Life of a Patriot', *The Irish Times*, 13 May 1960, p. 7.

21   Foy and Barton, *The Easter Rising* (2011), p. 174.

22   BMH WS 399 (Mary Josephine Mulcahy).

23   Lorcan Collins and Conor Kostick, 'New Monument to The O'Rahilly Unveiled', *History Ireland*, Vol. 13, No. 4 (July–August, 2005), p. 11; *The Irish Times*, 13 May 1960, p. 7.

24   FitzGerald, 'Inside the GPO', 7 April 1966, p. 9.

25   BMH WS 333 (Áine O'Rahilly).

26   Waters, 'Children of the Rising', 4 April 1991, p. 9.

27   Directed by Joseph MacDonagh, the Belfast Boycott was an attempt by the First Dáil in 1920– 21 to enforce a boycott of Belfast-manufactured goods that were being imported into southern Ireland, in protest against Unionist-inspired attacks on Catholics in Northern Ireland.

28   Bridie Clyne worked in Joe McGrath's office during the Truce period, and even though their politics differed in the Civil War, they remained close friends.

29   Thomas and Henry Coyle had three sisters, Annie, Teresa and Christina.

30   Ben Novick, *Conceiving Revolution: Irish Nationalist Propaganda during the First World War* (Four Courts Press, Dublin, 2001), p. 46.

31   McCoole, *Easter Widows* (2014), p. 285.

32   BMH MSP W2/4SP/198 (Thomas Coyle), Thomas Coyle to the Military Service Pensions Department, 15 February 1924.

33   *Ibid.*

34   *Ibid.*, Mrs Coyle to Séamus Byrne, Fianna Fáil, 24 November 1935.

35   Erected by the North Kerry Republican Soldiers' Memorial Committee.

36   BMH MSP W1/D208 (Michael Mulvihill), Margaret Mulvihill to J. Lyons Cork, 14 March 1947.

37   The other Shortis siblings were Patrick, Violet, Richard, Rosalie, Arnold and William.

38   J. J. O'Kelly (Sceilg), 'Kerry Heroes of the Rising', Brian Ó Conchubhair (ed.), *Kerry's Fighting Story 1916–1921, Told by the Men who Made It* (Mercier Press, Cork, 2009), p. 153.

39   Michael Mulvihill, 'Michael Mulvihill, 1879–1916', reprinted in *The Mulvihill Voice*, Vol. 17 (Spring 2010), p. 2.

40   BMH MSP W1/D208 (Michael Mulvihill).

41   Patrick O'Connor's siblings were Daniel, Thomas, John, Denis, Katie and Minnie.

42   Austin Kennan, 'Ballyduff Man's Part in the 1916 Rising', *The Kerryman*, 19 November 1966, p. 11.

43   *Ibid.*

44   Charlie Saurin, Shortis, Coyle and Séamus Daly stayed at the home of Michael O'Reilly in Foster Avenue in Ballybough on Monday evening, close to 'F' Company's outpost in Gilbey's; BMH WS 288 (Charles Saurin).

45   *The Kerryman*, 19 November 1966, p. 11.

46   Sceilg, 'Kerry Heroes of the Rising', in Ó Conchubhair (ed.), *Kerry's Fighting Story 1916–1921*: (2009) p. 151.

47   BMH WS 359 (Aoife de Burca).

48 Derek Molyneux and Darren Kelly, *When the Clock Struck in 1916: close quarter combat in the Easter Rising* (The Collins Press, Cork, 2015), p. 260.

49 BMH WS 153 (Éamonn T. Dore).

50 BMH MSP W1/D208 (Michael Mulvihill), Margaret Mulvihill to J. Lyons Cork, 14 March 1947.

51 Áine O'Rahilly testified that her sister Nell went to the morgue on Thursday 4 May, and there she found The O'Rahilly and 'Paddy Shortis of Ballybunion'; BMH WS 333 (Áine O'Rahilly).

52 BMH MSP W1/D208 (Michael Mulvihill), Mulvihill to Office of Adjutant General, 29 July 1923.

53 *Ibid.*, Mary Mulvihill to Sec., Ministry of Welfare, 10 May 1924.

54 *Ibid.*, Margaret Mulvihill to J. Lyons Cork, 14 March 1947. Lyons wrote a contribution to the 'Roddy the Rover Column' in *The Irish Press* about the circumstances of Mulvihill's death.

55 *Ibid.*, Margaret Mulvihill to Dan Spring, 4 July 1949.

56 *Ibid.*, Margaret Mulvihill to Sec., Department of Defence, 15 August 1953.

57 *Ibid.*, Margaret Mulvihill to Tom McEllistrim, TD, 22 March 1966.

58 *Ibid.*

59 *Ibid.*

60 Mossie Hartnett, *Victory and Woe: The West Limerick Brigade in the War of Independence* (UCD Press, Dublin, 2002), p. 156.

61 The inscription on the monument in the Republican Plot in Glasnevin Cemetery is an adaptation of a line from W. B. Yeats' 'Easter 1916', which reads: 'We know their dream; enough/To know they dreamed and are dead.'

62 BMH WS 1700 (Alphonsus O'Halloran).

63 Desmond Bowen and Jean Bowen, *Heroic Option: The Irish in the British Army* (Pen and Sword, Barnsley, 2005), p. 216.

64 Keith Jeffrey, *Ireland and the Great War* (Cambridge University Press, 2000), pp. 13–14.

65 *Ibid.*, p. 21.

66 BMH WS 251 (Richard Balfe).

67 Patrick Stephenson, *The Epic of the Mendicity* (Allen Library, Dublin).

68 BMH WS 251 (Richard Balfe). According to Captain Stephen Gwynn, Neilan had been 'strongly nationalist in his sympathies', cited in Bowen and Bowen (2005), p. 243. Lieutenant Neilan's younger brother Anthony fought in the Rising and was imprisoned in Knutsford, Cheshire, UK.

69 NLI MS 36,147; Patrick Stephenson (ed.), *Heuston's Fort: The Mendicity Institute, Easter Week 1916* (private publication, Dublin, 1966).

70 Paddy Stephenson interview on RTÉ documentary, *I Was There – Eyewitness 1916,* broadcast April 1955.

71 *The Irish Times*, 24 March 1984.

72 Stephenson, *Heuston's Fort* (1966).

73 Stephenson, *The Epic of the Mendicity.*

74 Foy and Barton, *The Easter Rising* (2011), p. 160.

75 The memorial is in Mornington House, which now comprises part of the hotel in Upper Merrion Street. It was home to the offices of the Land Commission in 1916, when Francis began work with the civil service.

76   W. B. Yeats, 'Easter 1916'.

77   A wooden Celtic Cross known as the Ginchy Cross was brought from France and erected in 1924 in College Green on Remembrance Sunday. The ceremony was moved to the Phoenix Park in 1926 after republican disturbances during the ceremonies at College Green.

78   The Dead Man's Penny, or 'Widow's Penny' was a commemorative medallion cast in bronze gunmetal, and issued to the next of kin of servicemen and women who had fallen in the Great War between 1914 and 1918.

79   President Michael D Higgins' keynote address at the Theatre of Memory Symposium at the Abbey Theatre on 16 January 2014. Available at: http://www.president.ie/en/media-library/speeches/keynote-address-by-president-michael-d.-higgins-at-the-theatre-of-memory-sy (accessed 31 July 2015).

'Keepers of the Flame'

1   Roy Foster, 'We Must not Politicise 1916 for Feel-good Purposes of the Present', *The Irish Times*, 27 December 2014.

2   Nuala O'Faolain, 'An Era Beyond Imaginative Reach', *The Irish Times*, 29 April 1991, p. 12.

3   Lucille Redmond, 'Commemorating 1916: How Miraculous that We Should Have Our Own Country in Our Own Hands', *The Irish Times*, 31 December 2014.

BIBLIOGRAPHY

BOOKS

Barton, Brian, *The Secret Court Martial Records of the 1916 Easter Rising* (The History Press, Stroud, 2010)

Béaslaí, Piaras, 'Edward Daly's Command, Dublin, 1916', in Brian Ó Conchubhair (ed.), *Limerick's Fighting Story 1916–21, Told by the Men Who Made It* (Mercier Press, Cork, 2009)

Béaslaí, Piaras, 'The North King Street Area', in Brian Ó Conchubhair (ed.), *Dublin's Fighting Story 1916–1921, Told by the Men Who Made It* (Mercier Press, Cork, 2009)

Bowen, Desmond and Bowen, Jean, *Heroic Option: The Irish in the British Army* (Pen and Sword Books Ltd, Barnsley, 2005)

Brennan, Robert, *Allegiance* (Browne & Nolan, Dublin, 1950)

Byrne, James Patrick, Coleman, Philip and King, Jason Francis (eds), *Ireland and the Americas: Culture, Politics, and History*, Vol. II (ABC-CLIO, Santa Barbara, CA, USA, 2008)

Caulfield, Max, *The Easter Rebellion: Dublin 1916* (Roberts Rinehart, Colorado, 1995)

Coogan, Tim Pat, *De Valera: Long Fellow, Long Shadow* (Arrow Books, London, 1995)

Coogan, Tim Pat, *The IRA* (HarperCollins, London, 1995)

Coogan, Tim Pat, *1916: The Easter Rising* (Phoenix, London, 2001)

Coogan, Tim Pat, *Michael Collins: The Man Who Made Ireland* (Palgrave, New York, 2002)

Coogan, Tim Pat, *Ireland in the Twentieth Century* (Hutchinson, London, 2003)

Costello, Francis, *The Irish Revolution and Its Aftermath, 1916–1923: Years of Revolt* (Irish Academic Press, Sallins, 2003)

Costello, Peter, *The Heart Grown Brutal: The Irish Revolution in Literature from Parnell to the Death of W. B. Yeats, 1891–1939* (Gill & Macmillan, Dublin, 1977)

Cottrell, Peter, *The Irish Civil War, 1922–1923* (Osprey Publishing, Oxford, 2008)

Daly, Madge, 'Con Colbert of Athea, Hero and Martyr', in Ó Conchubhair, Brian (ed.), *Limerick's Fighting Story, Told by the Men Who Made It* (Mercier Press, Cork, 2009)

Devoy, John, *Recollections of an Irish Rebel* (Charles D. Young Co., New York, 1929)

Doherty, Gabriel and Keogh, Dermot (eds), *1916: The Long Revolution* (Mercier Press, Cork, 2007)

Dudley Edwards, Owen and Pyle, Fergus (eds), *1916: The Easter Rising* (MacGibbon & Kee, London, 1968)

Dudley Edwards, Ruth, *Patrick Pearse: The Triumph of Failure* (Gollancz, London, 1977)

Dwyer, T. Ryle, *The Squad and the Intelligence Operations of Michael Collins* (Mercier Press, Cork, 2005)

Ferguson, Stephen, *'Self Respect and a Little Extra Leave': G.P.O. Staff in 1916* (An Post, Dublin, 2006)

Ferguson, Stephen, *The GPO: 200 Years of History* (Mercier Press, Cork, 2014)

Ferriter, Diarmaid, *Judging Dev: A Reassessment of the Life and Legacy of Éamon De Valera* (Royal Irish Academy, Dublin, 2007)

Findlater, Alex, *Findlaters: The Story of a Dublin Merchant Family (1774–2001)* (A&A Farmar, Dublin, 2001)

FitzGerald, Desmond, *Desmond's Rising: Memoirs 1913 to Easter 1916* (Liberties Press, Dublin, 2006)

Fitzpatrick, David, *Politics and Irish Life 1913–1921: Provincial Experiences of War and Revolution* (Cork University Press, 1998)

Foster, Roy, *Vivid Faces: The Revolutionary Generation in Ireland, 1890–1923* (Penguin, London, 2014)

Foy, Michael and Barton, Brian, *The Easter Rising* (The History Press, Stroud, 2011)

Gallagher, Mary, *16 Lives: Éamonn Ceannt* (The O'Brien Press, Dublin, 2014)

Gialanella Valiulis, Maryann, *Portrait of a Revolutionary: General Richard Mulcahy and the Founding of the Irish Free State* (University Press of Kentucky, Lexington, KY, USA, 1992)

Hanley, Brian, *The IRA: A Documentary History 1916–2005* (Gill & Macmillan, Dublin, 2010)

Hardiman, Adrian, 'Shot in Cold Blood: Military Law and Irish Perceptions in the Suppression of the 1916 Rebellion', in Gabriel Doherty and Dermot Keogh (eds), *1916: The Long Revolution* (Mercier Press, Cork, 2007)

Harrington, Niall C., *Kerry Landing, August 1922: An episode of the Civil War* (Anvil Books, Dublin, 1992)

Hartnett, Mossie, *Victory and Woe: The West Limerick Brigade in the War of Independence* (UCD Press, Dublin, 2002)

Hayes, Michael, 'Thomas MacDonagh and the Rising', in Francis X. Martin (ed.), *The Easter Rising 1916 and University College Dublin* (Browne & Nolan, Dublin, 1966)

Henry, William, *Éamonn Ceannt: Supreme Sacrifice* (Mercier Press, Cork, 2012)

Higgins, Roisín and Uí Chollatáin, Regina (eds), *The Life and After-Life of P. H. Pearse* (Irish Academic Press, Sallins, 2009)

Hopkinson, Michael (ed.), *Frank Henderson's Easter Rising: Recollections of a Dublin Volunteer* (Cork University Press, 1998)

Hopkinson, Michael, *Green Against Green: The Irish Civil War* (Gill & Macmillan, Dublin, 2004)

Hughes, Brian, *16 Lives: Michael Mallin* (The O'Brien Press, Dublin, 2013)

Jackson, Alvin, *Ireland 1978–1998* (Blackwell, Oxford, 1999)

Jeffrey, Keith, *Ireland and the Great War* (Cambridge University Press, 2000)

Jeffrey, Keith, *The GPO and the Easter Rising* (Irish Academic Press, Sallins, 2006)

Kautt, William H., *The Anglo-Irish War, 1916–1921: A People's War* (Praeger, London, 1999)

Kee, Robert, *The Green Flag: A History of Irish Nationalism* (Penguin, London, 2000)

Kenna, Shane, *16 Lives: Thomas MacDonagh* (The O'Brien Press, Dublin, 2014)

Laffan, Michael, *The Resurrection of Ireland* (Cambridge University Press, 1999)

Le Roux, Louis N., *Life of Patrick H. Pearse*, translated by Desmond Ryan (Phoenix Publishing, Dublin, 1932)

Lee, Joseph J., *Ireland 1912–85: Politics and Society* (Cambridge University Press, 1989)

Litton, Helen, *16 Lives: Edward Daly* (The O'Brien Press, Dublin, 2013)

Lynch, Diarmuid, *The IRB and the 1916 Insurrection* (Mercier Press, Cork, 1957)

Macardle, Dorothy, *The Irish Republic* (Gollancz, London, 1937)

MacDonagh, Thomas, *Through the Ivory Gate* (Sealy, Bryers & Walker, Dublin, 1902)

MacDonagh, Thomas, *Literature in Ireland: Studies in Irish and Anglo-Irish* (F. A. Stokes, New York, 1916)

MacLochlainn, Piaras F., *Last Words: Letters & Statements of the Leaders Executed after the Rising* (Kilmainham Jail Restoration Society, Dublin, 1971)

Martin, Francis X. (ed.), *The Easter Rising 1916 and University College Dublin* (Brown & Nolan, Dublin, 1966)

Matthews, Ann, *The Irish Citizen Army* (Mercier Press, Cork, 2014)

McCoole, Sinéad, *No Ordinary Women: Irish Female Activists in the Revolutionary Years 1900–1912* (The O'Brien Press, Dublin, 2008)

McCoole, Sinéad, *Easter Widows* (Doubleday, London, 2014)

McGarry, Fearghal, *Rebels: Voices from the Easter Rising* (Penguin Ireland, Dublin, 2011)

McGarry, Fearghal, *The Rising, Ireland: Easter 1916* (Oxford University Press, 2011)

McGough, Eileen, *Diarmuid Lynch: A Forgotten Irish Patriot* (Mercier Press, Cork, 2013)

Molyneux Derek and Darren Kelly, *When the Clock Struck in 1916: close quarter combat in the Easter Rising* (The Collins Press, Cork, 2015)

Mulcahy, Dan, 'Life and Death of Commandant Edward Daly', in Brian Ó Conchubhair (ed.), *Limerick's Fighting Story 1916–1921, Told by the Men Who Made It* (Mercier Press, Cork, 2009)

Novick, Ben, *Conceiving Revolution: Irish Nationalist Propaganda during the First World War* (Four Courts Press, Dublin, 2001)

O'Brien, Paul, *Crossfire: The Battle of the Four Courts, 1916* (New Island Books, Dublin, 2012)

Ó Brolcháin, Honor, *16 Lives: Joseph Plunkett* (The O'Brien Press, Dublin, 2012)

Ó Buachalla, Séamus (ed.), *A Significant Irish Educationalist: The Educational Writings of P. H. Pearse* (Mercier Press, Cork, 1980)

O'Callaghan, John, *16 Lives: Con Colbert* (The O'Brien Press, Dublin, 2015)

Ó Conchubhair, Brian (ed.), *Dublin's Fighting Story 1916–1921, Told by the Men Who Made It* (Mercier Press, Cork, 2009)

Ó Conchubhair, Brian (ed.), *Kerry's Fighting Story, 1916–1921, Told by the Men Who Made It* (Mercier Press, Cork, 2009)

Ó Conchubhair, Brian (ed.), *Limerick's Fighting Story 1916–21, Told by the Men Who Made It* (Mercier Press, Cork, 2009)

O'Donoghue, Florence (ed.), *Diarmuid Lynch, the IRB and the 1916 Insurrection* (Mercier Press, 1950)

O'Donoghue, Florence (ed.), *IRA Jailbreaks 1918–1921* (Mercier Press, Cork, 2010)

O'Hegarty, Patrick S., *The Victory of Sinn Féin* (Talbot Press, Dublin, 1924)

O'Keeffe, Jane O'Hea, *Recollections of 1916 and Its Aftermath: Echoes from History* (privately published, Ballyroe, Tralee, 2005)

O'Malley, Ernie, *The Singing Flame* (Anvil Books, Dublin, 1978)

O'Malley, Ernie, *On Another Man's Wound* (Mercier Press, Cork, 2013)

O'Rahilly, Aodogán, *Winding the Clock: O'Rahilly and the 1916 Rising* (Lilliput Press, Dublin, 1991)

Pašeta, Senia, *Irish Nationalist Women, 1900–1918* (Cambridge University Press, 2013)

Pearse, Mary Brigid, *The Home Life of Patrick Pearse: As Told By Himself, His Family and Friends* (Browne & Nolan, Dublin, 1934)

Ryan, Anne-Marie, *16 Dead Men: The Easter Rising Executions* (Mercier Press, Cork, 2014)

Ryan, Desmond (ed.), *The Collected Works of Padraic H. Pearse* (Phoenix Publishing Co., Dublin, 1924)

Ryan, Meda, *Michael Collins and the Women Who Spied for Ireland* (Mercier Press, Cork, 2006)

Stephenson, Patrick (ed.), *Heuston's Fort: The Mendicity Institute, Easter Week 1916* (private publication, Dublin, 1966)

Taylor, James W., *The 1st Royal Irish Rifles in the Great War* (Four Courts Press, Dublin, 2002)

White, Gerry, O'Shea, Brendan and Younghusband, Bill, *Irish Volunteer Soldier, 1913–1923* (Osprey Publishing, Oxford, 2013)

White, Richard, *Remembering Ahanagran* (Hill and Wang, New York, 1998)

Wills, Clair, *Dublin 1916: The Siege of the GPO* (Profile Books, London, 2010)

Yeats, William Butler, *Collected Poems* (Collier, New York, 1988)

Yeats, William Butler, *The Tower* (MacMillan & Co., London, 1928)

JOURNALS

Callan, Patrick, '*Rambles in Eirinn* by William Bulfin', *Studies: An Irish Quarterly Review*, Vol. 71, No. 284 (Winter 1982)

Carroll, F. M., 'De Valera and the Americans: The Early Years, 1916–1923', *The Canadian Journal of Irish Studies*, Vol. 8, No. 1 (June 1982)

Collins, Lorcan and Kostick, Conor, 'New Monument to The O'Rahilly Unveiled', *History Ireland*, Vol. 13, No. 4 (July–August 2005)

Ferriter, Diarmaid, 'In Such Deadly Earnest', *The Dublin Review*, No. 12 (Autumn 2003)

Fitzpatrick, David, 'James Connolly: A Full Life', *History Ireland*, Vol. 14, No. 2 (March/April 2006)

Lemass, Seán F., 'I Remember 1916', *Studies: An Irish Quarterly Review*, Vol. 55, No. 217 (Spring 1966)

MacDonagh, Donagh, 'Thomas MacDonagh', *An Cosantoir*, Vol. V, No. 10 (October 1945)

Martin, Francis X., 'Writings of Eoin MacNeill', *Irish Historical Studies*, Vol. 6 (March 1948)

McGarry, Fearghal, '"Too Many Histories"? The Bureau of Military History and Easter 1916', *History Ireland*, Vol. 19, No. 6 (November/December 2011)

McGuire, Charlie, 'Seán McLoughlin – the Boy Commandant of 1916', *History Ireland*, Vol. 14, No. 2 (March/April 2006)

Mulvihill, Michael, 'Michael Mulvihill, 1879–1916', *The Mulvihill Voice*, Vol. 17 (Spring 2010)

O'Donoghue, Florence, 'Plans for the 1916 Rising', *University Review*, Vol. 3, No. 19 (Spring 1963)

Ó Tuathaigh, Gearóid, 'Commemoration, Public History and the Professional Historian: An Irish Perspective', *Estudios Irlandeses*, No. 9 (2014)

Redmond, Lucille, 'The Lady Vanishes', *Skerries News*, Vol. 19, No. 8 (October 2008)

Scully, Séamus, 'Moore Street 1916', *Dublin Historical Record*, Vol. 39, No. 2 (March 1986)

Thornley, David, 'Patrick Pearse', *Studies: An Irish Quarterly Review*, Vol. 55, No. 217 (Spring 1966)

Thornley, David, 'Patrick Pearse and the Pearse Family', *Studies: An Irish Quarterly Review*, Vol. 60, No. 239/240 (Autumn/Winter 1971)

NEWSPAPER ARTICLES

Béalsaí, Piaras, 'The Fixing of the Date of the 1916 Rising', *Irish Independent*, 4 April 1952

Brennan, John, 'The O'Rahilly, The Life of a Patriot', *The Irish Times*, 13 May 1960

Byrne, Frank, 'Last Words Connolly Spoke to His Daughter', *Sunday Independent*, 16 April 1978

Carroll CSC, Rev P. J. 'Touching Memories of Easter Week', *Limerick Leader*, 8 October 1932

Dudley Edwards, Ruth, 'Willie Pearse – the loving shadow of his brother', *The Irish Press*, 10 November 1979

FitzGerald, Desmond, 'Inside the GPO', *The Irish Times*, 7 April 1966

Foster, Roy, 'We Must not Politicise 1916 for Feel-good Purposes of the Present', *The Irish Times*, 27 December 2014

Kennan, Austin, 'Ballyduff Man's Part in the 1916 Rising', *The Kerryman*, 19 November 1966, p. 11.

Kenny, Dave, 'Time for us to Draw on the Memory of the Heroes of 1916', *Irish Examiner*, 8 May 2013

Markievicz, Countess, 'James Connolly as I Knew Him', *The Nation*, 26 March 1927

McCoole, Sinéad, 'The Heroic Wives who were Left Behind in 1916', *Sunday Independent*, 23 April 2000

McCoole, Sinéad, 'Women were among the Chief Sufferers in the Ensuing Conflict', *The Irish Times*, 14 April 2006

Norgrove Hanratty, Emily, 'Destination Dublin Castle', *The Irish Press*, 8 April 1966

O'Faolain, Nuala, 'An Era beyond Imaginative Reach', *The Irish Times*, 29 April 1991

O'Kelly, Séamus G., 'Éamonn Ceannt: Rebel Piper', *Connacht Tribune*, 20 August 1955

Redmond, Lucille, 'Commemorating 1916: How Miraculous that We Should Have Our Own Country in Our Own Hands', *The Irish Times*, 31 December 2014

Ryan, Desmond, 'The Week the Nation Was Reborn', *The Irish Press*, 11 April 1955

Walsh, Sheila, 'Waiting for News at St Enda's', *The Irish Press*, 13 April 1966

Waters, John, '1916 Rising Honoured in Nature', *The Irish Times*, 18 April 2005

Newspapers

Connacht Tribune, Cork Constitution, Dublin Evening Mail, The Freeman's Journal, Irish Examiner, Irish Independent, The Irish Press, The Irish Times, The Kerryman, Limerick Leader, Nation, Southern Star, Sunday Independent, Ulster Herald, Westmeath Examiner

Websites

'Initial Statement by the Advisory Group on the Decade of Centenary Commemorations', 2012; www.decadeofcentenaries.com/statement

'Women of the Rising'; www.rte.ie/radio1/doconone/documentary-podcast-women-easter-rising-1916-cumann-mban.html

'Deirdre Morrissey, An Irishwoman's Diary', *The Irish Times*, October 1999; www.sallysmyth.com/deirdre_morrissey.html

'1916 in Context', Paper delivered by Kevin Whelan at conference entitled 'The 1916 Rising: Then and Now', Trinity College Dublin, 21 April 2006; www.theirelandinstitute.com/institute/p01-whelan_introduction_page.html

Fionnuala McHugh, 'My Life: Father Joseph Mallin', 13 September 2013; www.scmp.com/magazines/post-magazine/article/1308371/my-life-father-joseph-mallin

'Easter 1916 Witness Statements', 12 July 2012; www.easter1916.ie/index.php/rising/witnesses

'The Daly Family'; www.ul.ie/wic/content/daly-family#_ftn1The Daly Family

President Michael D. Higgins, keynote address at the Theatre of Memory Symposium at Abbey

Theatre, 16 January 2014; www.president.ie/en/media-library/speeches/keynote-address-by-president-michael-d.-higgins-at-the-theatre-of-memory-sy

MANUSCRIPT MATERIAL

Archer, Liam, 'My Services and Experiences in the Dublin General Post Office', unpublished memoir, courtesy of the Archer family

Bevan, Charles Stewart, 'Through the Valley', unpublished personal memoir, 1956, courtesy of the Bevan family

Bureau of Military History, Military Service Pensions and Witness Statements: www.bureauof militaryhistory.ie

NLI MS 21594 (Biographical note on Plunkett by his wife, Grace, 3 May 1923)

NLI MS 13069/1–9 (Ceannt papers)

NLI MS 15453 (Draft document of the surrender, 29 April 1916)

NLI MS 36147 (Patrick Stephenson (ed.), 'Heuston's Fort: The Mendicity Institution, Easter Week 1916', Dublin, 1966)

Stephenson, Patrick, *The Epic of the Mendicity* (Allen Library, Dublin)

ORAL HISTORY RECORDINGS

'1916 Rising', Oral History Collection, Irish Life and Lore, privately published 2013 (www. irishlifeandlore.com)

ADDITIONAL RECORDINGS DONATED FROM PRIVATE FAMILY ARCHIVES

John S. O'Connor interviewed by Proinsias Mac Aonghusa, for RTÉ documentary series, *The Week of the Rising*, April 1966. Donated by John O'Connor's daughter, Eileen Butterly, from the family collection

John O'Connor, Frank Shouldice and Thomas Sheerin, interviewed by John Caulhan, for WNAC Radio Boston, 1966. Donated by Eileen Butterly from the family collection

Fionán Lynch interviewed by the BBC, 1964. Donated by Dr Gearóid Lynch from the family's personal collection

ADDITIONAL RECORDED MATERIAL

'Women of the Rising', RTÉ Radio 1, Helena Molony interviewed by Donncha Ó Dulaing, first broadcast 16 April 1963

Documentary on One, *No. 3: Lessons in History*, RTÉ Radio 1, Simon Walker interviewed by Joe Duffy, first broadcast 20 July 2013

INDEX